Second Edition

KEY CONCEPTS
IN
MATHEMATICS

Though my friends are many, my close friends and dear family are few.
Three of life's miracles are with me every day: my wife, Julie, and our children, Jim and Lucy.
And, though I may not see them, the rest of my family and my close friends are with me every day, too.

Thank you for your love and for making me want to be a better person.

Second Edition

KEY CONCEPTS
IN
MATHEMATICS

STRENGTHENING STANDARDS
PRACTICE IN GRADES 6–12

TIMOTHY J. McNAMARA

CORWIN PRESS
A SAGE Publications Company
Thousand Oaks, CA 91320

For information:

Corwin Press
A Sage Publications Company
2455 Teller Road
Thousand Oaks, California 91320
www.corwinpress.com

Sage Publications Ltd.
1 Oliver's Yard
55 City Road
London EC1Y 1SP
United Kingdom

Sage Publications India Pvt. Ltd.
B-42, Panchsheel Enclave
Post Box 4109
New Delhi 110 017 India

Printed in the United States of America

Library of Congress Cataloging-in-Publication Data

McNamara, Timothy J.
Key concepts in mathematics: Strengthening standards practice in
grades 6–12 / Timothy J. McNamara. — 2nd ed.
      p. cm.
Includes bibliographical references and index.
ISBN 1-4129-3841-4 or 978-1-4129-3841-9 (cloth)
ISBN 1-4129-3842-2 or 978-1-4129-3842-6 (pbk.)
    1. Mathematics—Study and teaching (Middle school)—United States. 2. Mathematics—
Study and teaching (Secondary)—United States. 3. Problem-based learning. I. Title.
QA13.M388 2007
510.71′2—dc22

                                                          2006013310

This book is printed on acid-free paper.

06   07   08   09   10   10   9   8   7   6   5   4   3   2   1

Acquisitions Editor:	Cathy Hernandez
Editorial Assistant:	Charline Wu
Production Editor:	Melanie Birdsall
Typesetter:	C&M Digitals (P) Ltd.
Copy Editor:	Gillian Dickens
Indexer:	Ellen Slavitz
Graphic Designer:	Michael Dubowe

Contents

Preface

One of the provisions of the *No Child Left Behind* legislation is that every student in Grades 3 through 8 and those in a selected high school grade (as stipulated by each state) must pass yearly statewide assessments in mathematics. The good news for math teachers is that the National Council of Teachers of Mathematics, or NCTM, has produced a document that serves as a kind of de facto national curriculum that has guided states in the writing of standards upon which those assessments are based.

The bad news is that even with an influx of textbooks and materials that proclaim themselves to be "standards-based," those same math teachers have available to them very few examples of instructional techniques and insights that also reflect a standards-based philosophy. And the aforementioned book that the NCTM released, *Principles and Standards for School Mathematics* (2000), reads more like a series of teaching *pre*scriptions as opposed to more practical *de*scriptions.

What is needed for the everyday classroom is what this book, *Key Concepts in School Mathematics*, delivers. In its pages, the reader will find classroom-tested examples of standards-based lessons, hands-on activities, and graphing calculator applications and programs that may either be used verbatim or serve as an interpretation of a particular expectation to help the teacher pull his or her own standards-based lesson together.

A BRIEF OVERVIEW

The book joins forces with *Principles and Standards* and the rest of the mounting evidence from cognitive research that concludes that students are best taught math when they actually "do math" (Schoenfeld, 1985). The fact that one reads a book on riding a bicycle, for example, is no substitute for the experience of learning *how* to ride.

Key Concepts in Mathematics is a 10-chapter transitional supplement highlighting all 10 NCTM standards and affording many opportunities for students to "do math"—a resource that illustrates how to put guidelines into motion to move students toward a more inductive mode of thinking. There are two sections to the book: Chapters 1 through 5 (Content, or the skills-based, Standards) and Chapters 6 through 10 (Process, or the more abstract performance-based, Standards). The book is composed of inservice workshops, conference presentations, college seminars, and other direct input from experienced and highly esteemed colleagues.

TARGET AUDIENCE

One of the more ironic statements made by a participant at a workshop session recently hosted by yours truly was, "My students don't have time for thinking—they've got to get through the curriculum." What this time-challenged individual probably meant to say, however, was, "Yes, I see the need for creativity and for practicing critical-thinking problems with my students, but I've got a very tight schedule of topics to cover and almost no room available for such activities."

This person is echoing the pressure-filled sentiments felt by many in our profession of late—which is why *Key Concepts in Mathematics* might be a better fit in the everyday math classroom than at first thought. Its lessons and activities "compress" topic time, with lots of items either introduced or reviewed at once so that teachers do get some planning room at the end of a unit to review elusive topics or bring topics together with a real-world project. But those same lessons and activities also "connect" math concepts in some unique ways—encouraging better understanding, wider engagement, greater retention, and shorter review time prior to students' being subjected to taking the statewide assessments.

There are several potential audiences for whom *Key Concepts* can make a positive and immediate impact:

1. Preservice teachers and college instructors of such preservice courses

2. Beginning teachers incorporating a standards-based curriculum

3. Veteran teachers looking for fresh ideas that pull together old topics

4. Curriculum supervisors establishing more critical-thinking benchmarks

CALCULATORS IN USE

Because *Key Concepts in Mathematics* places such a high premium on participation, it follows that there will be numerous opportunities throughout the book in which some of today's available graphing calculator technology will play a strong supporting role. (Please be advised that the various technological applications and original programs will serve to enhance—and *never* replace—the mathematics in these pages.)

Three graphing calculators from the Texas Instruments line will be used: the TI-73 Explorer™, the TI-83 Plus, and the TI-84 Plus models.

Although interchangeable to a degree, the three calculators target different audiences. For example, the TI-73 Explorer is designed primarily for Grades 6 through 8, as it can be used with topics ranging from fractions through pre-algebra and has a wide array of data analysis and graphing features.

The TI-84 Plus is actually an improved (with greater memory capacity and preloaded applications) version of the older, but still very highly regarded and popular, TI-83 Plus model. Both are designed primarily for Grades 9 through 12—thereby useful with upper-level topics, including those in statistics and calculus—and are compatible with each other (which is why they will be referred to as "TI-83/84 Plus" throughout the book).

For those who might have occasion to use both the TI-73 and the TI-83/84 Plus, please locate the relevant input statement(s) in the left-hand column (steps for the TI-73) with the corresponding statement(s) in the right-hand column (steps for the TI-83/84 Plus):

TI-73		TI-83/84 Plus
1. 2nd MEM 6	=	2nd MEM 4
2. LIST	=	STAT 1
3. 2nd PLOT 1	=	2nd STAT PLOT 1
4. 2nd PLOT 4	=	2nd STAT PLOT 4
5. ZOOM 7	=	ZOOM 9

STARTING OVER

There are three steps involved for the TI-73 (and the corresponding steps for the TI-83/84 Plus in parentheses) that you can take to clear out all old input/output (the "Erase" phase) prior to doing something new with your graphing calculators:

1. Press 2nd PLOT, the number "4" (2nd STAT PLOT 4 for the TI-83/84 Plus), and ENTER to turn off old statistical graphs such as scatterplots, circle graphs, histograms, and so on.

2a. Press the "Y=" button, highlight with the arrow up/down to each previous entry, and CLEAR to remove all old functional graphs.

2b. In the rare case that a drawing such as a vertical line or a circle remains from past work, press DRAW, the number "1" (2nd DRAW 1 for the TI-83/84 Plus), and ENTER to remove it.

3. Press 2nd MEM, the number "6" (2nd MEM 4 for the TI-83/84 Plus), and ENTER to clear out all old lists from statistical tables.

Acknowledgments

Acknowledgments to those outstanding individuals who have made significant contributions to *Key Concepts in Mathematics* are found at the beginning of each of their units. When you are finished reading this book and trying out some of its ideas for yourself, I hope you have a much clearer vision of how the standards can directly, positively, and permanently affect your everyday math classroom.

Curt Boddie, Mathematics Teacher and Advisor (ret.)
Manhasset High School, Manhasset, NY

Sally Fischbeck, Professor of Mathematics (ret.)
Rochester Institute of Technology, Rochester, NY

Robin Fogarty, Educational Consultant/President
Robin Fogarty & Associates, Ltd., Chicago, IL

Abdus Sattar Gazdar, Editor, *Clear Mathematics*
Al-Khwarizmi Research Center, Frewville, South Australia, Australia

Ronald Greaves, Science Coordinator (ret.)
West Irondequoit Central Schools, Rochester, NY

Gerald Rising, Professor Emeritus of Mathematics Education
State University of New York at Buffalo, Buffalo, NY

Jim Ruddy, Professor of Mathematics
Concordia University, Montreal, Quebec, Canada

PUBLISHER'S ACKNOWLEDGMENTS

Corwin Press gratefully acknowledges the contributions of the following reviewers:

Carol Amos, Teacher Leader and Mathematics Coordinator
Twinfield Union School, Plainfield, VT

Fran Arbaugh, Assistant Professor of Mathematics Education
University of Missouri–Columbia, Columbia, MO

Jason Cushner, Lead Instructor
The Watershed School, Boulder, CO

Cathy Hewson, Mathematics Teacher
Rio Mesa High School, Oxnard, CA

Melissa Miller, Sixth-Grade Science and Mathematics Teacher
Randall G. Lynch Middle School, Farmington, AR

About the Author

Timothy J. McNamara is a private mathematics consultant specializing in K–12 systemic improvement efforts for schools and school districts nationwide.

Tim has served as both a math teacher and curriculum supervisor in the Western New York State region since 1975. Two of the schools where he has taught—Williamsville East High School near his hometown of Buffalo and Irondequoit High School near Rochester—have both been ranked in the Top 100 High Schools in America by *Newsweek* magazine.

Tim has taught students from middle-school grades through second-year undergraduate students but predominately at the senior high school level. He has taught all levels of ability, from remedial to gifted, and in both public and private school settings. He has also written articles for math teacher journals from several states and was founder and faculty editor for the Nichols School of Buffalo student mathematics publication, *The Nth Degree.*

He is a contributing member for a variety of professional organizations, including the National Council of Teachers of Mathematics (NCTM), and has facilitated countless conference workshops around the country (including five past NCTM national meetings since 1991) on topics ranging from problem solving and technological classroom applications, to hands-on algebra and geometry, to curriculum alignment and model teaching.

Tim was recognized in 1993 when he was honored as the New York State recipient of the prestigious Presidential Award for Excellence in Secondary Mathematics Teaching at ceremonies held in Washington, D.C. He was also a state finalist for the same award in 1990 and in 1991.

An accomplished three-sport athlete and coach, Tim was inducted into the Western New York Baseball Hall of Fame in 2002 and had a short appearance as a Pittsburgh Pirate in the 1983 baseball movie, *The Natural,* which starred Robert Redford and was filmed in Buffalo. He is also an avid runner, competing in and finishing the 2005 ING New York City Marathon and 2006 Nissan Buffalo Marathons.

He is married to his wife of 27 years, Julie, and they have two children—Jim, 22, and Lucy, 17. Tim's informational Web site is www.timmcnamara.com, and he can be reached via e-mail at improvek12math@timmcnamara.com.

Part I

Curriculum Content Standards

Number and Operations 1

According to the standards listed in *Principles and Standards for School Mathematics* (National Council of Teachers of Mathematics [NCTM], 2000), all students in Grades 6 through 12 should be able to do the following:

- Understand numbers, ways of *representing* numbers, relationships among numbers, and number systems

- Understand meanings of operations and how they *relate* to one another

- *Compute* fluently and make reasonable estimates

The Number and Operations Standard parallels the degrees of mathematical maturity students naturally develop as they move from kindergarten through Grade 12. Students first learn what numbers are and ways to represent numbers as objects or numerals or points on a number line. Students then examine relationships among numbers, their functionality within various rule-based systems, and, finally, the invaluable assistance they render in helping to solve problems.

This chapter includes the following activities: Flexible Arithmetic, Multiplying Integers, and Areas and Mental Arithmetic. Flexible Arithmetic allows students to experience firsthand how to decompose and compose numbers while at the same time gaining a greater appreciation for a variety of standard number properties. Multiplying Integers highlights the additive identity, symmetric, distributive, and commutative properties in a unique way so that students get a better sense as to why the rules of multiplying integers are the way they are. Areas and Mental Arithmetic extends one of the notable hands-on geometry lessons from the great mathematician and mathematics educator George Pólya (1951) into a thinking strategy for students to be able to perform two-digit-by-two-digit multiplication without the use of a calculator.

FLEXIBLE ARITHMETIC

> ## Grades 6–9
>
> This activity illustrates to students how to get answers in more than one way. The process promotes thinking mathematically about number properties. This activity correlates to the following highlighted expectation for students:
>
> - **Understand numbers, ways of *representing* numbers, relationships among numbers, and number systems**
> - Understand meanings of operations and how they *relate* to one another
> - *Compute* fluently and make reasonable estimates

In the article "On Problems With Solutions Attainable in More Than One Way," Pedersen and Pólya (1984) present the idea that students who are challenged to derive the results of routine computations in different ways tend to be more creative and inquisitive in their overall approach to learning mathematics. Presented here is this author's interpretative notion of flexible arithmetic and its use as a bridge to help all students naturally move their thinking from basic operations to more abstract number properties.

Use the following example as a demonstration, and then challenge students to take any two numbers and perform a range of similar operations on their own.

Since $6 \cdot 6 = 36$, then . . .

Distributive Property (Multiplication Over Addition): $a(b + c) = ab + ac$

How would you *rebuild* to arrive at 36?

$$6 \cdot 6 = 6 \cdot (4 + 2)$$
$$= (6 \cdot 4) + (6 \cdot 2) = 24 + 12 = 36$$

Distributive Property (Multiplication Over Subtraction): $a(b - c) = ab - ac$

How would you *reassess* to arrive at 36?

$$6 \cdot 6 = 6 \cdot (7 - 1)$$
$$= (6 \cdot 7) - (6 \cdot 1) = 42 - 6 = 36$$

Associative Property of Multiplication: $a(bc) = (ab)c$

How would you *regroup* to arrive at 36?

$$6 \cdot 6 = 6 \cdot (2 \cdot 3)$$
$$= (6 \cdot 2) \cdot 3 = 12 \cdot 3 = 36$$

Multiplicative Inverse (Reciprocal): Dividing by a = Multiplying by ($\frac{1}{a}$) Commutative Property of Multiplication: $ab = ba$ and Associative Property of Multiplication: $a(bc) = (ab)c$

How would you *rearrange* to arrive at 36?

$$6 \cdot 6 = 6 \cdot \left(\frac{18}{3} \right)$$
$$= 6 \cdot \left[18 \cdot \left(\frac{1}{3} \right) \right] = 6 \cdot \left[\left(\frac{1}{3} \right) \cdot 18 \right]$$
$$= \left[6 \cdot \left(\frac{1}{3} \right) \right] \cdot 18 = \left[\left(\frac{1}{3} \right) \text{ of } 6 \right] \cdot 18$$
$$= 2 \cdot 18 = 36$$

Distributive Property (Multiplication Over Addition): $a(b + c) = ab + ac$ and Commutative Property of Multiplication: $ab = ba$

How would you *rewrite* to arrive at 36?

$$6 \cdot 6 = 6 \cdot (3.5 + 2.5)$$
$$= 6 \cdot \left[\left(3 \text{ and } \frac{1}{2} \right) + \left(2 \text{ and } \frac{1}{2} \right) \right]$$
$$= 6 \cdot \left[\left(3 + \frac{1}{2} \right) + \left(2 + \frac{1}{2} \right) \right]$$
$$= \left[6 \cdot \left(3 + \frac{1}{2} \right) \right] + \left[6 \cdot \left(2 + \frac{1}{2} \right) \right]$$
$$= \left[(6 \cdot 3) + \left(6 \cdot \frac{1}{2} \right) \right] + \left[(6 \cdot 2) + \left(6 \cdot \frac{1}{2} \right) \right]$$
$$= [18 + (\text{half of } 6)] + [12 + (\text{half of } 6)]$$
$$= [18 + 3] + [12 + 3]$$
$$= 21 + 15 = 36$$

Distributive Property (Multiplication Over Addition): $a(b + c) = ab + ac$ or First Outside Inside Last (FOIL): $(a + b) \cdot (c + d) = ac + ad + bc + bd$ and Commutative Property of Multiplication: $ab = ba$

How would you *recall* to arrive at 36?

$$6 \cdot 6 = (4 + 2) \cdot (4 + 2)$$
$$= [4 \cdot (4 + 2)] + [2 \cdot (4 + 2)]$$
$$= [(4 \cdot 4) + (4 \cdot 2)] + [(2 \cdot 4) + (2 \cdot 2)]$$
$$= [16 + 8] + [8 + 4]$$
$$= 24 + 12 = 36$$

FOIL: $(a + b) \cdot (c + d) = ac + ad + bc + bd$ and Order of Operations: Parentheses/Exponents/Multiply or Divide/Add or Subtract (PEMDAS)

How would you *respond* to arrive at 36?

$$
\begin{aligned}
6 \cdot 6 &= (3 + 3) \cdot (3 + 3) \\
&= (3 \cdot 3) + (3 \cdot 3) + (3 \cdot 3) + (3 \cdot 3) \\
&= 4 \cdot (3 \cdot 3) \\
&= 4 \cdot 3^2 \\
&= 4 \cdot 9 = 36
\end{aligned}
$$

After introducing the flexible arithmetic concept, step back and allow students to create their own arithmetic relationships that illustrate the various number properties exhibited above. Tailor the degree of difficulty to match students' ability levels and willingness to explore different approaches.

CALCULATOR APPLICATION

Multiplication Facts

```
PROGRAM:FLSHCRDS
:Lbl 99
:randInt(1,10) → A
:randInt(1,10) → B
:Disp "WHAT_IS," A
:Disp "TIMES," B
:Pause
:Disp "_"
:Disp A × B
:Disp "_"
:Pause
:ClrScreen
:Goto 99
```

The application shown in the sidebar, using the TI-73 Explorer, is an original program titled "FLSHCRDS." Like Flash Cards, it is designed to help students practice and master multiplication facts through random number-generated multiplication problems:

NOTE: For help with any aspect of writing, editing, executing, or sharing programs, please refer to the Programming chapters in the Graphing Calculator Guidebooks, which accompany the TI-73 (Chap. 12) and the TI-83/84 Plus (Chap. 16).

Using the Application With Students

Your Input	Output (Example)
Press: **ON** **PRGM** (*Scroll down to* **FLSHCRDS**)	
ENTER	**prgmFLSHCRDS**

ENTER	**WHAT IS**
	     3
	 TIMES
	     4

ENTER	**WHAT IS**
	     3
	 TIMES
	     4
	     12

Your Input	**Output (Example)**

ENTER

WHAT IS
9
TIMES
7

ENTER

WHAT IS
9
TIMES
7
63

ENTER

(for a new question, etc.)

Instructional Ideas

1. There are a couple of reasons why two **Pause** steps were included in the "**FLSHCRDS**" program. First, for teachers working in a whole-class setting, using this program on one's overhead with a ViewScreen attachment allows for lots of questions to be posed rapid-fire for students seated around the room.

   Second, for those who wish to (or need to) work one-on-one, students can use the program and answer as many questions as circumstances warrant while practicing under direct adult supervision.

2. The **randInt(0,10)** steps were preset to generate random integers to be multiplied (or "multiplicands") between 0 and 10, inclusive. Those numbers can easily be adjusted higher or lower in the program (under "EDIT") to match student ability levels.

3. If any of your students need to reinforce their addition and/or subtraction skills, then this program can also be edited by first changing the word "TIMES" to either "PLUS" or "MINUS" and then replacing the "X" sign with either "+" or "−," respectively.

4. When you are finished and wish to escape the program, press the following:

2nd OFF

ON

CLEAR

MULTIPLYING INTEGERS

> ### Grades 6–8
>
> This activity shows students how to develop an example to justify the rule. Try simple arithmetic as an invitation to help your students recognize patterns and then to extend their thinking into more formal mathematical statements open to further inquiry and discussion. This activity correlates to the following highlighted expectation for students:
>
> - Understand numbers, ways of *representing numbers,* relationships among numbers, and number systems
> - **Understand meanings of operations and how they *relate* to one another**
> - *Compute* fluently and make reasonable estimates

In this activity, students explore a logical argument supported by combining four number properties—two new ones and two others from the previous activity:

- Additive identity property: $a + (-a) = 0$
- Symmetric property of equality: if $a = b$, then $b = a$
- Distributive property (multiplication over addition): $a(b + c) = ab + ac$
- Commutative property of multiplication: $ab = ba$

An effective instructional approach is to use the time-tested **scientific method.** First, consider Pólya's (1951) four-step interpretation of the scientific method: understand, plan, execute, and look back. A good way to help students remember those four steps is to use the mnemonic U-PLEX-L (*U*nderstand, *PL*an, *EX*ecute, *L*ook back).

Students should *understand,* for example, that $(+3) \cdot 0 = 0$ and that $(+2) + (-2) = 0$ by the additive identity property and then that $0 = (+2) + (-2)$ by the symmetric property of equality.

The *plan* is to substitute $(+2) + (-2)$ for 0. The *execution* is inherent in the distributive property phase.

The rule comes from the last, or *look back,* step. Reading vertically, note that $(+3) \cdot (+2) = (+6)$ but that $(+3) \cdot (-2)$ must be (-6), which is the whole essence of Rule 1: A positive times a negative is a negative.

Rule 1: A Positive Times a Negative Is a Negative

Since $(+3) \cdot 0 = 0$ (any nonzero integer times zero equals zero) and since $(+2) + (-2) = 0$, then

$$(+3) \cdot [0] = 0$$
$$(+3) \cdot [(+2) + (-2)] = 0 \text{ (substitution)}$$
$$[(+3) \cdot (+2)] + [(+3) \cdot (-2)] = 0 \text{ (distributive property)}$$
$$[(+6)] + [?] = 0$$

What must the value of *?* be to get an overall result of 0?
According to the additive identity property, $? = (-6)$.

Rule 2: A Negative Times a Negative Is a Positive

Since $(-2) \cdot 0 = 0$ and since $(+3) + (-3) = 0$, then

$$(-2) \cdot [0] = 0$$
$$(-2) \cdot [(+3) + (-3)] = 0 \text{ (substitution)}$$
$$[(-2) \cdot (+3)] + [(-2) \cdot (-3)] = 0 \text{ (distributive property)}$$
$$[(+3) \cdot (-2)] + [?] = 0 \text{ (commutative property)}$$
$$[(-6)] + [?] = 0$$

What must the value of *?* *have* to be to get an overall result of 0?
According to the additive identity property, $? = (+6)$.

One Step Further

Challenge students to uncover a signs pattern connecting both of the preceding rules. Encourage further exploration by having students use a four-function calculator for checking and by having them work through division problems.

- If the signs of both integers are the *same,* their product is *positive.*
- If the signs of both integers are *different,* their product is *negative.*

AREAS AND MENTAL ARITHMETIC

> ### Grades 6–10
>
> This activity clarifies that $a^2 - b^2 = (a + b) \bullet (a - b)$, which is the difference of two squares, and connects algebra and geometry. This activity correlates to the following highlighted expectation for students:
>
> - Understand numbers, ways of *representing* numbers, relationships among numbers, and number systems
> - Understand meanings of operations and how they *relate* to one another
> - ***Compute* fluently and make reasonable estimates**

The human brain is an incredibly powerful calculator and a much faster device than a four-function calculator. To help students tap that brainpower, share with them some of the secrets that you, as their teacher, possess. The following paper-cutting activity is a good way to reveal one of those secrets.

The activities of paper folding and paper cutting have been designed to help students see abstract concepts from algebra by touching, moving, and interpreting real objects of their own design (Sobel & Maletsky, 1988). The following activity provides a glimpse into a host of engaging opportunities for students to sharpen a wide variety of their mathematical skills.

Before you begin, make sure students understand that the area of a rectangle is measured in square units. It can be found in either of two ways:

1. Counting the number of square units within the rectangle *or* (if counting a discrete number of squares is not possible)

2. Using the formula $A = \text{length} \bullet \text{width} = l \bullet w$

Each student needs the following materials:

- One piece of square paper (size does not matter)
- Scissors
- A four-function calculator
- One piece of $8\frac{1}{2} \times 11$-inch paper
- A sharp pencil

Discovering the Secret

1. Using a square piece of paper, make a diagonal crease running from the top-left corner to the bottom-right corner. With the square open, label the left and top sides *a*. See Figure 1.1.

2. Mark a point about a third of the way up the diagonal from the bottom-right corner. Draw two perpendicular lines from that point. See Figure 1.1.

3. Cut along the two perpendicular lines you drew in Step 2 to detach a square from the bottom-right corner. Label the left and top edges of the just-removed square *b*. Label the remaining two sides of the new hexagon *a* – *b*. See Figure 1.2.

4. Cut the hexagon along the creased diagonal to make two congruent trapezoids.

5. Flip over the left-hand trapezoid, and slide the two trapezoids together to form a rectangle. See Figure 1.3.

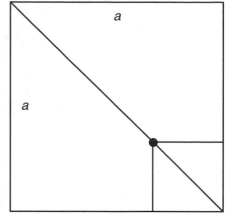

Figure 1.1

Once you work through the activity with students, share the following formula, or secret, with them:

If the hexagon (the original square piece of paper with the small square cut out of one corner) has area = $a^2 - b^2$

and

If the resulting rectangle (formed by flipping and sliding one of the two congruent trapezoids) has area = $(a + b) \cdot (a - b)$

and

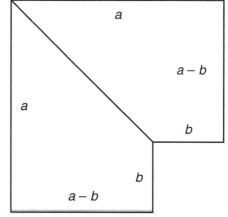

Figure 1.2

If the hexagon and the rectangle both have the same area

Then $a^2 - b^2 = (a + b) \cdot (a - b)$

An algebra student might recognize that formula as having resulted from factoring (the difference of two squares), but note how the formula is simply a summary of moving pieces of paper a certain way to make geometric figures and study their areas.

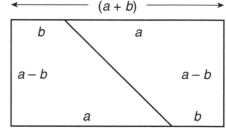

Figure 1.3

Performing Mental Arithmetic

With the paper-cutting process now complete, focus students' attention on how they can perform mental arithmetic (specifically, multiplying two-digit numbers by two-digit numbers) much more quickly than they can with a calculator. As a prerequisite exercise, challenge your students to identify all **perfect square** numbers from 1 to 625, inclusive. These numbers constitute one of the easiest and most prevalent groups of natural numbers for students to remember. These numbers continuously reappear throughout students' entire mathematical experience—from multiplication tables to area formulas to the Pythagorean Theorem to the Quadratic Formula and beyond.

Any number that is the product of the same two whole-number factors is a perfect square. Those numbers of 1 to 625, inclusive, are as follows:

1	16	49	100	169	256	361	484
4	25	64	121	196	289	400	529
9	36	81	144	225	324	441	576
							625

Now challenge students to solve the equation $22 \cdot 18 = ?$ by following these three steps:

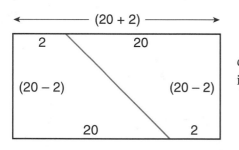

Figure 1.4

Step 1

Compute the **mean** (average) of 22 and 18. It may appear difficult at first, but the quickest and most efficient way to do this is to identify the middle number between 22 and 18, which is 20.

Step 2

Determine how far apart either 22 is from 20 *or* 20 is from 18. That "space" either way is 2.

Step 3

Try to imagine how the rectangle and the hexagon would look with the numbers 20 and 2 in place of the letters *a* and *b*, respectively. See Figures 1.4 and 1.5.

$$22 \cdot 18 = (20 + 2) \cdot (20 - 2)$$

Rearrange the rectangle to look like the hexagon again:

$$(20 + 2) \cdot (20 - 2) = 20^2 - 2^2$$
(area of big square minus little square)
$$= 400 - 4$$
$$= 396$$

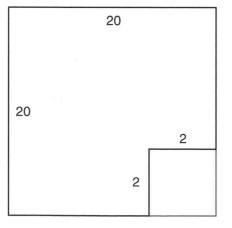

Figure 1.5

CALCULATOR APPLICATION

Perfect Squares

```
PROGRAM:PERFSQRS
:ClrScreen
:Disp "THE_FIRST_25"
:Disp "PERF._SQUARES"
:For (A, 1, 25, 1)
:Disp A²
:Pause
:End
```

Any number that is the product of the same two whole-number factors is referred to as a "perfect square." The subset of perfect squares from 1 to 625, inclusive, can be generated with the application at the right, an original program titled "**PERFSQRS**":

NOTE: The command "ClrScreen" for TI-73 users is the same as the command "ClrHome" for TI-83/84 Plus users.

Using the Application With Students

Your Input	Output
Press: **ON** **PRGM** (*Scroll down to* **PERFSQRS**)	
ENTER	prgmPERFSQRS
ENTER	THE FIRST 25 PERF. SQUARES 1
ENTER	THE FIRST 25 PERF. SQUARES 1 4
ENTER	THE FIRST 25 PERF. SQUARES 1 4 9
ENTER (*for the next perfect square, etc.*)	16 25 36 49 64

(Continued)

(Continued)

Your Input	**Output**
	81
	100
	121
	144
	169
	196
	225
	256
	289
	324
	361
	400
	441
	484
	529
	576
	625

Pressing **ENTER** after reading the last number in the list (625) yields:

prgmPERFSQRS

Done

Instructional Ideas

1. The **Pause** step included in the "**PERFSQRS**" program lets teachers working in a whole-class setting use this program on one's overhead with a ViewScreen attachment for either recitation or call-upon purposes.

    Students may not realize the importance of becoming very familiar with these numbers. But many situations exist—simplifying radicals, Pythagorean Theorem, and Quadratic Formula exercises, to name three—in which recognizing perfect squares makes the problem at hand much easier to solve.

2. An interesting sidelight to this list involves a sequence of increasing odd numbers. Note that each successive perfect square is the next odd-number difference away from its immediate predecessor. Starting from zero, $0 \underline{+1} = 1$, $1 \underline{+3} = 4$, $4 \underline{+5} = 9$, $9 \underline{+7} = 16$, $16 \underline{+9} = 25$, and so on.

    For a more visual explanation, please refer to the building of squares with two-color counting tiles in the "Visual Thinking" unit of Chapter 7.

3. As was the case with the "**FLSHCRDS**" program, the number 25 in this program can be adjusted according to student ability levels.

4. When you receive the **Done** statement and wish to escape,

    Press: **CLEAR**

    However, if you desire an immediate replay after being told you are done,

    Press: **ENTER**

Let's Review

Step 1: Find the middle number between the two given *multiplicands* (the two numbers being multiplied). This number is the same as the larger number in the paper hexagon.

Step 2: Count how far away that middle number is from either of the two multiplicands. This number is the same as the smaller number in the paper hexagon (one side of the cut-out square).

Step 3: Square the larger number (from Step 1) and subtract from it the square of the smaller number (from Step 2) to get the answer.

The following are some additional equations that you can use to challenge your students:

$$18 \cdot 12 = ?$$
Answer: $18 \cdot 12 = (15 + 3) \cdot (15 - 3) = 15^2 - 3^2 = 225 - 9 = 216$

$$23 \cdot 15 = ?$$
Answer: $23 \cdot 15 = (19 + 4) \cdot (19 - 4) = 19^2 - 4^2 = 361 - 16 = 345$

One Step Further

Test your students' estimation skills. Have them show that the number 9,991 is composite (that is, *not* prime).

Have students estimate and then visualize backward (recall "Discovering the Secret") and think from the hexagon to the rectangle.

$$9{,}991 = 10{,}000 - 9 = 100^2 - 3^2 = (100 + 3) \cdot (100 - 3) = 103 \cdot 97$$
$$a^2 - b^2 = (a + b) \cdot (a - b)$$

Algebra 2

According to the standards listed in *Principles and Standards for School Mathematics* (National Council of Teachers of Mathematics [NCTM], 2000), all students in Grades 6 through 12 should be able to do the following:

The Algebra Standard is a natural extension of numbers in that students progress from the certainty of constant values to the more abstract realm of variables. Just as with the Number and Operations Standard in the last chapter, experiencing algebra in the elementary grades helps foster an understanding that should be continuously strengthened throughout the later grades.

The first two activities are nontraditional yet engaging. In Fibonacci Patterns, students encounter a variety of interesting number and geometry patterns that allow them to use generalized thinking to develop and test formalized algebraic relationships. Constructing Logs is similar to Fibonacci Patterns, only in this activity, older students draw on their knowledge of scientific notation and three standard rules of logarithms to construct a better understanding of the origins of some log constants.

Visualizing Equations allows students to model and manipulate hands-on symbol representations within a rule-specific, problem-solving context. Students working with Straw Balances not only expand on the keep-two-sides-balanced model, but they are also invited to use their newly learned descriptive and predictive abilities in a host of interesting extended activities. The last activity, Finite Differences Equations, focuses on the notion of change—how to recognize it in a data set and how to use a pattern of change to reconstruct the equation that originally generated the given data.

FIBONACCI PATTERNS

Grades 6–11

This activity illustrates how a problem can create a number of patterns. It also provides an opportunity for students to build on their algebraic knowledge. This activity correlates to the following highlighted expectation for students:

- **Understand *patterns*, relations, and functions**
- Represent and analyze mathematical situations and structures using algebraic symbols
- Use mathematical models to represent and understand quantitative *relationships*
- Analyze *change* in various contexts

In the thirteenth century, Leonardo Fibonacci introduced the following rabbit reproduction problem (Garland, 1987):

> If a pair of adult rabbits is put into a walled enclosure to breed, how many pairs will there be in that enclosure after one year if, every month, each adult pair therein produces one new pair of rabbits (one male and one female) that matures and begins to bear young two months after its own birth? Assume that no rabbits in this enclosure die during the year.

This problem teaches naturally occurring **sequences** (two numbers add up to make a third, the second and third add up to make a fourth, the third and fourth add up to make a fifth, and so on). The notion of recursion (repeating) is illustrated by how many life systems actually reproduce.

Figure 2.1 and the accompanying question constitute a modern-day variation on Fibonacci's rabbit reproduction problem.

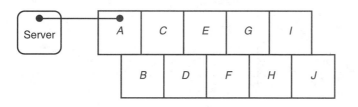

Figure 2.1

Show students Figure 2.1, and then explain that a defense company has hired a computer network specialist to wire a connection of computer stations for all 10 of its workers. As Figure 2.1 illustrates, first, the workers are ranked in importance from the office supervisor (*A*) down to the most recently hired worker (*J*). Second, every worker has at least two physically adjacent stations.

(Worker *F*, for example, has *four,* as his workstation borders coworkers *D, E, G,* and *H.*) Third, for reasons of national security, workers *B* through *J* may send information to the network server (the computer network's "mothership") from their computer only through the supervisor's (*A*) computer (as designated by the visible link).

Once the network is complete, input flows one way *into* the server, doing so on a seniority (decreasing-letter) basis. Input must also "go through channels," flowing first to a computer physically adjacent to one's location. For example, worker *B* (assistant supervisor) may send files to the server only one way (through worker *A*). Worker *C* may send files to the server using either one of two routes: from worker *C* to worker *A* (and on to the server) *or* from worker *C* to worker *B* to worker *A* (and on to the server).

As you work down the line, input can flow via several possible permutations. A permutation is any arrangement of numbers (or letters, objects, or events) in which *order* is also important.

Getting back to the computer network scenario, ask students how many possible paths (or permutations) files may take to get to the server from worker *J*.

First, have students consider some general methods of thinking, or heuristics (Pólya, 1951). The term *heuristics* is synonymous with the concept of thinking strategies, and there are several that you can encourage potential problem solvers to learn. Those include the following (in no particular order): guess and check, make a table, look for a pattern, make an organized list, solve a simpler problem, work backward, draw a picture, plot points, and visualize a graph and/or write an equation (play "guess my rule").

One problem-solving strategy for the computer network scenario would be to consider the first stages of the problem, organize those results in a table, and see if a pattern presents itself therein.

Initiating Worker	Paths to Server (S)	Total Permutations
A	*direct line (to S)*	1
B	B-A-S	1
C	C-A-S C-B-A-S	2
D	D-B-A-S D-C-A-S D-C-B-A-S	3
E	E-C-A-S E-C-B-A-S E-D-B-A-S E-D-C-A-S E-D-C-B-A-S	5

Upon analyzing the results in the final Total Permutations column, students will see that adding the first two numbers (1 and 1) yields the third number (2), that adding the second and third numbers (1 and 2) yields the fourth number (3), and so on.

Point out to students that any ordered set of quantities in which numbers are generated using some predetermined underlying rule is called a sequence.

Beginning with the numbers 1 and 1, the Fibonacci Sequence comprises numbers formed by the sum of the two preceding ones:

$$1, 1, 2, 3, 5, 8, 13, 21, 34, 55\ldots$$

Therefore, by matching the numbers in the Fibonacci Sequence here to the results from the Total Permutations column, the answer to "How many possible paths, or permutations, may files take to get to the server from worker *J*?" would be the same as the 10th number (corresponding to worker *J*) in the sequence—that is, 55 paths.

Magic Sum (Grades 7–9)

Students can sharpen their mental arithmetic ability and reinforce some algebra skills with this interesting activity that extends what they learned with the above Fibonacci Sequence.

Each student needs the following materials:

- One piece of lined 8½ × 11-inch paper
- A four-function calculator
- A sharp pencil

To illustrate the "Magic Sum" to your students, you might have a conversation such as the one that follows:

Teacher: Turn on your calculators, and add the first 10 numbers of the Fibonacci Sequence (highlighted above). You should get the sum 143.

Students verify that result: $1 + 1 + 2 + 3 + 5 + 8 + 13 + 21 + 34 + 55 = 143$.

(NOTE: The term for the sum of the numbers in a sequence is a **series**.)

Teacher: Now, let's pick two numbers other than 1 and 1, such as 4 and 8, to help us build a new 10-number Fibonacci Sequence. Put your calculators aside until you're done.

Students: $S_1 = 4, 8, 12, 20, 32, 52, 84, 136, 220, 356$.

(NOTE: S_1 is read "*S* sub one" and represents the first arithmetic series [or summation].)

Teacher allows students to figure out the sequence first before putting numbers up on the blackboard.

Teacher: If you add those 10 numbers on your calculator, you should get a sum of 924.

Students: Wait a minute! You knew the answer already because you picked the first two numbers before class and then used your own calculator to add them!

Teacher: OK. I need two volunteers to choose any two numbers, starting with numbers from 1 to 10. We will then each make another 10-number Fibonacci Sequence and then add up all 10 numbers without anyone using a calculator.

For the sake of illustration, suppose one volunteer selects 9 and a second volunteer selects 6. The Fibonacci Sequence that all students should write on their papers (and the teacher following on the blackboard) is as follows:

$$S_2 = 9, 6, 15, 21, 36, 57, 93, 150, 243, 393.$$

Teacher: If you add the 10 numbers on your calculator, you should get a sum of 1,023.

Students: How did you do that so fast? What's the trick?

Teacher: Just multiply the seventh number of the sequence by 11.

Students verify results with their calculators.

Students: Why does that work?

The teacher uses the following One Step Further to explain why this works.

One Step Further

Use a different notation for the numbers in any 10-number Fibonacci Sequence: F_1 = the first number, F_2 = the second number, F_3 = the third number, and so on. This 10-number Fibonacci Sequence would look as follows: F_1, F_2, F_3, F_4, F_5, F_6, F_7, F_8, F_9, F_{10}.

Note also that since the first two numbers do not *necessarily* have to be 1 and 1 (although in the traditional Fibonacci Sequence, they are), it is possible to let $F_1 = a$ and $F_2 = b$ for any first two numbers. Since $F_3 = F_1 + F_2$, it then follows that $F_3 = a + b$, and so on. The first 10 numbers of the general Fibonacci Sequence would then be represented in a more abstract way:

$$F_1 = a$$
$$F_2 = b$$
$$F_3 = F_1 + F_2 \rightarrow F_3 = a + b$$
$$F_4 = F_2 + F_3 \rightarrow F_4 = a + 2b$$
$$F_5 = F_3 + F_4 \rightarrow F_5 = 2a + 3b$$
$$F_6 = F_4 + F_5 \rightarrow F_6 = 3a + 5b$$
$$F_7 = F_5 + F_6 \rightarrow F_7 = 5a + 8b$$
$$F_8 = F_6 + F_7 \rightarrow F_8 = 8a + 13b$$
$$F_9 = F_7 + F_8 \rightarrow F_9 = 13a + 21b$$
$$F_{10} = F_8 + F_9 \rightarrow F_{10} = 21a + 34b$$

The sum for this general Fibonacci Sequence is as follows:

$$F_1 + F_2 + F_3 + \ldots + F_{10} = 55a + 88b$$
$$= 11 \bullet (5a + 8b)$$
$$= 11 \bullet (F_7)$$

Refer back to the exchange between teacher and students.

The sum for S_1 = 4, 8, 12, 20, 32, 52, 84, 136, 220, 356 would be as follows:
$$= 84 \bullet 11 = 84 \bullet (10 + 1) = (84 \bullet 10) + (84 \bullet 1) = 840 + 84$$
$$= 840 + (100 - 16) = (840 + 100) - 16 = 940 - 16 = 924$$

The sum for S_2 = 9, 6, 15, 21, 36, 57, 93, 150, 243, 393 would be as follows:
$$= 93 \bullet 11 = 93 \bullet (10 + 1) = (93 \bullet 10) + (93 \bullet 1) = 930 + 93$$
$$= 930 + (100 - 7) = (930 + 100) - 7 = 1030 - 7 = 1023$$

With a little practice, you can recall this approach or come up with your own algorithm for multiplying mentally by 11. Some students can learn to do this fairly easily, but it might be a bit of a reach for others.

Another Step Further

One may also take any four consecutive numbers from anywhere in any Fibonacci Sequence—call them A, B, C, and D—and show that the difference of the squares of the two means (the two middle numbers) equals the product of the extremes:

$$C^2 - B^2 = A \bullet D$$

For an algebra class participation review, have each student select any four numbers from the F_1, F_2, F_3, F_4, F_5, F_6, F_7, F_8, F_9, F_{10} sequence. For example, denoting $F_2 = A$, $F_3 = B$, $F_4 = C$, and $F_5 = D$:

$$
\begin{aligned}
C^2 - B^2 &= A \bullet D \\
F_4^2 - F_3^2 &= F_2 \bullet F_5 \\
(a + 2b)^2 - (a + b)^2 &= b \bullet (2a + 3b) \\
[(a + 2b)(a + 2b)] - [(a + b)(a + b)] &= \\
[a^2 + 4ab + 4b^2] - [a^2 + 2ab + b^2] &= \\
2ab + 3b^2 &= 2ab + 3b^2
\end{aligned}
$$

Interesting Math Fact

Consider the following Fibonacci Sequence: 1, 1, 2, 3, 5, 8, 13, 21, 34, 55, 89, 144, . . .

1. There is one perfect cube ($8 = 2^3$) and two perfect squares (1 and 144).

2. Every third number is divisible by 2.

    Every fourth number is divisible by 3.

    Every fifth number is divisible by 5.

    Every sixth number is divisible by 8.

    Every seventh number is divisible by 13, etc.

3. Square each number in the sequence:

    1, 1, 4, 9, 25, 64, 169, 441, 1,156, 3,025, 7,921, 20,736, . . .

Assuming 0 comes before the first 1, add its adjacent number pairs:

1, 2, 5, 13, 34, 89, 223, . . .

NOTE: Every number in this "hybrid sequence" is the 1st, 3rd, 5th, 7th, 9th, 11th, and so on, of the original Fibonacci Sequence.

Discovery Zone (Grades 9–11)

This section requires students to know some first- and second-year algebra but extends into number relationships and geometric applications (including compass and straightedge constructions).

Each student needs the following materials:

- One piece of lined 8½ × 11-inch paper
- One piece of unlined 8½ × 11-inch paper
- A four-function calculator
- A compass
- A straightedge (e.g., ruler)
- A sharp pencil

Challenge students to identify the positive number "x," whose value is equal to one more than its reciprocal. In other words, solve for x in the equation $x = \left(\frac{1}{x}\right) + 1$.

$$x = \left(\frac{1}{x}\right) + 1 \rightarrow x^2 = 1 + x \quad \rightarrow \text{(by the \textbf{Quadratic Formula})}$$

$$x = \frac{(1 + \sqrt{5})}{2}$$

It is advisable for the reciprocal $\left(\frac{1}{x}\right) = \frac{2}{1+\sqrt{5}}$ to be rationalized, which leads to the value of $\left(\frac{1}{x}\right) = \frac{\sqrt{5}-1}{2}$.

The Golden Section is a geometric proportion seen most prominently in ancient Greek art and architecture. In this activity, students can re-create the construction that Greek mathematicians used to draw, and they can measure precisely those same values for x and for $\left(\frac{1}{x}\right)$.

In Figure 2.2, line segment AB is divided at point C such that $\frac{AB}{AC} = \frac{AC}{CB}$.

Figure 2.2

The longer segment AC is thus defined as the **mean proportional** between the entire segment (AB) and the shorter segment (CB).

If you consider the line segment AB to be of unit length ($AB = 1$) and let $AC = y$ (making $CB = 1 - y$), then, by definition,

$$\frac{1}{y} = \frac{y}{1-y} \rightarrow y^2 + y - 1 = 0 \rightarrow y = \frac{\sqrt{5}-1}{2} = \frac{1}{x} \quad (\text{or } xy = 1)$$

NOTE: The negative root found in using the Quadratic Formula here is extraneous in terms of geometric length.

1. Have students use a four-function calculator to evaluate x and y (both to the nearest thousandth).

    Answer: $x = \dfrac{1 + \sqrt{5}}{2} \approx 1.618$ and $y = \dfrac{\sqrt{5} - 1}{2} \approx 0.618$

2. Then have students run the traditional Fibonacci Sequence out to 20 places.

    Answer: 1, 1, 2, 3, 5, 8, 13, 21, 34, 55, 89, 144, 233, 377, 610, 987, 1,597, 2,584, 4,181, 6,765

3. Then have them divide the 20th number (6,765) by the 19th number (4,181) in that sequence, and then have them do the same for the reciprocal of those two values.

    Answers: $6,765 \div 4,181 = 1.618$ and $4,181 \div 6,765 = 0.618$

4. Have students repeat Step 3 for the following sequences:

    $S_1 = 4, 8, 12, 20, 32, 52, 84, 136, 220, 356, 576, 932, 1,508, 2,440, 3,948, 6,388, 10,336, 16,724, 27,060, 43,784$

    Answers: $43,784 \div 27,060 = 1.618$ and $27,060 \div 43,784 = 0.618$

    $S_2 = 9, 6, 15, 21, 36, 57, 93, 150, 243, 393, 636, 1,029, 1,665, 2,694, 4,359, 7,053, 11,412, 18,465, 29,877, 48,342$

    Answers: $48,342 \div 29,877 = 1.618$ and $29,877 \div 48,342 = 0.618$

5. Ask students the following: What do you notice about the answers in Steps 1, 3, and 4?

6. Ask students another question: What happens when you multiply 1.618×0.618?

CALCULATOR APPLICATION

Fibonacci Sequences

PROGRAM:FIBONNOS	:Disp "_"	:Disp F, G, H, I, J
:ClrHome	:A + B → C	:Pause
(*NOTE:* ClrScreen *for* TI-73 *users*.)	:B + C → D	:ClrHome
	:C + D → E	:Disp
:Disp "PICK_ANY_TWO"	:Disp A, B, C, D, E	"THE_MAGIC_SUM_=_", A
:Disp "NATURAL_NUMBERS"	:Pause	+ B + C + D + E + F + G +
	:Disp "_"	H + I + J
:Disp "_"	:Disp "AND"	:{A, B, C, D, E, F, G, H, I, J} → L1
:Input "1ST_CHOICE_=_",A	:Pause	:I + J → K
:Disp "_"	:D + E → F	:{B, C, D, E, F, G, H, I, J, K} → L2
:Input "2ND_CHOICE_=_",B	:E + F → G	
:Pause	:F + G → H	:Pause
:ClrHome	:G + H → I	:L1/L2 → L3
:Disp "10_FIBONACCIS:"	:H + I → J	

This program, written for TI-83/84 Plus users, allows a student to pick any two numbers and quickly create his or her own 10-number Fibonacci Sequence.

The program (titled "FIBONNOS") actually produces three successive screens when executed. Those three screens are delineated by the placement of the two Pause steps (which forces the student to have to press ENTER to go from screen to screen).

The FIBONNOS program actually performs three interrelated functions:

1. lists the first 10 Fibonacci Sequence numbers,

2. computes the Magic Sum, and

3. computes and lists the ratios of each Fibonacci Sequence number to its immediate successor (allowing the user to view the approximate value of the Golden Ratio, ≈ 0.618, as a limit).

The program begins by asking what two natural (counting) numbers we wish to start with in order to generate 10 numbers in the Fibonacci Sequence. Here, we are using the numbers "1" and "1" to be consistent with the defense company computer network example seen earlier (but any two number choices will work):

Your Input	**Output**
Press: **ON** **PRGM** (*Scroll down to* **FIBONNOS**)	**prgmFIBONNOS**
ENTER	**PICK ANY TWO NATURAL NUMBERS:**

(Continued)

(Continued)

Your Input	Output
1 ENTER	**1ST CHOICE = 1**
1	**2ND CHOICE = 1**

ENTER **ENTER**	**10 FIBONACCIS:** 1 1 2 3 5

ENTER **ENTER**	**AND** 8 13 21 34 55

ENTER	**THE MAGIC SUM =** **143**

ENTER	**{1 .5 .66666666 . . .}**

The last entry, {1   .5   .66666666 . . .}, is significant because it indicates that data have been pasted into a table. The table can be accessed by pressing

STAT

ENTER

Note that the very last entry in the L3 column can be rounded to the aforementioned 0.618.

But even more interesting is how, reading the L3 column from top to bottom, the values "approach" 0.618 from both directions (1 is higher than 0.618, .5 is lower than 0.618, .6667 is higher but closer, .6 is lower but closer, etc.). This effect of squeezing, or approaching, a particular value is key to understanding the concept of limit, one of the chief building blocks of calculus.

L1	L2	L3
1	1	1
1	2	.5
2	3	.66667
3	5	.6
5	8	.625
8	13	.61538
13	21	.61905
21	34	.61765
34	55	.61818
55	89	.61798

One Step Further

This extension uses some compass-and-straightedge construction moves, which are required in most states. The activity helps connect a geometry piece (in which answers are exact) with the previous arithmetic/algebra piece (in which answers are rounded but still very close to those in the geometry extension).

Provide each student with two 1×1 cardboard squares. Instruct students to put them together to create a 1×2 rectangle. See Figure 2.3.

Then have students draw a diagonal line from the top left-hand corner to the bottom right-hand corner. Have students label the diagonal AB and label the bottom left-hand corner (vertex) C. They now have a right triangle ACB. See Figure 2.4.

Since ACB is a right triangle, students may use the Pythagorean Theorem ($c^2 = a^2 + b^2$) to say that $(AB)^2 = 1^2 + 2^2$. (The following *proves* that $AB = \sqrt{5}$.)

Next, take a compass, place its pivot point on A, and swing an arc down from point D to lay off $AE = 1$ along the diagonal (leaving the rest of the diagonal = $EB = \sqrt{5} - 1$).

NOTE: To lay off an arc means that sweeping the compass down with its point on A and its pencil on D, the arc will cross AB at point E, which effectively makes $AD = AE = AC = 1$.

Then, using the compass and a straightedge, construct the **perpendicular bisector** of line segment EB (which makes point F the midpoint of EB). Thus,

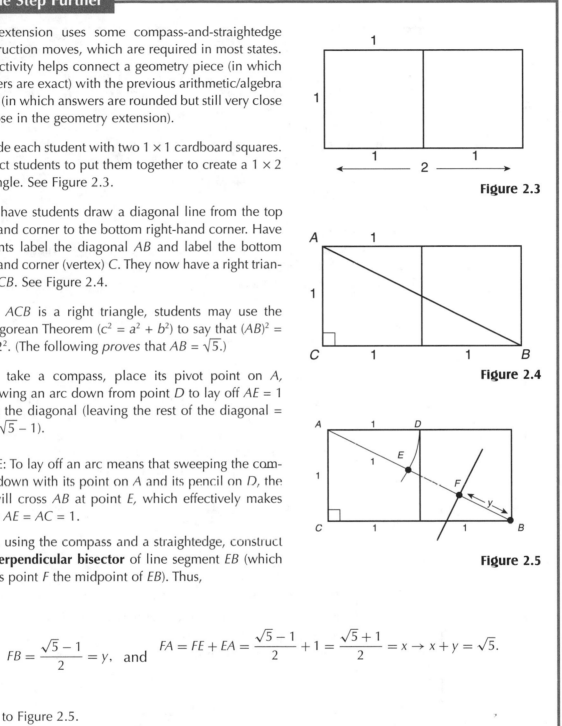

Figure 2.3

Figure 2.4

Figure 2.5

$$FB = \frac{\sqrt{5}-1}{2} = y, \quad \text{and} \quad FA = FE + EA = \frac{\sqrt{5}-1}{2} + 1 = \frac{\sqrt{5}+1}{2} = x \rightarrow x + y = \sqrt{5}.$$

Refer to Figure 2.5.

CONSTRUCTING LOGS

Grades 11–12

This activity is adapted from an abridged version of a lecture given at the State University of New York at Buffalo by one of America's most respected mathematics educators, Gerald Rising, PhD.

This activity helps students develop a feeling for what logs are and a means of estimating their values. It also gives students another opportunity to use such heuristics (Pólya, 1951) as make a table, look for a pattern, solve a simpler problem, and work backward. This activity correlates to the following highlighted expectation for students:

- Understand *patterns*, relations, and functions
- **Represent and analyze mathematical situations and structures using algebraic *symbols***
- Use mathematical models to represent and understand quantitative *relationships*
- Analyze *change* in various contexts

x	$y = \log x$
1	0.00
2	0.30
3	0.48
4	0.60
5	0.70
6	0.78
7	
8	0.90
9	0.96
10	1.00
11	
12	1.08
13	
14	
15	1.18
16	1.20
17	
18	1.26
19	
20	1.30

Figure 2.6

Given that a log is (=) an exponent, set up this activity by giving each student a chart similar to the one shown in Figure 2.6, but missing the y-column numbers (see the appendix for a full-page blackline master of the Log Chart).

Start with the following two entries:

$\log 1 = \log_{10} 1 = 0.00$
$(10^0 = 1)$
$\log 10 = \log_{10} 10 = 1.00$
$(10^1 = 10)$

What students do not realize is that they can predict the remaining y-column values (*without* a calculator) by combining the logs of the first two prime numbers (2 and 3), scientific notation, and some well-timed applications of three basic log rules:

1. $\log (A \cdot B) = \log A + \log B$
2. $\log \left(\dfrac{A}{B}\right) = \log A - \log B$
3. $\log A^N = N \log A$

For example, $\log 2 = ?$

$2^{10} = 1{,}024 = 1.024 \cdot 10^3$ (scientific notation)

$\log 2^{10} = \log (1.024 \cdot 10^3)$ (substitution)

$= \log 1.024 + \log 10^3$

$= \log 1.024 + 3 \log 10$ (Log Rules 1 and 3 above)

$= \text{"almost 0"} + 3 \cdot 1$ (since $\log 10 = 1$)

$10 \log 2 \approx 0 + 3$ (Log Rule 3)

$\log 2 \approx \dfrac{3}{10} \approx 0.30$ (add $\log 2 = 0.30$ to the chart)

Now, how about $\log 3 = ?$

$3^9 = 19{,}683$

$= 20{,}000 \cdot (19{,}683/20{,}000)$ (multiplicative identity: $20{,}000 \cdot 1/20{,}000 = 1$)

$\log 3^9 = \log (20{,}000 \cdot \text{"almost 1"})$ (substitution)

$\approx \log 20{,}000 + \log 1$ (Log Rule 1)

$\approx \log (2 \cdot 10^4) + 0$ (scientific notation and since $\log 1 = 0$)

$9 \log 3 \approx \log 2 + \log 10^4$ (substitution and Log Rules 1 and 3)

$\approx 0.30 + 4 \log 10$ (since $\log 2 = 0.30$ and Log Rule 3)

$\approx 0.30 + 4 \cdot 1$ (since $\log 10 = 1$)

≈ 4.30

$\log 3 \approx \dfrac{4.30}{9} \approx 0.48$ (add $\log 3 = 0.48$ to the chart)

One Step Further

Students already have log 1 = 0, log 2 = 0.30, log 3 = 0.48, and log 10 = 1. Instruct students to fill in the blanks using this information, the three rules of logs, and those aforementioned thinking strategies.

1. Integrate log 2: Since

$$\log 4 = \log 2^2 = 2 \log 2 \approx 2 \cdot 0.30 = 0.60$$

$$\log 8 = \log 2^3 = 3 \log 2 \approx 3 \cdot 0.30 = 0.90$$

$$\log 16 = \log 2^4 = 4 \log 2 \approx 4 \cdot 0.30 = 1.20$$

$$\log 5 = \log \left(\frac{10}{2}\right) = \log 10 - \log 2 \approx 1 - 0.30 = 0.70$$

2. Integrate log 3: Since 6 = 2 • 3,
   log 6 = log (2 • 3) = log 2 + log 3 ≈ 0.30 + 0.48 = 0.78

   Now, think of 12 = either 4 • 3 or 6 • 2
   log 12 = log (4 • 3) = log 4 + log 3 ≈ 0.60 + 0.48 = 1.08

   or = log (6 • 2) = log 6 + log 2 ≈ 0.78 + 0.30 = 1.08

   Since 15 = 5 • 3 → log 15 = log 5 + log 3 ≈ 0.70 + 0.48 = 1.18

   Now, think of 18 = either 9 • 2 or 6 • 3
   log 18 = log 9 + log 2 *or* log 6 + log 3 ≈ 1.26

3. Interpolate logs of prime numbers by averaging

$$\log 7 \approx \frac{\log 6 + \log 8}{2} \approx 0.84$$

$$\log 11 \approx \frac{\log 10 + \log 12}{2} \approx 1.04$$

$$\log 13 \approx \frac{\log 12 + \log 14}{2} \approx 1.11, \text{ etc.}$$

Since 14 = 7 • 2 → log 14 = log (7 • 2) = log 7 + log 2 ≈ 0.84 + 0.30 = 1.14

4. Expand the chart:

   log 20 = log 10 + log 2 ≈ 1 + 0.30 = 1.30
   log 25 = log 5² = 2 log 5 ≈ 2 • 0.70 = 1.40
   log 30 = log 10 + log 3 *or* log 6 + log 5 ≈ 1.48
   log 36 = . . . Think of the possibilities!

VISUALIZING EQUATIONS

Grades 6–10

Gaining wide acceptance as a means to differentiating instruction, the theory of multiple intelligences (Gardner, 1993) suggests that a teacher can create a more engaging classroom environment by identifying students' intelligences and by planning activities that more closely match students' thought processes. Figure 2.7 provides examples for each of the eight intelligences.

Visual/Spatial	Images, graphics, drawings, sketches, maps, charts, doodles, pictures, spatial orientation, puzzles, designs, looks, appeal, mind's eye, imagination, visualization, dreams, nightmares, films, videos
Logical/Mathematical	Reasoning, **deductive** and **inductive** logic, facts, data, information, spreadsheets, databases, sequencing, ranking, organizing, analyzing, proofs, conclusions, judging, evaluations, assessments
Verbal/Linguistic	Words, wordsmiths, speaking, writing, listening, reading, papers, essays, poems, plays, narratives, lyrics, spelling, grammar, foreign languages, memos, bulletins, newsletters, newspapers, e-mail, faxes, speeches, talks, dialogues, debates
Musical/Rhythmic	Music, rhythm, beat, melody, tunes, allegro, pacing, timbre, tenor, soprano, opera, baritone, symphony, choir, chorus, madrigals, rap, rock, rhythm and blues, jazz, classical, folk, ads, jingles
Bodily/Kinesthetic	Art, activity, action, experiential, hands-on, experiments, try, do, perform, play, drama, sports, throw, toss, catch, jump, twist, twirl, assemble, disassemble, form, re-form, manipulate, touch, feel, immerse, participate
Interpersonal/Social	Interact, communicate, converse, share, understand, empathize, sympathize, reach out, care, talk, whisper, laugh, cry, shudder, socialize, meet, greet, lead, follow, gangs, clubs, charisma, crowds, gatherings, twosomes
Intrapersonal/ Introspective	Self, solitude, meditate, think, create, brood, reflect, envision, journal, self-assess, set goals, plot, plan, dream, write, fiction, nonfiction, poetry, affirmations, lyrics, songs, screenplays, commentaries, introspection, inspection
Naturalist	Nature, natural, environment, listen, watch, observe, classify, categorize, discern patterns, appreciate, hike, climb, fish, hunt, snorkle, dive, photograph, trees, leaves, animals, living things, flora, fauna, ecosystem, sky, grass, mountains, lakes, rivers

SOURCE: Adapted with permission from *Problem-Based Learning and Other Curriculum Models for the Multiple Intelligences Classroom* by Robin Fogarty, copyright ©1997 Corwin Press.

Figure 2.7   Gardner's Eight Intelligences

This activity demonstrates an interpretation of how to tap a student's visual/spatial intelligence to make solving a **linear equation** more understandable. It is a solid physical interpretation of solving linear equations associated with equations written in mathematical language. This activity correlates to the following highlighted expectation for students:

- Understand *patterns*, relations, and functions
- Represent and analyze mathematical situations and structures using algebraic *symbols*
- **Use mathematical models to represent and understand quantitative *relationships***
- Analyze *change* in various contexts

Equ-Cube Game

Each student needs the following materials:

- A ruler
- An abundant supply of four-color (white, black, green, and red) inter-locking cubes (any supply of objects in four colors will suffice)
- A graphing calculator (for a later lesson extension)

NOTE: The idea of the Equ-Cube game is to manipulate cubes and interpret—*not* to write out the equations traditionally.

To play the Equ-Cube game, each student receives a set of colored interlocking cubes. Students should have access to 6 to 10 cubes of each color. If supplies are low in a classroom, pair off students. Each colored cube carries its own meaning as follows:

White Cube (W) = Positive Variable (x)

Black Cube (B) = Negative Variable (x)

Green Cube (G) = Positive Constant (number)

Red Cube (R) = Negative Constant (number)

Some of the colored cubes neutralize another color:

A White cancels a Black ($W + B = 0$).
A Green cancels a Red ($G + R = 0$).

Walk through the Equ-Cube game with your class by showing students how to solve the following equation: $5x + 2 = 3x - 2$. Since x is a White cube, the object of the game is for one side to have only White cubes and the other side to have either Green or Red cubes. (A *side* is defined as one of the two work areas a student has on his or her desk when a ruler is placed down vertically in front of the student.)

Students must keep in mind four rules.

Rule 1

If the *same* cube color appears on both sides of the equation, then an equal number of cubes of that color may be removed from both sides.

Translate the given equation, $5x + 2 = 3x - 2$, into the representation shown in Figure 2.8. (The solid black line in the middle is the ruler, which represents the equal sign of the equation.)

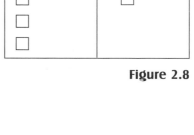

Figure 2.8

According to Rule 1, the student should be able to remove the same number of White cubes—three from each side of the work area (see Figure 2.9). Students should now be able to translate the cubes that remain into $2x + 2 = -2$.

Rule 2

Make one side contain only White cubes.

Rule 3

If cubes of neutralizing colors (White with Black, Green with Red) appear on either side of the equation, then pair them off and remove them.

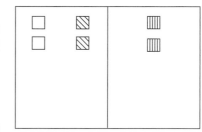

Figure 2.9

Rule 4

If you add cubes of one color on one side, you must also add the same number of cubes of that color to the other side.

By Rule 2, since there are no Black cubes anywhere and only White cubes on the left, students can isolate the White cubes. To accomplish this, have them add two Red cubes to pair off with the two Green cubes (Rule 3) that are already in place (see Figure 2.10).

Remind students that adding two Red cubes on the left side means they must balance the right side by adding two Red cubes (Rule 4).

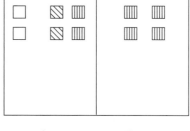

Figure 2.10

Note how Green and Red were paired off and removed from the left side of the work area (see Figure 2.11). The result in abstract terms is $2x = -4$, but "reading" the cubes indicates that for every White, there are two Reds: $x = -2$.

The following is a second question, presented in two-column format. Figures 2.12 through 2.16 represent the work area of a student solving the question by playing the Equ-Cube game (with the first figure representing the translation of terms into color cubes and the equal sign into a ruler). The left-hand column solves the question in the more traditional way.

The challenge is to cover up the right-hand column and *interpret* what the moves in this particular Equ-Cube game actually mean (see Figures 2.12 to 2.16).

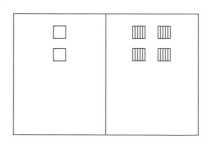

Figure 2.11

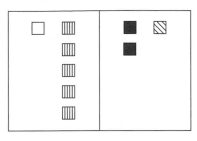

Solve for x:

$$x - 5 = -2x + 1$$

Figure 2.12

$$\begin{array}{rcl} x - 5 &=& -2x + 1 \\ +2x & & +2x \end{array}$$

Figure 2.13

$$3x - 5 = +1$$

Figure 2.14

$$\begin{array}{rcl} 3x - 5 &=& +1 \\ +5 & & +5 \end{array}$$

Figure 2.15

$$3x = +6$$
$$\frac{3x}{3} = \frac{+6}{3}$$
$$x = 2$$

Figure 2.16

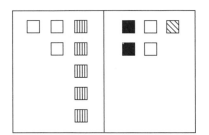

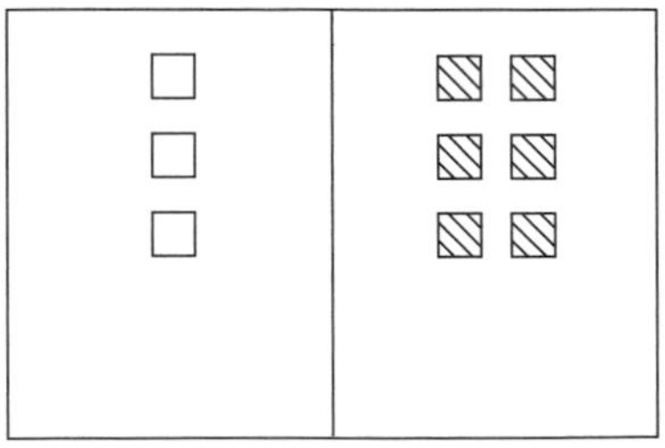

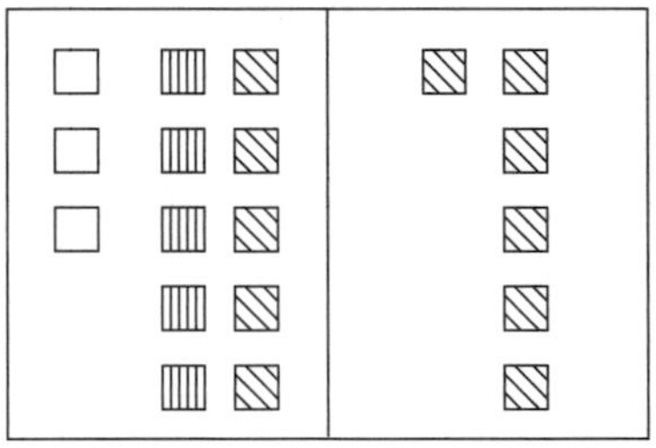

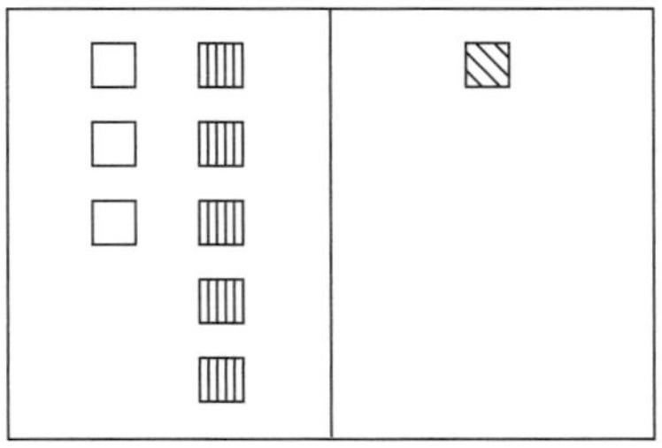

CALCULATOR APPLICATION

Three More Ways to Solve Linear Equations

X	Y1	Y2
−2	−8	−8
−1	−3	−5
0	2	−2
1	7	1
2	12	4
3	17	7
4	22	10

X = −2

NOTE: The Equ-Cube game and, of course, standard algebraic reasoning (transposing) are not the only two ways to solve a linear equation. Recall that the point of this section is to target students' visual intelligence, and a graphing calculator is intended to enhance (and not be a substitute for) the students' learning experience.

Students may use either the TI-73 or the TI-83/84 Plus to solve the equation $5x + 2 = 3x - 2$ for x more creatively.

One method begins by calling (the left side) **$5x + 2 = $ Y1** and (the right side) **$3x - 2 = $ Y2.** The TI-73 can then be used in detective-like fashion to check the answer found earlier ($x = -2$) by following the steps listed below to create the table at the left:

Using the Application With Students

Your Input (TI-73)	**Output**

Press: **ON**

2nd FORMAT

(*Select* **AxesOn**)

2nd PLOT 4

ENTER —— PlotsOff   Done

CLEAR

Go to the **Y=** *screen*

(*and* **CLEAR** *all old lines*)

Y1= (*Type in* **5x + 2**)

ENTER

Y2= (*Type in* **3x − 2**)

Plot1 Plot2 Plot3
\Y1= 5X + 2
\Y2= 3X − 2
\Y3=
\Y4=

ZOOM 4 —— *Result:* Two lines in the first quadrant do not meet but seem to get closer to each other as they move back toward the origin.

ZOOM 6 —— *Result:* The two lines do meet in the third quadrant (which means that the answer for x will be negative).

2nd TBLSET

(*Select* **0, 1, Auto, Auto**)

2nd TABLE

(*Push* **ArrowUp** *to* **x = −2**)

(Continued)

(Continued)

Since the table on the previous page indicates that **Y1 = Y2** when $x = -2$, we conclude that the point $(-2, -8)$ is the common point (and verified by the **ZOOM 6** visual function), and hence the answer to the equation $5x + 2 = 3x - 2$ is $x = -2$.

A second method demonstrates how the TI-83/84 Plus can go one step further by using its built-in intercept finder to pinpoint the answer (refer to Figure 2.17):

Your Input (TI-83/84 Plus)   Output

(NOTE: **2nd STAT PLOT 4** is the equivalent of **2nd PLOT 4** for TI-73 users.) Repeat all the steps above up to and including **ZOOM 6** (and *skip* **ZOOM 4**). Then, rather than go to **2nd TBLSET** or **2nd TABLE,**

Press: **2nd CALC 5**

Now, move the cursor with **ArrowLeft** until you are *close* to the point of intersection (but not directly on it). Then,

Press: **ENTER ENTER ENTER**

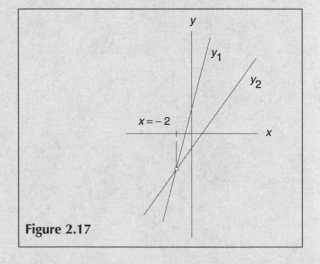

Figure 2.17

Intersection
$x = -2$ $y = -8$
(Figure 2.17)

A third and final use of the calculator involves a new program titled "LINEQTWO," whose secret is nothing more than being able to solve the literal equation $ax + b = cx + d$ for x. After transposing so that terms containing variables and those that are constants move to separate sides of the equation, factoring out the common variable and dividing both sides by the subsequent coefficient quantity reveals $x = (d - b) \div (a - c)$:

PROGRAM:LINEQTWO

:ClrHome

(*NOTE:* ClrScreen *for TI-73 users.*)

:Disp "SOLVE_EQUATIONS"

:Disp "OF_THE_FORM"

:Disp "_"

:Disp "AX_+_B_=_CX_+_D"

:Pause

:ClrHome

:Disp "FOR_AX_+_B"

:Disp "____=_CX_+_D:"

:Disp "_"

:Input "A_=_",A

:Input "B_=_",B

:Disp "_"

:Input "C_=_",C

:Input "D_=_",D

:Pause

:ClrHome

:Disp "X_=_",(D-B) / (A-C) → Frac

:Disp "_"

Your Input	Output
Press: **ON** **PRGM** (*Scroll down to* **LINEQTWO**)	prgmLINEQTWO
ENTER	
ENTER	**SOLVE EQUATIONS** **OF THE FORM** *AX + B = CX + D*
ENTER	**FOR** *AX + B* = *CX + D:* *A* = 5 *B* = 2 *C* = 3 *D* = –2
Recall: 5*x* + 2 = 3*x* – 2 **5 ENTER** **2 ENTER** **3 ENTER** **–2 ENTER**	
ENTER **ENTER**	*X* = –2 **Done**

STRAW BALANCES

> ### Grades 6–10
>
> This simple, yet powerful, activity is adapted from a lesson developed by Ronald Greaves, K–12 science coordinator for the West Irondequoit School District near Rochester, New York.
>
> This activity helps students develop the concepts of inverse and direct relationships using a physical model. This activity correlates to the following highlighted expectation for students:
>
> - Understand *patterns*, relations, and functions
> - Represent and analyze mathematical situations and structures using algebraic *symbols*
> - **Use mathematical models to represent and understand quantitative relationships**
> - Analyze *change* in various contexts

Each student needs the following materials:

- Two 6-inch straws
- Tape
- One piece of 12-inch string (small gauge)
- Scissors
- Six to 10 paper clips
- A metric ruler
- A four-function calculator
- One piece of 8½ × 11-inch lined paper
- One piece of graph paper
- A sharp pencil

Have students take two straws, place them end to end, and carefully connect them by wrapping a small piece of tape around the point where the two straws meet. (Make sure the two 6-inch straws combine to make as straight a 12-inch length as possible.) Then have students use a 12-inch piece of string (you may want to precut these before class) and another small piece of tape and carefully attach the string to the middle of the two straws they just taped together.

You may consider providing older students with needle and thread to poke string through the point where the two straws meet and to help them create a more sensitive balance. (Tell students to tie a knot at the short end of the thread to prevent slippage.) For a variety of safety reasons, however, this option is not recommended for younger students.

When held at arm's length by the long end of the string, each student's straw should dangle parallel to the floor. (If it does not, have students add a small piece of tape to the higher side to give it a little more weight.) Once students achieve balance with their straws, instruct them to take a small piece of masking tape and tape the long end of the string to the edge of their desks so that their straws dangle parallel to the floor.

Then ask students the following questions:

1. What does it mean (in mathematical terms) for your straw to be balanced?

    Answer: It's parallel to the floor.

2. Take one paper clip and slide it over one end of your straw (anywhere between the string and the end). What happened?

    Answer: The straw balance dips on one side.

3. Slide a second paper clip over the other end. If you want to achieve straw balance with both of these paper clips, what must you do?

    Answer: Slide over the second paper clip so that its distance from the center string is exactly the same as the first clip's distance from the center string.

4. Link (hook) a third paper clip onto one of the two clips already being used. If you want to achieve straw balance with all three of the paper clips, now what must you do?

    Answer: Move the two on one side closer to the center string.

5. Assuming that your straw is balanced, take your metric ruler and measure the distance from the center string (fulcrum) to the one paper clip and then from the center string to the two linked paper clips on the other side of your straw. Record your measurements.

    Answer: The single paper clip should be twice as far away from the fulcrum as the two linked clips are.

6. Write an equation with all four of the numbers you now have.

    Answer: Two variables (in this case, let x = number of linked paper clips and y = distance in centimeters from the center string) are inversely proportional to each other if their product is always the same (k = a constant):

    $$(xy)_{\text{left side}} = (xy)_{\text{right side}} = k$$

7. Predict how far away from the center string on the left two linked paper clips would have to be to balance three linked paper clips 4 centimeters away from the center string on the right. Then, actually conduct the experiment to test your findings.

Answer: $2 \cdot 6 = 3 \cdot 4$

Five Steps Further

1. Have students compare the Straw Balance activity with the Equ-Cube game. Both activities involve the hands-on solution of equations. While the Straw Balance is limited to multiplication and division, it *does* make allowance for decimals and fractions.

2. It is important to recognize interdisciplinary connections to science when appropriate. Here, **inverse proportionality** can be applied to environmental science (e.g., the more population in a confined environment, the less resources per living unit) and to physical science (e.g., Boyle's law states that decreasing the volume of a balloon increases the balloon's pressure).

    In the Straw Balance activity, increasing one variable on one side of the equation (number of paper clips) meant that students had to decrease the other variable (the distance from the center) to retain balance with the other side. In other words, as one variable increases (e.g., population in the environment or the pressure one creates by sitting on a balloon to demonstrate Boyle's law), the other variable decreases (e.g., available resources in the environment or the volume inside of that pressed-upon balloon).

3. Suppose that $x = 1$ paper clip was $y = 12$ centimeters away from the center string. Challenge your algebra class to do two things:

    a. Give all possible whole-number permutations of x and y that will balance (in this case, $xy = 12$). When $x = 2$, $y = 6$; when $x = 6$, $y = 2$; when $x = 3$, $y = 4$; when $x = 4$, $y = 3$; when $x = 12$, $y = 1$; and when $x = 1$, $y = 12$. In other words, as one variable increases in value, the other decreases—just as the increase in the number of paper clips means a decrease in how far away they can be from the center.

    b. Using graph paper and a pencil, draw an equilateral hyperbola (see Figure 2.18).

    c. To check the accuracy of your graph, let the graphing calculator "String the Beads" for you. The process involves highlighting points on a scatterplot and then running a selected function through them in a sewing-like fashion:

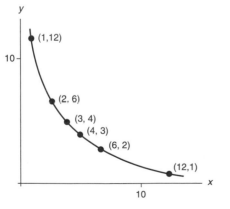

Figure 2.18

Your Input (TI-73)   **Output**

Press: **ON**

2nd FORMAT

(*Select* **AxesOn**)

2nd PLOT 4

(*NOTE:* 2nd STAT PLOT 4
for TI-83/84 users.)

ENTER

PlotsOff	Done

CLEAR

Go to the **Y =** *screen*

(*and* **CLEAR** *all old lines*)

2nd MEM 6

(*NOTE:* 2nd MEM 4 *for
TI-83/84 users.*)

ENTER

ClrAllLists	
	Done

CLEAR

LIST

(*NOTE:* STAT 1 *for
TI-83/84 users.*)

(*Push* **ArrowLeft** *so that
the black block is directly
under the* **L1** *heading*)

1 ENTER 2   ENTER

3 ENTER 4   ENTER

6 ENTER 12 ENTER

(*Push* **ArrowRight** *so that
the black block is directly
under the* **L2** *heading*)

12 ENTER 6 ENTER
4   ENTER 3 ENTER
2   ENTER 1 ENTER

L1	L2	L3
1	12	-----
2	6	
3	4	
4	3	
6	2	
12	1	
-----	-----	
L2(7) =		

2nd QUIT

2nd PLOT 1

(*NOTE:* 2nd STAT PLOT 1
for TI-83/84 users.) (*Select:*
On, Scatterplot, L1, L2, Bead)

(*NOTE: All list headings are found
under* **2nd STAT** *for TI-73 users
or* **2nd LIST** *for TI-83/84 users.*)

ZOOM 7

(*NOTE:* **ZOOM 9**
for TI-83/84 users.)

Go to the **Y** = *screen*
Y1= (*Type in* **12 ÷ x**)

GRAPH

Result: Since the graph "strings the beads," **Y = 12 ÷ x** (or the more familiar **xy = 12**), is the correct rule (or function) for this problem.

4. The number of paper clips used in this unit thus far has conveniently been chosen as a factor of 12. Now change the number of paper clips to get results that involve decimals (through actual measurements) and mixed numbers (through algebraic substitutions).

   a. Place 2 paper clips 6 cm away from the fulcrum on one side. On the other side, measure with the ruler to see how far away

5, 8, 9, and 10 clips, respectively, would need to be positioned to achieve straw balance:

Results: 5 paper clips are 2.4 cm away, 8 paper clips are 1.5 cm away, 9 paper clips are about 1.3 cm away, and 10 paper clips are 1.2 cm away. Those increasing clips/decreasing distances should be consistent with the inverse relationship described thus far.

b. Now see if that real-life data match what we know algebraically. If we return to the **Y1 = 12 ÷ x** form of our equation, it should follow that

For 5 paper clips: Y = $12 \div 5 = 2\frac{2}{5} =$ **2.4 cm**

For 8 paper clips: Y = $12 \div 8 = 1\frac{1}{2} =$ **1.5 cm**

For 9 paper clips: Y = $12 \div 9 = 1\frac{1}{3} =$ **about 1.3 cm**

For 10 paper clips: Y = $12 \div 10 = 1\frac{1}{5} =$ **1.2 cm**

c. Return to the graphing calculator (TI-73) for some quick checking. Right after the **GRAPH** command, provide some new input:

2nd PLOT 4

ENTER

(Screen will say Done—the beads will disappear)

CLEAR

ZOOM 7

(The graph of $xy = 12$ now appears by itself)

TRACE

*(and then type any integer from 1 to 12, inclusive—let's try **5**)*

ENTER

Result: Along the bottom of the screen, read **$x = 5\ y = 2.4$** (or, 5 paper clips would have to be placed 2.4 cm away from the fulcrum).

Press: **CLEAR**

TRACE (Type a new integer)

ENTER for more

5. Hang two baskets (with pipe cleaners and ketchup cups) from both sides of the straw balance. Suppose that $x = 1$ penny in one cup balances $y = 5$ beads in the other cup, $x = 2$ pennies in one cup balance $y = 10$ beads in the other cup, and so on.

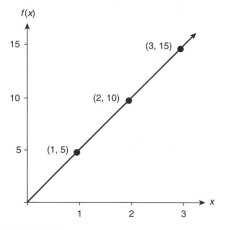

Figure 2.19

Since the baskets are a set distance away from the center on each side, students can think in terms of normal balancing—that is, increasing the number of items placed into one basket means a proportionate increase in items that must go into the other basket. Notice how as one variable goes up, so does the other—similar to the representative straight line when students graph the two variables (see Figure 2.19). The line represents **direct proportionality** (one quantity changes by the same factor as another: $y = 5x$), in which the number of beads in one cup is a function of (or depends on) the number of pennies in the other cup.

FINITE DIFFERENCES EQUATIONS

Grades 8–12

Pick up a traditional secondary mathematics textbook and turn to any section in the book. The order by which material is presented usually follows a prescribed script: introduction, formulas or rules, examples, and in-class and homework exercises. This is the packaged-for-consumption deductive pattern—moving from generalities (formulas) to specifics (examples)—and is the antithesis of the growing amount of do-math-to-know-more-math research (NCTM, 2000).

In fact, working professionals will be quick to tell you how out of touch deductive thinking is with the real world. Outside the classroom, data are generated, people create and test hypotheses based on that data, and general trends or patterns are (hopefully) identified to guide strategic direction. This is more in line with inductive reasoning—moving from specifics to generalities—and serves do-math participation learning much better.

This activity comes from a branch of study known as **discrete mathematics** (Sandefur, 1995) and poses the following backward dilemma: Given a set of ordered pairs (points) organized in table form, find the equation of the function generating that table. The solution strategy is twofold:

1. Determine the Nth finite level of common differences from the y-values in the table.

2. Solve a system of simultaneous equations to identify coefficients that will be used to pinpoint the unknown function.

This activity is especially useful as a review for solving either a two-equation–two-variable (Algebra I) or a three-equation–three-variable (Algebra II) system of simultaneous equations. Make sure you plan backward as well: Decide on the answer (whether a linear or a quadratic function), and then make a table for the students (see the TI-83/84 Plus extension at the end of this activity). Be sure the x-values are separated by a constant amount when writing the table used by the students. This activity correlates to the following highlighted expectation for students:

- Understand *patterns*, relations, and functions
- Represent and analyze mathematical situations and structures using algebraic *symbols*
- Use mathematical models to represent and understand quantitative *relationships*
- **Analyze *change* in various contexts**

Algebra I Example (Grades 8–10)

The key element to understand is that given a constant difference among x-values in a given chart of data, the Nth constant difference of the y-values will determine the degree of the function that you seek. In this example, the first differences of the y-values are constant—meaning that the function that generated this data set is a first-degree (linear) function.

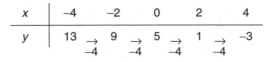

(1st Differences = → Linear Function)

Goal: Find the values of *a* and *b* to identify function $y = ax + b$.

Process: Pick any two points from the table above, and substitute *twice* for *x* and *y* to create a system:

$$(-4, 13): -4a + b = 13 \text{ (Equation 1)}$$
$$(-2, 9): -2a + b = 9 \text{ (Equation 2)}$$
$$(\text{Equation 1} - \text{Equation 2}): -2a = 4 \rightarrow a = -2$$
$$\text{Substitute back: When } a = -2, b = 5$$

Function (Answer): $y = -2x + 5$

To check your answer on the TI-83/84 Plus, be sure to perform the Erase Phase before inputting the following:

Y1 = −2x + 5

2nd TBLSET

   (*Select* **TblStart**) = − 4

         ΔTbl (**"change by"**) = 2

         Auto

         Auto)

2nd TABLE

Algebra II Example (Grades 10–12)

Since this problem exhibits a *second* common difference among the *y*-terms, the sought-after function is second degree in nature—that is, it will be quadratic. Incidentally, had the *third* differences been common, then the function that would have generated that data set would have been cubic, and so on.

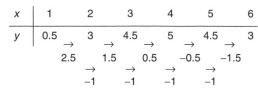

(2nd Differences = → Quadratic Function)

Goal: Find the values of a, b, and c to identify function $y = ax^2 + bx + c$.

Process: Pick any three points from the table above, and substitute three times for x and y to create a system:

$$(2, 3): 4a + 2b + c = 3 \text{ (Equation 1)}$$
$$(4, 5): 16a + 4b + c = 5 \text{ (Equation 2)}$$
$$(6, 3): 36a + 6b + c = 3 \text{ (Equation 3)}$$
$$\text{(Equation 1 − Equation 2)}: -12a - 2b = -2 \text{ (Equation A)}$$
$$\text{(Equation 2 − Equation 3)}: -20a - 2b = 2 \text{ (Equation B)}$$

$$\text{(Equation A − Equation B)}: 8a = -4 \rightarrow a = -\frac{1}{2}$$

Substitute back into "A-B" equation system: $b = 4$
Substitute back into "1-2-3" equation system: $c = -3$

Function (Answer): $y = \left(-\dfrac{1}{2}\right)x^2 + 4x - 3$

Again, to check your answer on the TI-83/84 Plus, make sure to perform the Erase Phase before you input the following:

Y1 = −.5x^2 + 4x − 3

2nd TBLSET

   (*Select* **TblStart**) = 1

   Δ**Tbl ("change by")** = 1

   Auto

   Auto)

2nd TABLE

(Screen should match the previous table)

Geometry 3

As the Algebra Standard did previously, the Geometry Standard represents another extension of the Number and Operations Standard, only this time within a more concrete framework of shapes and structures and the analysis of geometric characteristics and relationships. To see things from a geometric perspective means that students can build and manipulate mental images both on paper and with software. This allows them to develop reasoning and justification skills from grade to grade and to appreciate the precision of formal proofs at the secondary level.

The Algebraic Geometry activity promotes the notion that combining established knowledge with multiple approaches (as found in algebra) allows students to deduce information and discover important connections. That algebra-geometry partnership is also on display in the Points Across the Grades activity, in which coordinate geometry and a basic knowledge of transformations provide another avenue for students to deepen their understanding—this time around the area of a triangle. In the Tessellation Insights activity, transformational geometry returns the favor to its Euclidean counterpart by using line and rotational symmetry, scales, and movement to demonstrate a sweeping variety of geometric relationships.

This chapter concludes with a tribute to George Pólya (1951). The Triangle "Mushrooms" (a term he coined himself) activity extends similar triangles and the Pythagorean Theorem into some interesting directions of discovery for students.

ALGEBRAIC GEOMETRY

Grades 6–10

Geometric relationships become clearer and much more appreciated by students when students can actually follow logical arguments using equations and substitutions. This activity presents some theorems that are provable algebraically. This activity correlates to the following highlighted expectation for students:

- **Analyze characteristics and properties of two- and three-dimensional geometric shapes and develop mathematical *arguments* about geometric relationships**
- Specify locations and describe spatial relationships using *coordinate geometry* and other representational systems
- Apply *transformations* and use symmetry to analyze mathematical situations
- Use visualization, spatial reasoning, and geometric *modeling* to solve problems

Theorem 1: If you extend one side of a triangle to form an exterior angle, then the measure of the exterior angle is equal to the sum of the measures of the two angles inside the triangle furthest away from it (or the sum of the measures of its two remote interior angles).

Use the following example to illustrate this theorem to students (see also Figure 3.1):

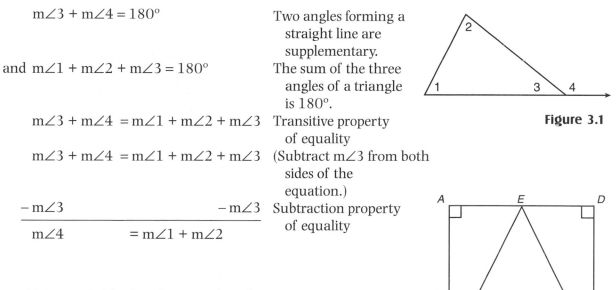

$m\angle 3 + m\angle 4 = 180°$	Two angles forming a straight line are supplementary.
and $m\angle 1 + m\angle 2 + m\angle 3 = 180°$	The sum of the three angles of a triangle is 180°.
$m\angle 3 + m\angle 4 = m\angle 1 + m\angle 2 + m\angle 3$	Transitive property of equality
$m\angle 3 + m\angle 4 = m\angle 1 + m\angle 2 + m\angle 3$	(Subtract m∠3 from both sides of the equation.)
$-m\angle 3 \qquad\qquad\qquad -m\angle 3$	Subtraction property of equality
$m\angle 4 \qquad = m\angle 1 + m\angle 2$	

Figure 3.1

Theorem 2: The two base angles of an isosceles triangle are congruent.

To illustrate this theorem to students, first define an **isosceles triangle** as a triangle that has two congruent sides (called legs). The third side of the triangle is referred to as the base, and two base angles are formed where the base intersects the two legs.

Figure 3.2

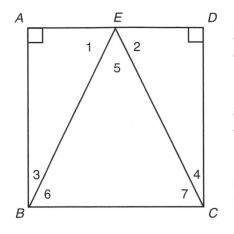

Figure 3.3

Draw a square and label the corners *A*, *B*, *C*, and *D*. Label *E* as the midpoint of segment $\overline{AD}$, and draw a line from *E* to *B* and from *E* to *C* to form three triangles (Δ). Refer to Figure 3.2.

Δ*EAB* and Δ*EDC* are congruent by side-angle-side (SAS).

Since corresponding parts of congruent triangles are congruent (CPCTC), segments $\overline{EB}$ and $\overline{EC}$ are congruent, making Δ*EBC* an isosceles triangle.

Now label the angles of the triangle to match Figure 3.3.

By CPCTC, angle 3 = angle 4. Also, since angles *B* and *C* of square *ABCD* are right angles, angle 3 + angle 6 = 90° and angle 4 + angle 7 = 90°.

Therefore, the following argument proves that the two base angles of the *BEC* isosceles triangle are congruent:

If	$m\angle 3 + m\angle 6 = 90°$	Definition of complementary angles
and	$m\angle 4 + m\angle 7 = 90°$	Definition of complementary angles
then	$m\angle 3 + m\angle 6 = m\angle 4 + m\angle 7$	Transitive property of equality
	$m\angle 3 + m\angle 6 = m\angle 4 + m\angle 7$	($m\angle 3 = m\angle 4$ by CPCTC. Subtract equal angles from both sides of the equation.)

$$
\begin{array}{cc}
-m\angle 3 & -m\angle 4 \\
\hline
m\angle 6 & = m\angle 7
\end{array}
$$

Subtraction property of equality

Theorem 3: The measure of an inscribed angle is equal to half the measure of the intercepted arc (the subtended angle of the circle).

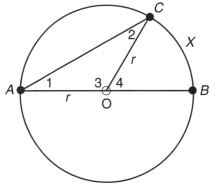

Figure 3.4

First, explain to students that an **inscribed angle** is an angle in which the vertex lies directly on the circle and in which the sides are chords of the circle.

Given circle *O*, draw **diameter** $\overline{AB}$ and label a third point *C* on the circle, as shown in Figure 3.4. Let the measure of arc $\overset{\frown}{CB} = x$. Now draw segment $\overline{CO}$, making it the third side of new triangle *AOC*. By definition, both $\overline{CO}$ and $\overline{AO}$ are radii, making $CO = AO = r$. Label *A* as angle 1, *C* as angle 2, and angle *AOC* as angle 3 (all inside the triangle). Then lable angle *COB* outside the triangle as angle 4. Note that angle 4 is a central angle.

central $m\angle 4 = $ arc x	Definition of a central angle
$m\angle 3 + m\angle 4 = 180°$	Two angles forming a straight line are supplementary.
$m\angle 3 + x = 180°$	By substitution.

$$
\begin{array}{cc}
 & -x \quad -x \\
\hline
m\angle 3 & = 180° - x
\end{array}
$$

Now, let angle 1 = *y*. Because Δ*AOC* is isosceles (two of its sides are radii), angle 2 must also = *y* (Theorem 2). Since angle 1 + angle 2 + angle 3 = 180°:

$$y + y + (180° - x) = 180°$$
$$\underline{ -180° \qquad -180°}$$
$$2y - x = 0$$
$$2y = x$$
$$y = \left(\frac{1}{2}\right)x$$

Y is the measure of the inscribed angle 1, and *x* is that of the intercepted arc *CB* (Quod Erat Demonstrandum [QED]).

Theorem 4: The measure of the circumference of a circle (in degrees) is 360°.

Inscribe regular hexagon ABCDEF (all sides congruent), and divide the hexagon into six equilateral triangles (all angles = 60°). Since each central angle is equal in measure to the arc it subtends, $6 \times 60° = 360°$.

Note also that since $C = 2\pi r$, and letting $r = 1$, then $C = 2\pi (1) = 2\pi$. Thus, if $2\pi = 360°$, then $\pi = 180°$ (a useful conversion in unit circle trigonometry). Refer to Figure 3.5.

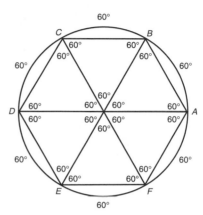

Figure 3.5

Theorem 5: If one side of an inscribed triangle is also the diameter of the circle, then the inscribed triangle is a right triangle.

(This theorem is also known as Ptolemy's Theorem.)

For Theorem 5, $\triangle ABC$ is inscribed in such a way that side *AB* passes through center *O*, making *AB* a diameter. Since diameters cut circles in half, arc *AB* becomes a semicircle = 180°. Thus, angle *ACB* is an inscribed angle (= one half the subtended arc), and $\triangle ABC$ is a right triangle (see Figure 3.6).

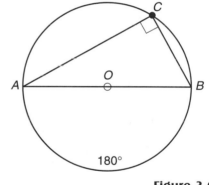

Figure 3.6

Theorem 6: The median drawn to the hypotenuse of a right triangle measures half the length of that hypotenuse.

Now draw **radius** *CO* (see Figure 3.7). Since $\triangle ABC$ is right, side *AB* becomes its hypotenuse because a radius always measures half of a diameter. ($\overline{AB}$ is also the diameter.)

Theorem 7: The sum of the interior angles of a regular polygon = (n – 2) × 180°; the sum of the exterior angles of any regular polygon = 360°.

Students need to understand that formulas do not just fall out of the sky—they come from somewhere, usually as an extension of some other idea. After all, humans created mathematics—the operative word being *created*.

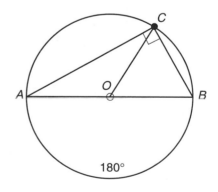

Figure 3.7

Use the Interior and Exterior Angles of a Regular Polygon worksheet (see Figure 3.8 and refer to the appendix for a full-page blackline master) to prove Theorem 7. As students work line by line across the worksheet, it is hoped that they will get a sense of the patterns of the arithmetic in each line that will lead to discovery of the various formulas along the right-hand column.

Interior and Exterior Angles of a Regular Polygon

Derive formulas for the interior and exterior angles of a regular polygon.

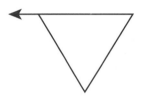 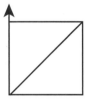 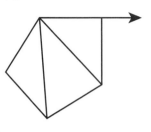

Directions: Fill in the last column (Regular *N*-gon) and the last row of this chart.

Figures	Equilateral Δ	Square	Regular Pentagon . . .	Regular N-gon
1. Number of diagonals drawn from a given vertex	0	1	2	$N - 3$
2. Number of interior triangles	1	2	3	$N - 2$
3. Number of degrees in sum of the interior angles	180°	360°	540°	$(N - 2) \bullet 180°$
4. Number of degrees in any one interior angle	$\dfrac{180}{3} = 60°$	$\dfrac{360}{4} = 90°$	$\dfrac{540}{5} = 108°$	$\dfrac{(N - 2) \bullet 180°}{N}$
5. Number of degrees in any one supplementary exterior angle	120°	90°	72°	$180° - \left[\dfrac{(N - 2) \bullet 180°}{N} \right]$ $= \dfrac{360°}{N}$
6. . . . Times the number of sides	360°	360°	360°	360°

Figure 3.8

In line 1, students should notice that the number of diagonals is always 3 less than the number of sides in the given figure. In line 2, the number of interior triangles that students can draw from one vertex is always 2 less than the number of sides in the given figure. Since students already know that the sum of the angles of a triangle = 180°, line 3 illustrates the first part of Theorem 7: The sum of the interior angles of a regular polygon = $(n - 2) \cdot 180°$. As an extension, note how line 4 takes the answers from line 3 and divides each answer by the number of sides in the given figure. Hence, some geometry books will even make note of the following formula: *The measure of each interior angle of a regular polygon = [(n − 2) • 180°] ÷ n.*

The answers for line 5 are just the supplements (subtract from 180°) of the answers from line 4. Students can find the answers in line 6 by multiplying the answers from line 5 by the number of sides in the given figure. All yield 360° (which is the second part of Theorem 7: *The sum of the exterior angles of any regular polygon = 360°*).

What troubles students is simple memorizing for tests. Learning the *where from* and *why* makes learning the *how* much easier and promotes a genuine and deeper understanding of mathematics.

POINTS ACROSS THE GRADES

> ### Grades 7–11
>
> This activity provides a comprehensive look at a variety of ways to deal with the area of a triangle at various levels of sophistication. This activity correlates to the following highlighted expectation for students:
>
> - Analyze characteristics and properties of two- and three-dimensional geometric shapes and develop mathematical *arguments* about geometric relationships
> - **Specify locations and describe spatial relationships using *coordinate geometry* and other representational systems**
> - Apply *transformations* and use symmetry to analyze mathematical situations
> - Use visualization, spatial reasoning, and geometric *modeling* to solve problems

One of the hallmarks of a good problem is its ability to be solved by a variety of methods. Students—for that matter, their teacher—should rate themselves along a scale of understanding in direct relation to the number of potential strategies that produce positive results during the solution process.

Recall that one of the criteria listed in the introduction for a good problem was one that you could solve through multiple strategies. The same holds true for a good problem solver: "Students who are challenged to derive the results of routine computations differently tend to be more creative and more inquisitive in their overall approach to learning math" (Pedersen & Pólya, 1984, p. 218).

In a more practical sense, suppose students are faced with a problem that contains no immediate or obvious way to determine a solution. If students have only one strategy available and are unable to make any inroads into solving the problem using that one solution method, then they are in trouble. If, however, students are able to recall two, three, or even four strategies that they may apply to the situation, then their odds for solving the problem increase dramatically. That is the hallmark of true problem solvers.

In theory, then, the further along students are in their formal study of mathematics, the more competent problem solvers they should become. The following activity presents a coordinate geometry question that is an example of how you can help students in the recall process. The progression of grade levels shows that the further along in grade sequence a student progresses, the more solution strategies are available. Hence, the good problem solver not only learns the new approach at the appropriate grade level but also should take advantage of being able to recall previous strategies. The key point for you to emphasize is facilitating student recall.

Consider the following coordinate geometry question and how the same student progressing from Grade 7 through Grade 11 might approach it:

Find the area of a triangle (in square units) in which the coordinates are A (−1, −1), B (5, 7), and C (−3, 3). Refer to Figure 3.9.

Figure 3.9

The area of a rectangle is measured in square units. Students can find it using one of the following two methods:

1. Counting the number of smaller squares within the original square *or* (if counting a discrete number of squares is not possible)

2. Using the formula $A = \text{length} \cdot \text{width} = l \cdot w$

Since a triangle is half of a rectangle, the area of a triangle is as follows:

$$A = \left(\frac{1}{2}\right) \text{length} \cdot \text{width} = \left(\frac{1}{2}\right) \text{base} \cdot \text{height} = \left(\frac{1}{2}\right) b \cdot h$$

Fundamentals (Grade 7)

Frame (or box in) triangle ABC ($\triangle ABC$) with a rectangle (or, in this case, a square). Compute the area of the square frame, and then subtract from it the sum of the areas of the three right triangles that border $\triangle ABC$ (see Figure 3.10).

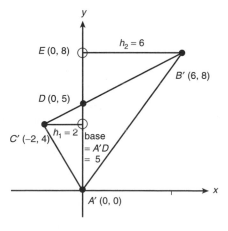

Area of square $= 8 \cdot 8 = 64$

Area of $\triangle 1 = \left(\frac{1}{2}\right) 4 \cdot 8 = 16$

Area of $\triangle 2 = \left(\frac{1}{2}\right) 2 \cdot 4 = 4$

Area of $\triangle 3 = \left(\frac{1}{2}\right) 6 \cdot 8 = 24$

Figure 3.10

Area of $\triangle ABC = (\triangle ABC) = 64 - (16 + 4 + 24) = 64 - 44 = 20$

Transformations (Grade 8)

Translate, or shift, $\triangle ABC$ by $(x + 1, y + 1)$ to $\triangle A'B'C'$. Segment $A'D$ serves as the base for *both* $\triangle A'C'D$ and $\triangle A'B'D$ (the y-axis effectively divides $\triangle ABC$ in two). The key point to emphasize is to move one point of the original triangle to shift to the origin, which then informs students what the exact shift factors will be for the other two points of the original triangle (see Figure 3.11).

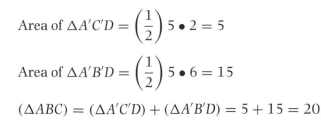

Area of $\triangle A'C'D = \left(\frac{1}{2}\right) 5 \cdot 2 = 5$

Area of $\triangle A'B'D = \left(\frac{1}{2}\right) 5 \cdot 6 = 15$

Figure 3.11

$(\triangle ABC) = (\triangle A'C'D) + (\triangle A'B'D) = 5 + 15 = 20$

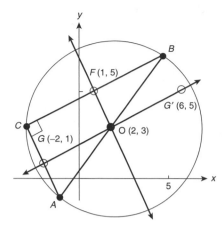

Figure 3.12

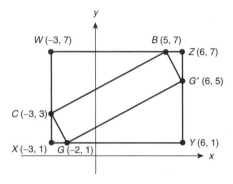

Figure 3.13

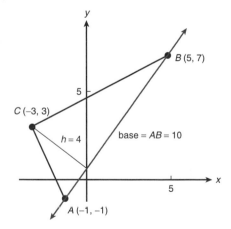

Figure 3.14

Geometry (Grade 9)

Construct perpendicular bisectors of sides $\overline{BC}$ and $\overline{AC}$ for $\triangle ABC$. Label the intersection of the bisectors point O. Draw a circle passing through points A, B, and C with the center at point O. Since side $\overline{AB}$ passes through O, $\overline{AB}$ must be a diameter of the circle *and also* the hypotenuse of right $\triangle ABC$ (by Theorem 5 in Algebraic Geometry). Refer to Figure 3.12.

The key point to emphasize is that given any three points and the triangle they form, the intersection of the perpendicular bisectors of any two of the three sides of that triangle constitutes the center of the triangle's circumscribed circle.

Distance Formula (Point to Point) $\sqrt{(x_2 - x_1)^2 + (y_2 - y_1)^2}$

Base $AC = \sqrt{20}$ and height $BC = \sqrt{80}$:

$$(\triangle ABC) = \left(\frac{1}{2}\right)\sqrt{20} \bullet \sqrt{80} = 20$$

Alternative Solution

This is an alternative solution that may be of interest to students. The essence of the problem is to "chop off" little triangle AGO and rotate it counterclockwise (another Grade 8-type transformation students would recognize as turning) so that point A is now on top of point B. The result is that big original triangle ABC is reshaped into rectangle $BCGG'$; the areas of the two are the same, only it's no longer in the shape of a big triangle.

Students can then determine the area of this new rectangle (see Figure 3.13) using the framing strategy from the Grade 7 discussion.

Algebra II (Grade 10)

With two points A and B and the slope of

$$\overleftrightarrow{AB} = \frac{4}{3},$$

determine the general form of line $AB(4x - 3y + 1 = 0)$. Use the Distance Formula from the preceding section to find the length of base $= AB = 10$, but to find the height, employ the Distance Formula that follows (see also Figure 3.14).

Distance Formula (Point to Line) $\dfrac{|Ax_1 + By_1 + C|}{\sqrt{A^2 + B^2}}$

With point C and line AB:

$$\frac{|4(-3) + (-3)(3) + 1|}{\sqrt{4^2 + (-3)^2}} = \frac{|-20|}{5} = 4 = h$$

$$(\triangle ABC) = \left(\frac{1}{2}\right)10 \bullet 4 = 20$$

Precalculus (Grade 11)

Each student needs the following materials to solve this problem:

- Five sheets of $8\frac{1}{2} \times 11$-inch lined paper
- Five sheets of graph paper
- A straightedge
- A compass
- A sharp pencil

The **slope of a line** (or line segment) reveals how the value of y changes as the value of x changes. For any two points—(x_1, y_1) and (x_2, y_2)—on the line:

$$\text{Slope} = \frac{\text{change in } y}{\text{change in } x} = \frac{y_2 - y_1}{x_2 - x_1}$$

Step 1

Find the center of circle O with one of two different methods.

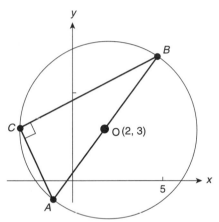

1. The slope of side $BC = \frac{1}{2}$ (making the slope of perpendicular bisector $OF = -2$).

    Using the point-slope form of a line $[y - y_1 = m(x - x_1)] \rightarrow y = -2x + 7$.

    The slope of side $AC = -2$ (making the slope of perpendicular bisector $OG = \frac{1}{2}$).

    Again using the point-slope form

    $$[y - y_1 = m(x - x_1)] \rightarrow y = \left(\frac{1}{2}\right) x + 2.$$

    By the transitive property of equality,

    $$-2x + 7 = y = \left(\frac{1}{2}\right) x + 2 \rightarrow -2x + 7 = \left(\frac{1}{2}\right) x + 2 \rightarrow x = 2, y = 3.$$

Figure 3.15

    Since the perpendicular bisectors of two sides of an inscribed triangle intersect at the center of its circumcircle, the center of circle O is $(2, 3)$. Refer to Figure 3.15.

2. Refer back to Finite Differences Equations in Chapter 2. Recall that an inductive process was described whereby students could use given data to identify the function from which that data originated.

    The general equation of a conic section is $Ax^2 + Bxy + Cy^2 + Dx + Ey + F = 0$.

    For circles, let $A = C = 1$ and $B = 0$ before substituting in for x and y:

    $$(-1, -1): 1 + 1 - D - E + F = 0 \rightarrow -D - E + F = -2$$
    $$(5, 7): 25 + 49 + 5D + 7E + F = 0 \rightarrow 5D + 7E + F = -74$$
    $$(-3, 3): 9 + 9 - 3D + 3E + F = 0 \rightarrow -3D + 3E + F = -18$$

    Solving the system of equations for D, E, and F: $D = -4$, $E = -6$, and $F = -12$.

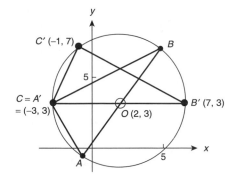

Figure 3.16

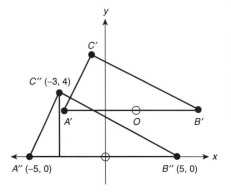

Figure 3.17

To pinpoint the location of the circle, change the general form of the equation ($x^2 + y^2 - 4x - 6y - 12 = 0$) into standard form by completing the square:

$$(x - 2)^2 + (y - 3)^2 = 5^2 \rightarrow \text{radius} = 5 \text{ and center: } (2, 3)$$

Step 2

Use transformations to center $\triangle ABC$ to find ($\triangle ABC$). Rotate $\triangle ABC$ clockwise about point O so that diameter $A'B'$ of $\triangle A'B'C'$ is parallel to the x-axis. An equivalent transition rule for each point is ($x \pm 2$, $y \pm 4$) and is clarified by studying Figure 3.16 more closely.

Then translate $\triangle A'B'C'$ under the rule ($x - 2$, $y - 3$), which corresponds to shifting point O onto the origin. Using the x-axis to support the base, ($\triangle A''B''C''$) is found by counting the base from point A'' to point B'' (= 10) and the perpendicular height from point C'' to the x-axis (= 4). Refer to Figure 3.17.

$$(\triangle A''B''C'') = \left(\frac{1}{2}\right) 10 \bullet 4 = 20$$

CALCULATOR APPLICATION

Drawing Circles

One of the features that both the TI-73 and the TI-83/84 Plus graphing calculators have is the ability to draw circles. Using the "String-the-Beads" idea described back in Chapter 2 (in the unit "Straw Balances"), we shall plot points *A*, *B*, and *C* and then draw the circumcircle identified previously:

Using the Application With Students

<table>
<tr><th>Your Input (TI-73)</th><th>Output</th></tr>
</table>

*Begin by erasing all old work, as detailed in the "Straw Balances" unit. All steps up to and including the **LIST** command should be repeated. Then,*

L1	L2	L3
−1	−1	-----
5	7	
−3	3	
-----	-----	

L2(7) =

(*Push **ArrowLeft** so that the black block is directly under the **L1** heading*)

Press: −1 ENTER 5 ENTER

          −3 ENTER

(*Push **ArrowRight** so that the black block is directly under the **L1** heading*)

Press: −1 ENTER 7 ENTER

          3 ENTER

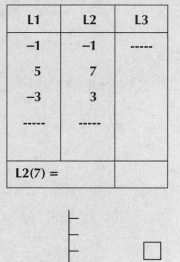

          2nd QUIT

          2nd PLOT 1

(*Select **On, Scatterplot, L1, L2, Bead***)

          ZOOM 7

          ZOOM 5

          2nd QUIT

          DRAW 6
          2, 3, 5)
          ENTER

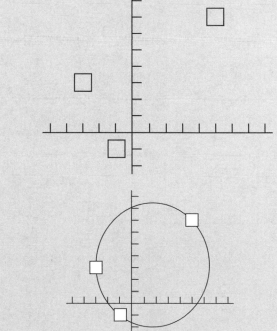

NOTE: The numbers 2, 3, and 5 above stand for, in order, the center of the circle (2, 3) and the length of its radius (5).

Consider: Add more points to your graphs for a more dramatic effect. For example, from Figure 3.16, we could have added *B'* (7, 3) and *C'* (−1, 7) to the **L1** and **L2 LISTS**.

TESSELLATION INSIGHTS

Grades 6–10

This activity is adapted from an activity presented by Jim Ruddy, Loyola High School, Montréal, Quebec. It dramatically illustrates why all students should be exposed to hands-on mathematics whenever possible, regardless of grade level.

In this activity, students apply transformations and symmetry to create a **tessellation** that produces an entire spectrum of Euclidean properties and theorems. The activity is an outstanding vehicle to introduce or to review a range of Euclidean ideas. This activity correlates to the following highlighted expectation for students:

- Analyze characteristics and properties of two- and three-dimensional geometric shapes and develop mathematical *arguments* about geometric relationships
- Specify locations and describe spatial relationships using *coordinate geometry* and other representational systems
- **Apply *transformations* and use symmetry to analyze mathematical situations**
- Use visualization, spatial reasoning, and geometric *modeling* to solve problems

Each student needs the following materials:

- One piece of unlined 8½ × 11-inch piece of paper
- Three colored marking pens (blue, red, and green)
- A school-provided plastic ruler (to ensure uniformity of the cardboard cutouts)
- A teacher-provided cutout cardboard scalene triangle (in which the height = the width of the ruler)
- A sharp pencil

Figure 3.18

1. Take the cardboard triangle and label it with a blue 1, a red 2, and a green 3. Refer to Figure 3.18.

2. Using the ruler and pencil, draw six parallel lines widthwise across a piece of paper.

   NOTE: The space between any two consecutive lines must equal the width of the ruler.

3. Beginning at the left-hand end of the second line, lay the cutout triangle down on the paper so that its base (longest side, containing angles 1 and 3) rests on the second line and so that angle 2 (the apex of the triangle) barely contacts the first line (see Figure 3.19).

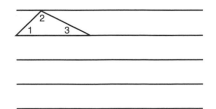

Figure 3.19

4. Trace the cardboard triangle *as many times as possible* between the first and second lines. This involves rotating the triangle a

half-turn (180°) each time as you continue tracing across the paper (see Figure 3.20).

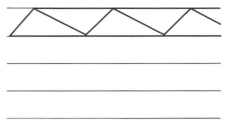

Figure 3.20

5. When you run out of room going from left to right, resume the process between the second and third lines (see Figure 3.21).

   NOTE: Trace the first triangle upside down (i.e., angle 2 should barely touch the third line).

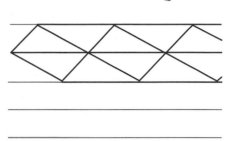

Figure 3.21

6. When you run out of room the second time, take the colored marking pens and color-label the angles of the traced triangles the same way the cardboard is labeled (see Figure 3.22).

7. With the ruler and the pencil, extend the diagonal lines that have been formed so far down to the sixth line (see Figure 3.23).

8. Complete the figure by repeating Step 6 and color-labeling all the angles in the remaining triangles (between the third and fourth lines, the fourth and fifth lines, and the fifth and sixth lines) to match those on the cardboard triangle (see Figure 3.24).

Figure 3.22

In a tessellation, a pattern of shapes is repeated over and over to cover some specified area. The shapes (in this case, triangles) must fit together perfectly so that there are no gaps or overlaps.

An abundance of geometric theorems jumps out of this tessellation. The following is a partial list of various properties and theorems from Euclidean geometry. During or after a unit of study, ask students which of the following rules apply. For example, after covering a unit on angles, ask if students can see from their tessellation the rule that an exterior angle of a triangle = the sum of its two remote interior angles.

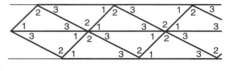

Area

1. The area of a triangle = half the area of a parallelogram.

2. (traced between lines 3 and 5) A triangle formed by joining the midpoints of a similar triangle = one quarter the area of that triangle.

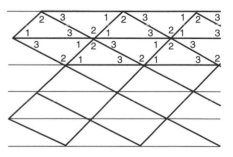

Figure 3.23

Length

3. A midline of a triangle = half its parallel base.

4. The median of a trapezoid = half the sum of its parallel bases.

Angles

5. An exterior angle of a triangle = the sum of its two remote interior angles (a replay from Algebraic Geometry).

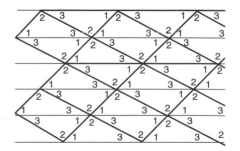

Figure 3.24

6. A straight angle = 180°.

7. The sum of the three angles of a triangle = 180°.

8. The measure of a circle = 360° (six angles at any one vertex).

9. The sum of the exterior angles of any polygon = 360° (a replay from Points Across the Grades).

Congruency

10. Vertical angles are congruent.

11. Supplements of congruent angles are also congruent.

12. Opposite angles of a parallelogram are congruent.

13. The diagonal of a parallelogram divides it into two congruent triangles (by angle-side-angle [ASA]).

Two Lines Are Parallel if and Only if . . .

14. the interior angles on the same side of the transversal are supplementary.

15. corresponding angles are congruent.

16. alternate interior angles are congruent.

Transformations

17. Rotation preserves **orientation.**

TRIANGLE "MUSHROOMS"

Grades 7–11

A true scholar and master teacher of mathematics, as well as a prolific lecturer and writer on the subject, George Pólya (1951) became synonymous with problem solving as the means for teaching and learning mathematics well before his ideas were generally accepted and adapted during the past 20 years. For most, *problem solving* is a misleading term in its inherent emphasis of process over product, but in Pólya's eyes, the solution was not so much an end but rather an invitation to explore other similar problems and their subsequent solutions.

Today's teachers are pressured to race through a prescribed course syllabus, but these clusters of insightful problems that Pólya dubbed "mushrooms" (NCTM, 1989b) remain nonexistent in written materials and professional inservice. But even in the current research climate of reflection and metacognition, consider how far ahead of his time Pólya truly was when he wrote, "Look around when you have got your first mushroom or made your first discovery; they grow in clusters" (NCTM, 1989b, p. 197). The opportunities for deeper understanding through mushrooms have thus far taken a backseat to topic coverage.

This activity provides an example of how exploring triangle relationships can lead to a cluster of other mathematical situations with a creative thread running through them. This activity correlates to the following highlighted expectation for students:

- Analyze characteristics and properties of two- and three-dimensional geometric shapes and develop mathematical *arguments* about geometric relationships
- Specify locations and describe spatial relationships using *coordinate geometry* and other representational systems
- Apply *transformations* and use symmetry to analyze mathematical situations
- **Use visualization, spatial reasoning, and geometric *modeling* to solve problems**

Figure 3.25

Making a slight change in what is known to create a solution leads to some unexpected discoveries. If you want students to be creative, you need to give them the opportunity to use what they know to discover some new applications for some old mathematical tools.

Have students turn a right triangle so that its hypotenuse becomes its base. Then have them draw an altitude from the right angle to the hypotenuse, dividing the original right triangle into two smaller right triangles (labeled ΔI and ΔII). Angles 1 and 2 are complementary (add up to 90°), and $x + y = c$ (see Figure 3.25).

Remind students that two triangles are similar when each of the following is true:

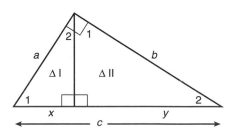

Figure 3.25

1. Their corresponding angles are congruent.

2. Their corresponding sides are in proportion.

By the **Angle-Angle Postulate** (AAP): $\Delta I \sim \Delta II \sim$ original Δ.

Hypotenuse: Side across from angle 2 ($\Delta I \sim$ original Δ) $\rightarrow \dfrac{a}{x} = \dfrac{x+y}{a}$

$$a^2 = x^2 + xy$$

Hypotenuse: Side across from angle 1 ($\Delta II \sim$ original Δ) $\rightarrow \dfrac{b}{y} = \dfrac{x+y}{b}$

$$b^2 = xy + y^2$$

Adding the left-hand sides and right-hand sides of the two equations yields the Pythagorean Theorem (Loomis, 1968):

$$a^2 + b^2 = x^2 + xy + xy + y^2 = x^2 + 2xy + y^2 = (x+y)^2 = c^2$$

Figure 3.26

Theorem 1: The product of the segments of one chord equals the product of the segments of the other chord.

Figures 3.25 and 3.26 demonstrate the learning possibilities for a student familiar with similar triangles who is willing to extend that idea. When the two great building blocks of geometry (triangles and circles) are finally brought together, the mathematics gets moving.

Have students draw a circle and two intersecting chords. Then have them draw dotted lines and label the angles per Figure 3.26.

The angles labeled 1 are congruent because they are vertical, and the angles labeled 2 are congruent because they are inscribed and subtend the same minor arc. (The angles labeled 3 would be congruent the same way but subtend a different minor arc.)

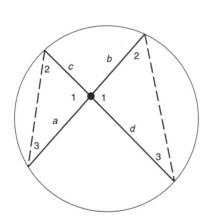

Figure 3.26

By AAP, the two triangles are similar, and, hence, $\dfrac{c}{a} = \dfrac{b}{d}$ or $a \bullet b = c \bullet d$.

Figure 3.27: The Law of Cosines

Now ask students how the formula relating the products of the segments formed by two intersecting chords can help them derive one of the most powerful laws in trigonometry (Nelson, 1993).

Refer to Figure 3.27. Circle B has inscribed right ΔCEF and diameters $CE = DG = 2a$. Note how sides in ΔABC are labeled, and since $\overline{BG}$ is a radius, $AG = BG - BA = a - c$. In ΔCEF,

$$\cos C = \frac{CF}{CE} = \frac{FA + AC}{CE} = \frac{FA + b}{2a} \rightarrow 2a \cos C - b.$$

From Figure 3.26 (two chords intersecting at point A), $(DA) \times (AG) = (CA) \bullet (AF)$ or $(a+c) \bullet (a-c) = b \bullet (2a \cos C - b) \rightarrow c^2 = a^2 + b^2 - 2ab \cos C$ (the Law of Cosines).

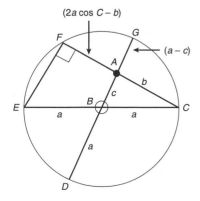

Figure 3.27

Figure 3.28

Now ask students how the formula relating the products of the segments formed by two intersecting chords can help them derive the most famous theorem in geometry.

Have students draw a circle and its vertical diameter. Then have them draw a horizontal chord intersecting the diameter at a point *not* at the center of the circle and draw a radius from either endpoint of the horizontal chord. (Call it c = hypotenuse of resulting right $\triangle$.) Label the base of the resulting $\triangle = b = \frac{1}{2}$ the horizontal chord (making the entire chord = $2b$). If a = height of the $\triangle$, then the longer segment of the diameter = $(c + a)$, and the shorter segment = $(c - a)$. Refer to Figure 3.28.

If $(c + a) \cdot (c - a) = b \cdot b$, then $c^2 - a^2 = b^2$ or $a^2 + b^2 = c^2$.

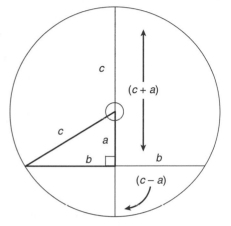

Figure 3.28

Figure 3.29

Simply stated, the converse of the theorem from Figure 3.29 is $b^2 = (c + a) \cdot (c - a)$.

Have students draw a circle and an inscribed right triangle such that leg b is a tangent line (one intersecting point) to the circle, leg a is a radius, and hypotenuse c lies along its diameter (as shown in Figure 3.29). Next, have students label the part of the hypotenuse that is also a radius of the circle a, which makes the part of the hypotenuse outside the circle $c - a$. Then, have them extend the hypotenuse from the center of the circle in the opposite direction to create a horizontal secant line (two intersecting points) to the circle. Since that extension is also a radius (label it a), the length of the entire secant line should finally be labeled $c + a$.

Now have students write the Pythagorean Theorem and change it somewhat by performing two algebraic procedures:

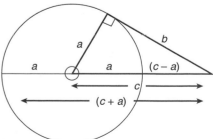

Figure 3.29

1. Subtract a^2 from both sides, so that $b^2 = c^2 - a^2$.

2. Factor $c^2 - a^2 = (c + a) \cdot (c - a)$.

If students return to Figure 3.29 and apply $b^2 = (c + a) \cdot (c - a)$, they should notice the following:

- $b^2 =$ the length of the tangent line squared.
- $(c + a) =$ the length of the secant line.
- $(c - a) =$ the external segment (that portion of the secant line found outside the circle).

> *Theorem 2: If a tangent and a secant to a circle intersect at an exterior point, the tangent squared equals the product of the secant and its external segment.*

The operation that students just performed uses converse reasoning. Students worked backward by starting at the end (the Pythagorean Theorem), wiggling it algebraically (What if we subtracted a^2 and then factored?), and deriving a common theorem from geometry (the tangent-secant theorem) in an unexpected way. This activity attempts to establish the notion of guided discovery for students, as opposed to strict memorization.

Figure 3.30

This is a second converse process, starting with the Pythagorean Theorem, that ends with a formula for finding the area of a circumscribed right triangle (note the inscribed circle within) (Loomis, 1968).

To start, advise students that the positioning of the only inscribed circle possible (there is only one other circle possible by geometric proof beyond the scope of this problem) contains a critical square whose sides equal the radius of the circle.

Refer to Figure 3.30. Since each side of square $CDOF =$ radius r, $BF = BC - FC = a - r$ and $AD = AC - DC = b - r$.

Points D, E, and F are where the sides of the circumscribed $\triangle$ are tangent to the circle (and, hence, perpendicular to the radii).

By the "Hypotenuse-Leg" Theorem, $\triangle BOE$ Matches $\triangle BOF$, and $\triangle AOD$ matches $\triangle AOE \rightarrow BE = BF = a - r$ and $AE = AD = b - r$.

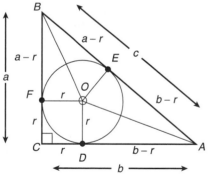

Figure 3.30

Since $AB = BE + AE$, $c = a + b - 2r$, or $r = \dfrac{a + b - c}{2}$. Note that the semiperimeter $S = \dfrac{a + b + c}{2}$.

$$a^2 + b^2 = c^2 \rightarrow a^2 + b^2 - c^2 = 0 \rightarrow a^2 + \mathbf{2ab} + b^2 - c^2 = \mathbf{2ab}$$

$$\rightarrow (a + b)^2 - c^2 = 2ab \rightarrow \frac{(a + b)^2 - c^2}{4} = \frac{2ab}{4}$$

$$\rightarrow \left(\frac{a + b + c}{2}\right) \cdot \left(\frac{a + b - c}{2}\right) = \left(\frac{1}{2}\right) ab \rightarrow S \bullet r = (\triangle ABC)$$

Theorem 3: The area of a circumscribed
right triangle is the product of its semiperimeter
and the radius of the inscribed circle.

Encourage students to make a sort of visual confirmation of the beauty of the formula just derived. Since they just proved area $= S \bullet r$, rewrite it as $r \bullet S$ and substitute for S the following:

$$r \bullet S = r \bullet \left[\frac{a+b+c}{2} \right] \text{(by definition of the semiperimeter)}$$

$$= \left(\frac{1}{2} \right) r[a+b+c] \text{ (by multiplicative inverse)}$$

$$= \left[\left(\frac{1}{2} \right) r \bullet a \right] + \left[\left(\frac{1}{2} \right) r \bullet b \right] + \left[\left(\frac{1}{2} \right) r \bullet c \right] \text{(by distributive property)}$$

Now have students draw line segment CO and substitute each of the following in the preceding step:

$$\left[\left(\frac{1}{2} \right) r \bullet a \right] = \text{area of triangle } COB$$

$$\left[\left(\frac{1}{2} \right) r \bullet b \right] = \text{area of triangle } COA$$

$$\left[\left(\frac{1}{2} \right) r \bullet c \right] = \text{area of triangle } BOA$$

Since the areas of these three triangles make up the area of the *entire* large triangle ABC, students have proven that $S \bullet r =$ the area of the circumscribed right triangle (the converse of Theorem 3).

Measurement 4

According to the standards listed in *Principles and Standards for School Mathematics* (National Council of Teachers of Mathematics [NCTM], 2000), all students in Grades 6 through 12 should be able to do the following:

- Understand measurable *attributes* of objects and the units, systems, and processes of measurement

- Apply appropriate techniques, *tools*, and formulas to determine measurements

The Measurement Standard is important to any student interested in how mathematics actually connects with the outside world. Besides its essential relationship to all four of the other content standards (numbers, algebra, geometry, and data analysis and probability), measurement facilitates student access to a wide spectrum of ideas among many other intelligences: linguistic, artistic, musical, physical, and, of course, scientific.

Hands-on experiences permeate this chapter. The Sorting It All Out activity takes students beyond merely sorting objects and encourages an understanding of set theory through applications of the **Counting Principle** and **Venn diagrams.** The Easy as Pi activity reviews various aspects of the circle (diameter, radius, circumference, and area) to help students gain a better idea of the meaning behind the elusive 3.14 value of pi. The final activity, Reflections on Trig, combines some of the basic concepts of reflection with that of the unit circle in an analog-clock setting that allows students to conjure up visual imagery of various relationships in trigonometry.

SORTING IT ALL OUT

> **Grades 6–8**
>
> Derided as a poster child for the demise of the "New Math" movement in U.S. education in the late 1950s and 1960s, the Venn diagram and its accompanying geometry have recently been resurrected through useful applications in such fields as psychology (mind map) and sociology (graphic organizer). In this activity, students use manipulatives to develop Venn diagrams. This activity correlates to the following highlighted expectation for students:
>
> - **Understand measurable *attributes* of objects and the units, systems, and processes of measurement**
> - Apply appropriate techniques, *tools*, and formulas to determine measurements

A Venn diagram is a pictorial representation using a rectangle and combinations of interlocking and/or separate circles. It is drawn in such a way as to represent operations found in set theory.

For example, suppose you have the set $U = \{1, 2, 3, \ldots, 20\}$. The universal set ($U$) represents the counting numbers from 1 to 20. In a classic Venn diagram structure, all of those numbers would be inside a rectangular "corral" to exclude all the other possible numbers (e.g., those greater than 20, 0, negatives, fractions, radicals, pi). In other words, you would create a subset of the counting numbers 1 through 20 with this rectangle.

Now create some even smaller subsets. Let $A = \{1, 2, 3, 4, 5\}$. Let $B = \{5, 6, 7, 8, 9\}$. Let $C = \{10, 11, 12\}$. To visualize these sets inside the rectangular corral, draw the two interlocking circles for A and B (use the shared number 5 as the intersection of A and B) and also a third and disconnected circle for C. All the other numbers in the universe (all the teens and the number 20) still rattle around inside the corral but are not part of any of the three circles. They are designated as complements to the union = $\{1, 2, 3, \ldots, 12\}$ and would be categorized as = $\{13, 14, 15, \ldots, 20\}$ in set form.

You can get even more creative. Suppose you let new set $D = \{1, 2, 3\}$. You would draw a circle inside of A but not touching the interlocking region that A shares with B. Hence, the intersection of A and $D = D$, and the union = A. However, the establishment of the rectangle is critical to a classic Venn diagram illustration, and the circles therein can do any number of things without necessarily interlocking. (For example, dropping the 5 from set B would have created separate circles A, B, and C inside the corral.)

For the following activity, each student needs the following materials:

- Three 30-centimeter lengths of precut string (students knot the ends of each piece of string to make circles)
- One envelope with predetermined sets of 32 cutout or hand-pressed figures inside (of different sizes, colors, and shapes)

NOTE: You will need to prepare a class set of envelopes each containing 32 cutout or hand-pressed figures. You can use thin, colored sheets of craft foam, construction paper, or other material of your choosing. This activity uses the following key for sizes, colors, and shapes:

> *Size:* large (uppercase) and small (lowercase)
> *Color:* blue (*b*), green (*g*), red (*r*), yellow (*y*)
> *Shape:* circle (*c*), diamond (*d*), square (*s*), and triangle (*t*)

For example:

> *BC* = large blue circle
> *bc* = small blue circle
> *GD* = large green diamond
> *gd* = small green diamond

Step 1

Instruct students to extract the small blue diamond (*bd*) from their envelopes and lay it in front of them. Then ask them to extract a large yellow square (*YS*) and lay it in front of them. Repeat the selection process in a planned way several more times.

Make sure you predetermine which figures students should extract and in what order. Always repeat this teaser question: Without looking, can anyone tell me how many figures are in your envelope . . . and why? Then take out a large yellow triangle (*YT*), for example, from your envelope; ask your students to do the same; and repeat the question. Then take out another shape, perhaps a small green circle (*gc*), from your envelope; ask your students to do the same; and repeat the question. Continue this process with the rest of your pieces while your students organize the shapes on their desks.

After about the fifth selection, one of the students might begin to formulate the answer to your repeated question. Once students figure out the number is 32 and that there are two sizes, four colors, and four shapes, have them empty the contents of their envelopes on the desk and arrange all the figures in any way they desire. At this point, patrol the room going desk to desk and comment on all the various arrangements (most all of them perfectly satisfactory, mind you) before you introduce Figure 4.1.

The matrix in Figure 4.1 demonstrates how students can arrange colors by horizontal rows and shapes by vertical columns and can then stack smaller-size items atop their larger counterparts to achieve a sort of third dimension. However, because the matrix would be incomplete after only a small number of item extractions, students may be clever enough to notice that two sizes, four colors, and four shapes would mean 32 total items.

BC	BD	BS	BT
bc	bd	bs	bt
GC	GD	GS	GT
gc	gd	gs	gt
RC	RD	RS	RT
rc	rd	rs	rt
YC	YD	YS	YT
yc	yd	vs	vt

Key :
b or *B* = blue
g or *G* = green
r or *R* = red
y or *Y* = yellow

C = large circle
c = small circle
D = large diamond
d = small diamond
S = large square
s = small square
T = triangle
t = triangle

Figure 4.1

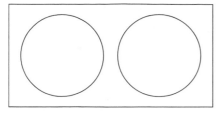

Figure 4.2

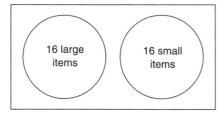

Figure 4.3

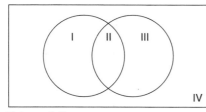

Figure 4.4

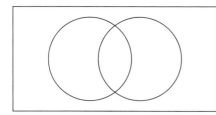

Figure 4.5

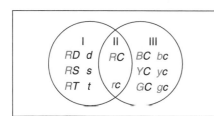

Figure 4.6

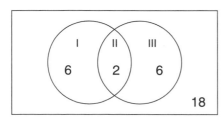

Figure 4.7

The Counting Principle states that if there are *K* distinct ways to describe one attribute and *L* distinct ways to describe another attribute and *M* distinct ways to describe a third attribute, then the highest possible number of items having all three attributes = *K • L • M*. Interestingly, many students will arrive at 32 for an answer (= 2 • 4 • 4) without any formal introduction to the Counting Principle.

Step 2

Instruct students to replicate a Venn diagram on their desks by taking two of their strings and forming separate circles (see Figure 4.2).

Choose one attribute, such as size (i.e., large and small), and have students arrange their 32 items (see Figure 4.3).

After students sort the pieces into large and small categories, challenge them to organize items using one of the other two attributes (i.e., color or shape). For example:

- Blue and nonblue = 8 and 24, respectively
- Squares and diamonds = 8 inside each circle and 16 inside the rectangle and not in any circle

Step 3

Now have students interlock the two circles to construct a Venn diagram that addresses *two* attributes (see Figure 4.4).

For the sake of clarity, reference each region with Roman numerals (see Figure 4.5).

Students will most likely question Region II. This is a good time to introduce the concept of intersection. Ask students to place both red circles in Region II. If Regions I and II represent items that are red, it follows that Region I by itself represents red items that are *not* circles. If Regions II and III represent all circles, then it follows that Region III by itself represents all circles that are *not* red (see Figure 4.6).

Figure 4.7 represents the actual *number* of items (**cardinality**) in each of the four regions. If students were working without a Venn diagram and simply added up the number of red items (8) and circles (8), the answer (16) would differ from the correct answer (6 + 2 + 6 = 14) found by adding up the numbers in Regions I through III.

The **Addition Formula** states that, given two sets A and B, N $(A$ or $B) = N(A) + N(B) - N(A$ and $B)$.

Students should now be able to check, back in Figure 4.7, numerically that the sum of $N(A)$, the number of items in the first circle (8), and $N(B)$, the number of items in the second circle (8), *less* the double-counted items, or those in the intersection Region II (2), will yield the same result ($8 + 8 - 2 = 6 + 2 + 6 = 14$). NOTE: A represents Regions I plus II, and B represents Regions II plus III.

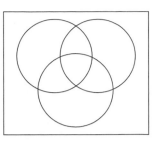

Figure 4.8

Step 4

Now have students interlock *three* circles (see Figure 4.8) to construct a Venn diagram that addresses three attributes. NOTE: With two attributes, number of regions = $2^2 = 4$, and with three attributes, number of regions = $2^3 = 8$. Thus, number of regions = 2^n, in which n = number of attributes being considered.

Instruct students to place the large green triangle in Region V. Refer to Figure 4.9 for placement.

Students can then properly place their remaining items (see Figure 4.10). Three large triangles that are *not* green go in Region IV, one green triangle that is *not* large goes in Region VI, and three large green items that are *not* triangles go in Region II.

Then, three triangles that are neither large nor green go in Region VII, three green items that are neither large nor a triangle go in Region III, and nine large items that are neither green nor a triangle go in Region I.

Nine items (bc, bd, bs, rc, rd, rs, yc, yd, and ys) remain and go in Region VIII (see Figure 4.11).

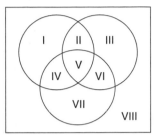

Figure 4.9

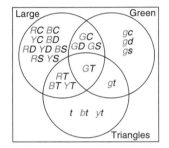

Figure 4.10

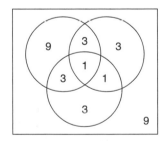

Figure 4.11

Interesting Math Fact

The *cardinality* (number of items) diagram (see Figure 4.12) is the exponential-form equivalent of the triple Venn diagram from Step 4 (in which $3^0 = 1$, $3^1 = 3$, and $3^2 = 9$). Students who have never worked with the zero-exponent concept (Regions V and VI) may wish to verify those results using a calculator.

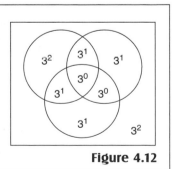

Figure 4.12

EASY AS PI

> ## Grades 6–11
>
> In any circle, regardless of its size, the **ratio** (a comparison of two quantities by division, usually in fraction form) of the circle's circumference (perimeter) to its diameter (one of the infinite number of chords that pass through the circle's center with their endpoints on the circle) is always the same number. That ratio is approximately 3.14 and is called π (the Greek letter pi). In this activity, students will discover the meaning behind the transcendental number π. This activity correlates to the following highlighted expectation for students:
>
> - Understand measurable *attributes* of objects and the units, systems, and processes of measurement
> - **Apply appropriate techniques, *tools*, and formulas to determine measurements**

Each student needs the following materials:

- A blank π Explorations Table (see the appendix for a full-page blackline master)
- One piece of unlined 8½ × 11-inch paper
- One piece of graph paper (¼-inch lined)
- A ball of string
- A metric ruler
- Scissors
- Tape
- A four-function calculator
- A sharp pencil

Ask each student to bring one circular-based can (i.e., a right circular cylinder) of some nonperishable food item to class. This should provide a variety of different-size cans for the entire class to use for the measurements in this activity. You may want to anticipate any possible shortfall by bringing a few of your own cans.

Part I: Finding π With Circumference and Diameter

1. Have students tape the end of the ball of string under the top rim of the can, wrap it around the rim once, and use the scissors to cut off that length. Then have them detach the string and pull it taut along the metric ruler to measure the circumference of the circular base of the can. Have them record the circumference (to the nearest tenth of a centimeter) on the π Explorations Table (see Figure 4.13).

π Explorations Table					
	Explorations	Object #1	Object #2	Object #3	Predict
Q1	**C** (circumference)				
	d (diameter)				
	$\dfrac{c}{d} = \pi$?				
Q2	**A₁** (inscribed sq.)				
	A₂ (circumscribed sq.)				
	$\dfrac{A_1 + A_2}{2} = A$				
	r (radius)				
	r² (radius squared)				
	$\dfrac{A}{r^2} = \pi$?				

Figure 4.13

2. Then have students apply the ruler directly to the circular base of the can to measure and record its diameter.

3. Next, have students place the can base down on the unlined 8½ × 11-inch piece of paper, trace the base (circle), and label it 1.

4. Instruct students to exchange cans and repeat Steps 1 and 2 with the second can. NOTE: Make sure students cut off and use a new piece of string for each circumference.

5. Also have students repeat Step 3 but label the second circle 2.

6. Have students exchange cans for a third time and repeat Steps 1 through 3, but label the third circle 3.

Question 1

Ask students the following question: According to the worksheet and for each circle that you traced, how close to the number π is each ratio of the circle's circumference divided by its diameter?

To answer Question 1, students should be asked to divide the circumference of each can's circular base by its corresponding diameter and enter the respective results (rounded to the nearest hundredth) into the π Explorations Table. Figure 4.14 is an example of a partially completed π Explorations Table.

π Explorations Table					
	Explorations	Object #1 (Can of Soup)	Object #2 (Can of Tuna)	Object #3 (Bulk Seed)	Predict (Coffee Can)
Q1	**C** (circumference)	21.4	27.0	36.4	
	d (diameter)	6.8	8.6	11.6	
	$\dfrac{c}{d} = \pi$?	3.15	3.14	3.14	
Q2	**A₁** (inscribed sq.)				
	A₂ (circumscribed sq.)				
	$\dfrac{A_1 + A_2}{2} = A$				
	r (radius)				
	r² (radius squared)				
	$\dfrac{A}{r^2} = ?$				

Figure 4.14

One Step Further

On a sheet of graph paper, have students plot each diameter along the horizontal axis and each circumference along the vertical axis. When they connect the dots, the resulting graph constitutes a linear function. Figure 4.15 is a diagram for the data listed in Figure 4.14.

For each point, students can multiply the diameter by the same number (π as the **constant of proportionality**) to arrive at the corresponding circumference. In coordinate geometry, however, that constant π would be recognized as the slope of the line $C = \pi d$.

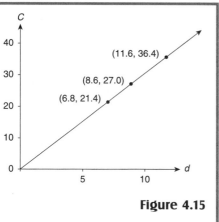

Figure 4.15

π Explorations Table					
	Explorations	Object #1 (Can of Soup)	Object #2 (Can of Tuna)	Object #3 (Bulk Seed)	Predict (Coffee Can)
Q1	C (circumference)	21.4	27.0	36.4	49.6
	d (diameter)	6.8	8.6	11.6	15.8
	$\frac{c}{d} = \pi$?	3.15	3.14	3.14	3.14
Q2	A_1 (inscribed sq.)				
	A_2 (circumscribed sq.)				
	$\frac{A_1 + A_2}{2} = A$				
	r (radius)				
	r^2 (radius squared)				
	$\frac{A}{r^2} = ?$				

Figure 4.16

Prediction 1

Hold up a larger circular item, such as a coffee can or a Frisbee, and inform students that the diameter of the object is, for example, 15.8 centimeters. Then ask students, based on the information gleaned thus far, to predict the circumference of the object.

Answer: 49.6 centimeters, which is the diameter times π, or 15.8 • 3.14

Then have students figure out how close the ratio is to the number π and fill in their tables. See Figure 4.16 for an example.

One Step Further

A. Find your answer in more than one way. Remember that solving problems in more than one way is the benchmark of deeper understanding. Pursuant to that concept, here are some other possible ways for students to arrive at a prediction (e.g., 49.6):

  1. Extend the graph. (Locate 15.8 along the horizontal axis, draw a line up to the line itself, and then draw over [left] to the vertical axis for an approximate answer.)

  2. Think of the formula $C = \pi d$ as the linear function $y = 3.14x$ and substitute 15.8 for x.

B. Given the circumference of a second particular circular item, predict its diameter.

CALCULATOR APPLICATION

Circumference of a Circle

Using the Application With Students

Use the TI-73 graphing calculator with the following steps:

Press: **ON**

2nd FORMAT

(*Select* **AxesOn**)

2nd PLOT 4

ENTER

CLEAR

Go to the **Y =** *screen*

(*and* **CLEAR** *all old lines*)

Y1 =   (*Type in* **2ndπX**)

MODE

(*Click off* **FLOAT** *and select the number* **1** *from the group* **0123456789**)

ZOOM 4   (**ZOOM 6** *on the TI-83/84 Plus*)

NOTE: If you now study the graph on either calculator, you'll see that any *x*-values (representing diameters) greater than 9.4 on the TI-73 or greater than 10 on the TI-83/84 Plus cannot be displayed. Their **WINDOWS** need cleaning!

(Continued)

(Continued)

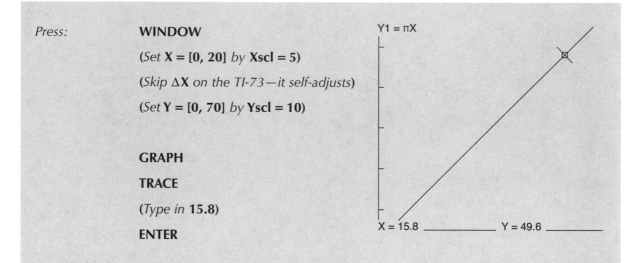

Press: **WINDOW**

(*Set* **X = [0, 20]** *by* **Xscl = 5**)

(*Skip* Δ**X** *on the TI-73—it self-adjusts*)

(*Set* **Y = [0, 70]** *by* **Yscl = 10**)

GRAPH

TRACE

(*Type in* **15.8**)

ENTER

Reading along the bottom of the screen:

$$x = 15.8 \; y = 49.6$$

NOTE: The *y*-value of 49.6 represents the circumference, rounded to the nearest tenth. Recall on the previous page that we clicked off **FLOAT** and chose the number **1** instead—indicative of our answer being automatically rounded to the first digit after the decimal point (the nearest tenth).

Part II: Finding π With Approximate Area and Radius Squared

Make sure students understand that the area of a square is measured in square units and can be found in either of two ways:

- Counting the number of smaller squares within the original square or (if counting a discrete number of squares is not possible)
- Using the formula $A = $ side $\bullet$ side $= s2$

7. Have students take the sheet of paper with the traced circles (from Steps 1–6) and draw an **inscribed square** (within) and a **circumscribed square** (outside) for Circle 1 (see Figure 4.17).

8. Instruct students to measure the length of one side of the inscribed square, using the metric ruler. After squaring that measurement (as per the definition above), have them enter the result in π Explorations Table for A_1 (the area of the inscribed square within the traced circular base of Object 1).

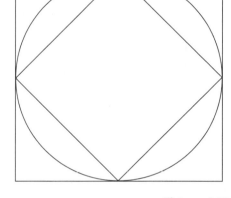

9. Have students perform the same operation for one side of the circumscribed square and enter the result in π Explorations Table for A_2 (the area of the circumscribed square outside the traced circular base of Object 1).

10. Instruct students to average A_1 and A_2 and enter the result in the π Explorations Table $[(A_1 + A_2)/ 2 = A]$ for Object 1.

Figure 4.17

11. Instruct students to take half of Object 1's diameter to determine its radius and enter the results in the π Explorations Table for r (radius). Finally, have students square the radius and enter the result in the π Explorations Table for r^2 (radius squared).

12. Have students repeat Steps 7 through 11 for Objects 2 and 3.

Question 2

Ask students the following question: According to the worksheet and for each circle that you traced, how close to the number π is each ratio of the circle's approximate (average) area divided by the square of its radius?

To answer Question 2, students should be asked to divide the approximate area of each can's circular base by the corresponding square of its radius and enter the respective results (rounded to the nearest hundredth) into the π Explorations Table. Figure 4.18 is the remaining data for the example π Explorations Table introduced in Steps 1 through 6 (see Figure 4.16).

π Explorations Table					
	Explorations	Object #1 (Can of Soup)	Object #2 (Can of Tuna)	Object #3 (Bulk Seed)	Predict (Coffee Can)
Q1	C (circumference)	21.4	27.0	36.4	49.6
	d (diameter)	6.8	8.6	11.6	15.8
	$\frac{c}{d} = \pi$?	3.15	3.14	3.14	3.14
Q2	A₁ (inscribed sq.)	23.04	37.00	92.54	
	A₂ (circumscribed sq.)	6.24	73.96	184.96	
	$\frac{A_1 + A_2}{2} = A$	34.64	55.48	138.75	
	r (radius)	3.4	4.3	6.8	
	r² (radius squared)	11.56	18.49	46.24	
	$\frac{A}{r^2} = ?$	3.00	3.00	3.00	

Figure 4.18

One Step Further

On the other side of the graph paper used for the One Step Further to Question 1, have students plot the radii for each object along the horizontal axis and the average area for each object along the vertical axis. When students connect the dots, the resulting graph constitutes a quadratic (parabolic) function. Figure 4.19 is a diagram for the Question 2 example.

What the shape of the graph implies is that for each point, the constant of proportionality (3) is multiplied by the square of the radius to arrive at the corresponding average area.

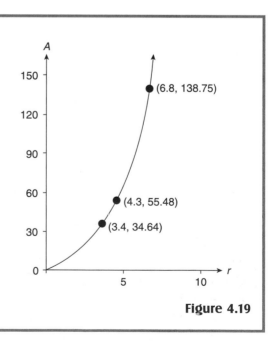

Figure 4.19

		Object #1 (Can of Soup)	Object #2 (Can of Tuna)	Object #3 (Bulk Seed)	Predict (Coffee Can)
	C (circumference)	21.4	27.0	36.4	49.6
	d (diameter)	6.8	8.6	11.6	15.8
Q1	$\dfrac{c}{d} = \pi?$	3.15	3.14	3.14	3.14
	A$_1$ (inscribed sq.)	23.04	37.00	92.54	125.44
	A$_2$ (circumscribed sq.)	46.24	73.96	184.96	249.64
	$\dfrac{A_1 + A_2}{2} = A$	34.64	55.48	138.75	187.23
	r (radius)	3.4	4.3	6.8	7.9
	r^2 (radius squared)	11.56	18.49	46.24	62.41
Q2	$\dfrac{A}{r^2} = ?$	3.00	3.00	3.00	3.00

π Explorations Table heads the table.

Figure 4.20

Prediction 2

Hold up the larger circular item from Prediction 1 and remind students that the diameter of the object is, for example, 15.8 centimeters. Then ask students, based on the information gleaned thus far, to predict the area of the circular base of that object.

Answer: 187.23 square centimeters—take half of 15.8 = 7.9, square the result, and then multiply 62.41 • 3, which yields the answer 187.23

Ask students to complete the Predict column on their tables before answering. Figure 4.20 is the remaining data for the example π Explorations Table (see Figure 4.18).

One Step Further

A. Given the area of a second particular circular item, predict its radius.

B. Construct the inscribed and circumscribed squares with compass and straightedge:

- Pick any three points on the circle and draw two chords.
- Construct two perpendicular bisectors (meeting at the center of the circle).
- With one on-circle point and center point, extend this radius to make a diameter.
- Draw a perpendicular bisector of this diameter through its midpoint (center of the circle).

CALCULATOR APPLICATION

Area of a Circle

```
PROGRAM:AREACIRC
:ClrScreen
:Lbl 99
:Input "RADIUS_=_", R
:π × R² → A
:Disp "AREA_=", round
(A, 2)
:Disp "_"
:Disp "_"
:Pause
:Goto 99
```

1. Start by finding the areas of the circles using the standard $A = \pi R^2$.

2. For any of the radii R above, the areas A of those corresponding circles can quickly be checked with the application at the left, an original program titled **"AREACIRC"**:

3. If you consider the last row ("Q2") of the completed π Explorations Table in Figure 4.20, you'll notice that every entry for $A \div r^2$ (the ratio of the calculated area of the circle to the square of its radius) is 3.00.

The fact that that ratio is incorrect—it, of course, *should* be 3.14 (or, to be even more precise, π)—should lead you to a quick conclusion. Since measuring the radius and the sides of two squares is fairly direct, the reason why our ratio is 3.00 and not 3.14 lies with the formula we used to determine the area.

Upon examination and comparison, it turns out that the area of the circumscribed (outside) square is somewhat closer to the actual area of the circle than the area of the inscribed (inside) square—although both are clearly wrong. The circle's area still resides somewhere in between the two extremes, but computing that area by using the average of the two squares' areas would work only if it were exactly halfway between the other two.

Using the Application With Students

Your Input	Output
Press: **ON**	
PRGM	
(*Scroll down to* **AREACIRC**)	
ENTER	prgmAREACIRC
ENTER	RADIUS =
(*Type in* **7.9**)	RADIUS = 7.9
ENTER	AREA =
	196.07

(Continued)

(Continued)

Your Input	Output
Options	
You may now either	
Press:	**ENTER** (*for new data entry*)
or	
Press:	**2nd OFF** **ON** **CLEAR** (*to escape the program*)

PROGRAM:APPROXPI

:Lbl 99

:Disp "AREA_INSQUARE"

:Input "___=_", P

:Disp "_"

:Disp "AREA_OUTSQUARE"

:Input "___=_", Q

:Disp "_"

:$(3 \times P + 4 \times Q) / 7 \to A$

:Input "RADIUS_=_", R

:Disp "_"

:$A / R^2 \to B$

:Disp "A / R^2_=", round (B, 2)

:Disp "_"

:Disp "_"

:Pause

:Goto 99

After some trial and error, a better (but still imperfect) formula involves creating a slight weighted advantage for the area of the outside square over the area of the inside square: [(3 × inside square's area) + (4 × outside square's area)] ÷ 7. The calculations can get a bit tedious—which is why another program for the graphing calculator is being proposed to include our new formula.

Notice in the original program titled **"APPROXPI"** that the command containing the formula is but the halfway point of the process. The radius still needs to be folded in before the ratio of the area to the square of the radius can be determined.

Your Input	**Output**

Press: **ON**
　　　　　PRGM
　　　　　(*Scroll down to* **APPROXPI**)
　　　　　ENTER

> prgmAPPROXPI

　　　　　ENTER

> AREA INSQUARE
>
> =

(*From* **Predict** *column, type in* **125.44**)
　　　　　ENTER

> AREA INSQUARE
>
> = 125.44
>
> AREA OUTSQUARE
>
> =

(*Type in* **249.64** *from beneath that*)
　　　　　ENTER

> AREA INSQUARE
>
> = 125.44
>
> AREA OUTSQUARE
>
> = 249.64
>
> RADIUS =

(*Skip down and type in* **7.9**)
　　　　　ENTER

> AREA INSQUARE
>
> = 125.44
>
> AREA OUTSQUARE
>
> = 249.64
>
> RADIUS = 7.9
>
> $A / R^2 =$
>
> 　　　3.15

Options

As before, press either:

> **ENTER** (*for* **new** *data entry*)

or

> **2nd OFF**
>
> **ON**
>
> **CLEAR** (*to* **escape** *the program*)

REFLECTIONS ON TRIG

> ## Grades 10–12
>
> This activity explores trigonometry relations through transformations. It is a good visual representation of the trigonometry identities. This activity correlates to the following highlighted expectation for students:
>
> - Understand measurable *attributes* of objects and the units, systems, and processes of measurement
> - **Apply appropriate techniques, *tools*, and formulas to determine measurements**

Trigonometry is the study of the relations between the sides and angles of triangles. It is a clear extension of Euclidean geometry traditionally taught in an algebraic way. Thus, it was not uncommon for visual learners in the past to have difficulty with the subject, prompting creative mathematicians to write and U.S. textbook companies to publish alternatives to rote pedagogy that de-emphasize simple memorization in favor of true understanding.

For the purposes of this activity, the combination of transformational geometry techniques (specifically reflection) with some of the essentials of Euclidean geometry and trigonometry will serve to bring trigonometry relationships into a more visible light, beginning with these three sets of formulas:

1. Complementary angles: $\cos(90° - \theta) = \sin\theta$
   $\sin(90° - \theta) = \cos\theta$

2. Negative angles: $\cos(-\theta) = \cos\theta$
   $\sin(-\theta) = -\sin\theta$

3. Supplementary angles: $\cos(180° - \theta) = -\cos\theta$
   $\sin(180° - \theta) = \sin\theta$

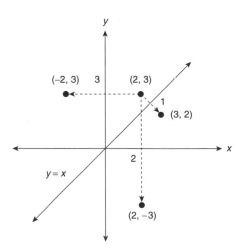

Complementary-Negative-Supplementary (CNS) Angle Formulas

Each student needs the following materials:

- CNS Angle Formulas worksheet (see the appendix for a full-page blackline master)
- A sharp pencil

Show students Figure 4.21 and ask them to identify (in general terms) the rules of point reflection.

Figure 4.21

The following are the correct responses:

1. Reflection over the line $y = x$:
   $(x, y) \rightarrow (y, x)$
   x- and y-coordinates switch

2. Reflection over the x-axis:
   $(x, y) \rightarrow (x, -y)$
   y-coordinate changes sign

3. Reflection over the y-axis:
   $(x, y) \rightarrow (-x, y)$
   x-coordinate changes sign

Then ask students to use basic trigonometry to recall how the definitions of both the **sine** and **cosine of an acute angle** θ change from Figure 4.22 to Figure 4.23 when the hypotenuse of the right triangle is set $= 1$:

$$\cos \theta = \frac{x}{r} = \frac{x}{1} = x \quad \text{and} \quad \sin \theta = \frac{y}{r} = \frac{y}{1} = y.$$

Now ask students to combine two concepts into one process. For each of the Trigonometry Angle Formulas (highlighted in the introduction to this activity) and their accompanying figures here, students begin by drawing an angle (θ) in which the initial side is on the x-axis and the terminal side is in the first quadrant, represented by the ray drawn to the point $(\cos \theta, \sin \theta)$ on the unit circle.

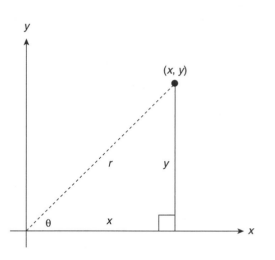

Figure 4.22

Complementary Angle Formulas

Have students use the CNS Angle Formulas worksheet (see Figure 4.24; see the appendix for a full-page blackline master) to complete the following steps:

1. In the first circle on the worksheet, label the x- and y-axes.

2. Identify and label the third line in the picture.

   Answer: the line $y = x$

3. Assuming that this is a unit circle (the length of either ray $= 1$), find the angle being measured from the x-axis to the first ray encountered counterclockwise and label it θ.

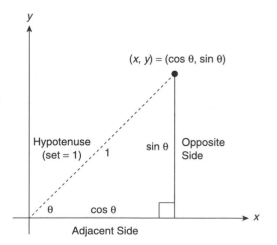

Figure 4.23

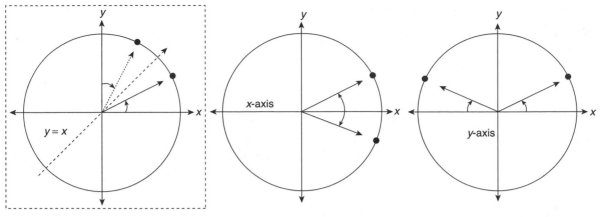

Figure 4.24

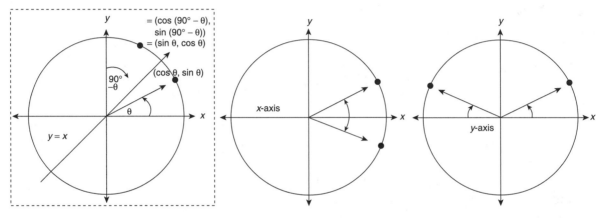

Figure 4.25

4. What are the coordinates of the point at the tip of this ray along the unit circle?

   Answer: the point $(\cos \theta, \sin \theta)$

5. Now find the angle being measured from the y-axis to the other ray. How should it be labeled?

   Answer: $90° - \theta$

6. What are the coordinates of the point at the tip of this ray along the unit circle?

   Answer: the point $(\cos (90° - \theta), \sin (90° - \theta))$

7. Now suppose you notice that the two points along the unit circle are reflections of each other over the line $y = x$. Starting at the point labeled

(cos θ, sin θ), could you determine a "reflective" way to label the point on the other side of $y = x$?

>   **Answer:** Since x- and y-coordinates switch, call it (sin θ, cos θ).

>   Refer to Figure 4.25 to see what students' worksheets should look like.

8.   If you equate the two labels for that point (match up the two x-coordinates, match up the two y-coordinates), what do you notice?

>   **Answer:** $\cos(90° - θ) = \sin θ$, and $\sin(90° - θ) = \cos θ$

Negative Angle Formulas

Have students use the CNS Angle Formulas worksheet (see Figure 4.26; see the appendix for a full-page blackline master) to complete the following steps:

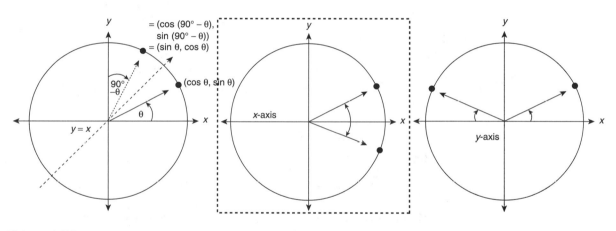

Figure 4.26

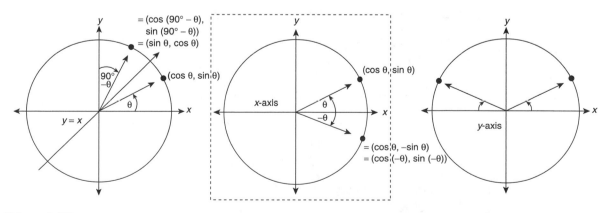

Figure 4.27

1. In the second circle on the worksheet, label the x- and y-axes.

2. Assuming that this is a unit circle (the length of either ray = 1), find the angle being measured from the x-axis to the first ray encountered counterclockwise and label it θ.

3. What are the coordinates of the point at the tip of this ray along the unit circle?

    Answer: the point $(\cos \theta, \sin \theta)$

4. Now find the angle being measured from the x-axis clockwise to the other ray. How should it be labeled?

    Answer: $-\theta$

5. What are the coordinates of the point at the tip of this ray along the unit circle?

    Answer: the point $(\cos (-\theta), \sin (-\theta))$

6. Now suppose you notice that the two points along the unit circle are reflections of each other over the x-axis. Starting at the point labeled $(\cos \theta, \sin \theta)$, could you determine a "reflective" way to label the point on the other side of the x-axis?

    Answer: Since the y-coordinate changes sign, call it $(\cos \theta, -\sin \theta)$. Refer to Figure 4.27 to see what students' worksheets should look like.

7. If you equate the two labels for that point (match up the two x-coordinates, match up the two y-coordinates), what do you notice?

    Answers: $\cos (-\theta) = \cos \theta$, and $\sin (-\theta) = -\sin \theta$

NOTE: Cosine is thus defined as an **even function** (symmetric to the y-axis) and sine as an **odd function** (symmetric to the origin).

Supplementary Angle Formulas

Have students use the CNS Angle Formulas Worksheet (see Figure 4.28; see the appendix for a full-page blackline master) to complete the following steps:

1. In the third circle on the worksheet, label the x- and y-axes.

2. Assuming that this is a unit circle (the length of either ray = 1), find the angle being measured from the positive x-axis to the first ray encountered counterclockwise and label it θ.

3. What are the coordinates of the point at the tip of this ray along the unit circle?

    Answer: the point $(\cos \theta, \sin \theta)$

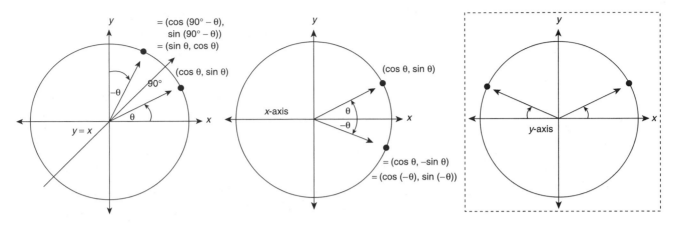

Figure 4.28

4. Now find the angle being measured from the negative *x*-axis clockwise to the other ray. How should it be labeled?

   Answer: $180° - \theta$

5. What are the coordinates of the point at the tip of this ray along the unit circle?

   Answer: the point $(\cos(180° - \theta), \sin(180° - \theta))$

6. Now, suppose you notice that the two points along the unit circle are reflections of each other over the *y*-axis. Starting at the point labeled $(\cos\theta, \sin\theta)$, could you determine a "reflective" way to label the point on the other side of the *x*-axis?

   Answer: Since the *x*-coordinate changes sign, call it $(-\cos\theta, \sin\theta)$.

   Refer to Figure 4.29 to see what students' worksheets should look like.

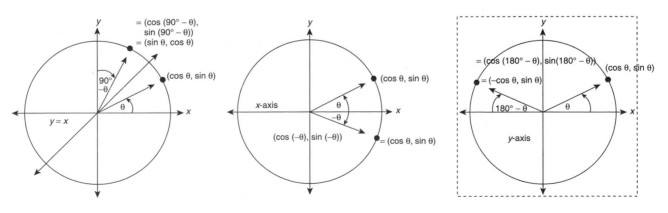

Figure 4.29

7. If you equate the two labels for that point (match up the two *x*-coordinates, match up the two *y*-coordinates), what do you notice?

> **Answers:** $\cos(180° - \theta) = -\cos\theta$, and $\sin(180° - \theta) = \sin\theta$

NOTE: The sines of supplementary angles are equal—a critical piece of information used to solve problems correctly involving the Law of Sines.

The Coordinate Clock

In this exploration, students take each hour number on an analog (face) clock and give it trigonometric value coordinates. Process 1 involves identifying trigonometric values on the *x*- and *y*-axes (corresponding to the face clock at 12, 3, 6, and 9 o'clock), and Process 2 involves identifying trigonometric values at all of the other numbers on the face clock (at 1, 2, 4, 5, 7, 8, 10, and 11 o'clock).

Each student needs the following materials:

- 12-3-6-9 O'Clock worksheet (see the appendix for a full-page blackline master)
- Degree Time Table (see the appendix for full-page blackline master)
- 1-2-4-5-7-8-10-11 O'Clock worksheet (see the appendix for a full-page blackline master)
- A ruler
- A sharp pencil

Process 1: 12-3-6-9 O'Clock

In the first circle of the 12-3-6-9 O'Clock worksheet (see Figure 4.30; see the appendix for a full-page blackline master), have students mark the four compass points of the face of a circular clock (12, 3, 6, and 9 o'clock) with a pencil.

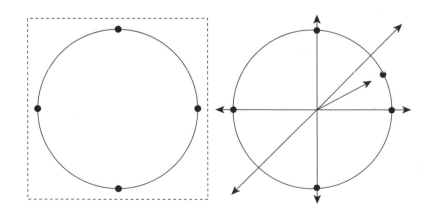

Figure 4.30

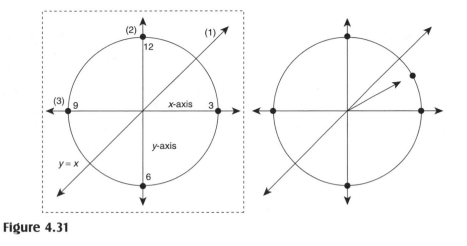

Figure 4.31

Then have students draw the three lines of reflection (identified in CNS Angle Formulas) directly on that clock face. Refer to Figure 4.31 for an example.

Next, ask students to complete the Degree Time Table. Figure 4.32 illustrates the answers students should get (see the appendix for a blank blackline master). The first column represents the degrees at each specified point on the unit circle reading counterclockwise from 3:00 (= 0°).

Degrees	Time	(1) Over $y = x$	(2) Over x-axis	(3) Over y-axis
0°	3:00	12:00	3:00*	9:00
90°	12:00	3:00	6:00	12:00*
180°	9:00	6:00	9:00*	3:00
270°	6:00	9:00	12:00	6:00*

Figure 4.32

Ask students what interesting patterns emerge from reading the columns in the answer key. One is the alternation of the **identity element** (represented with an asterisk) in the Over x-axis and the Over y-axis columns.

The other involves the loss of orientation as one reads either column 1, 2, or 3. Note that even though trigonometry clearly defines angles along the unit circle in a counterclockwise direction, each of the read-down columns contains a clockwise pattern (e.g., column 2 reads 3, 6, 9, 12).

Instruct students to return to the 12-3-6-9 O'Clock worksheet. Using the second circle, they should replace the clock face numbers with the coordinates of those points along the unit circle (recall radius = 1) that are on either the x- or y-axis (see Figure 4.33). Remind students that they can label any other point along the unit circle with the standard (x, y) or, more desirable here, with $(\cos\theta, \sin\theta)$.

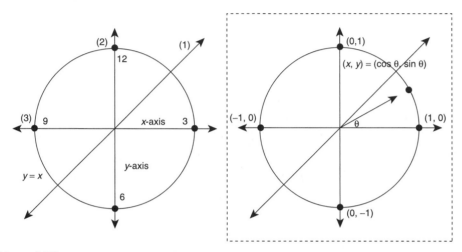

Figure 4.33

Two fairly common patterns should become apparent. First, since $x = \cos\theta$, the values for the cosine of $0°$, $90°$, $180°$, $270°$, and $360°$ $(= 0°)$ are $\{1, 0, -1, 0, \text{ and } 1\}$, respectively. Similarly, for $y = \sin\theta$, the respective values are $\{0, 1, 0, -1, \text{ and } 0\}$. These **quadrantal angle values** take on importance when students face graphing cosine and sine waves.

Process 2: 1-2-4-5-7-8-10-11 O'Clock

Have students use the 1-2-4-5-7-8-10-11 O'Clock worksheet (see the appendix for a full-page blackline master) to fill in the in-between numbers on the face of a clock. Refer to Figure 4.34.

Since there are 12 numbers on the face, each sector between numbers would $= \frac{360°}{12} = 30°$. For example, beginning at 3:00 and moving counterclockwise, 1:00 would represent $60°$ on the unit circle. Ask students the following: What is the cosine and sine of $60°$?

On the reverse side of the worksheet, have students draw a **unit equilateral triangle** (all angles = $60°$, and all sides = 1). Remind students of the three things the perpendicular bisector can do: It bisects the top angle, bisects the base, and equals $\frac{\sqrt{3}}{2}$ (using the Pythagorean Theorem). See Figure 4.35.

Figure 4.34

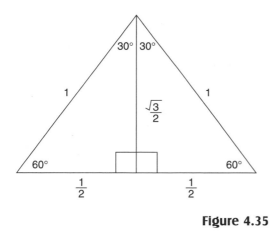

Figure 4.35

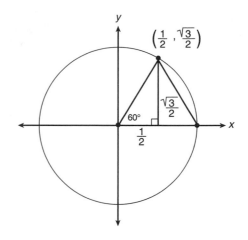

Figure 4.36

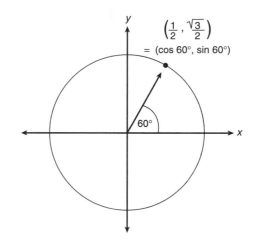

Figure 4.37

Have students turn the 1-2-4-5-7-8-10-11 O'Clock worksheet back over and transcribe the labeled unit equilateral triangle into the first quadrant (the triangle's top angle should touch the unit circle at 1:00) into the third circle. As shown in Figure 4.36, students can label the 1:00 point with $\left(\frac{1}{2}, \frac{\sqrt{3}}{2}\right)$.

Remind students that all points along the unit circle are defined such that $x = \cos\theta$ and $y = \sin\theta$, where θ = a central angle of rotation. Therefore, according to Figure 4.37, $\cos 60° = \frac{1}{2}$ and $\sin 60° = \frac{\sqrt{3}}{2}$.

Now ask students the following: How does knowing the three rules of point reflection listed earlier in the discussion on CNS Angle Formulas allow you to discover values for some other numbers on the circular clock face (e.g., 2:00, 5:00, 11:00)?

Have students use the 1-2-4-5-7-8-10-11 O'Clock worksheet (see the appendix for a full-page blackline master) to complete the following steps:

1. Reflect the 1:00 point $\left(\frac{1}{2}, \frac{\sqrt{3}}{2}\right)$ over the line $y = x$. Flipping 1:00 ($= 60°$) over the line now places the point at 2:00 ($= 30°$).

   Since x- and y-coordinates *switch*, $\cos 30° = \frac{\sqrt{3}}{2}$ and $\sin 30° = \frac{1}{2}$. See Figure 4.38.

2. Next, have students reflect the 1:00 point $\left(\frac{1}{2}, \frac{\sqrt{3}}{2}\right)$ over the y-axis. Flipping 1:00 ($= 60°$) over the y-axis now places the point at 11:00 ($= 120°$).

   Since the y-coordinate changes sign, $\cos 120° = -\frac{1}{2}$ and $\sin 120° = \frac{\sqrt{3}}{2}$. See Figure 4.39.

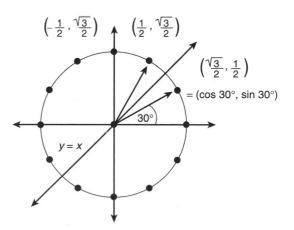

Figure 4.38

3. Finally, have students reflect the 1:00 point $\left(\frac{1}{2}, \frac{\sqrt{3}}{2}\right)$ over the *x*-axis. Flipping 1:00 (= 60°) over the *x*-axis now places the point at 5:00 (= 300°).
   Since the *x*-coordinate changes sign, $\cos 300° = \frac{1}{2}$ and $\sin 300° = -\frac{\sqrt{3}}{2}$. See Figure 4.40.

4. Students should now be able to complete the worksheet for the cosine and sine values at 10:00 (= 150°), 8:00 (= 210°), 7:00 (= 240°), and 4:00 (= 330°).

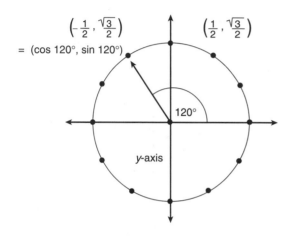

Figure 4.39

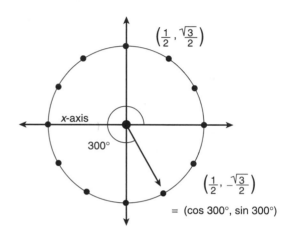

Figure 4.40

Data Analysis and Probability 5

The Data Analysis and Probability Standard, the last of the five content standards, easily affords students their best access to mathematical applications that affect their daily lives. For example, the availability of brand-name merchandise is usually the result of various forms of customer surveys. The election of local, state, and national candidates is the result of political strategies crafted around polling data gathered and analyzed closely throughout a campaign. Advances in the field of medicine are the result of painstaking research and experimentation.

The Johnny Appleseed activity helps students familiarize themselves with their own real-world data and follow them through the organizational, interpretative (graph-making), and predictive phases of statistical analysis. The 100-Yard Field activity organizes that same data, yet graphs them in a couple of different ways (one of which is technological) so that students may gauge for themselves what characteristics of the data they want to highlight and what type of graph would perform that task most efficiently. The ability to interpret data organized in a grid lies at the heart of the Mind Your P's & C's activity, which helps students visualize the difference between a permutation and a combination.

Probability is the theme of the last two activities. In the Bag of Beads activity, students encounter the idea that individual outcomes might be difficult to predict but that the frequency of various outcomes is not. In the 1–3–3–1 Pattern activity, students consider 10 seemingly unrelated scenarios (many probability based) that touch on all five content standards but are nonetheless linked by the recognition of a simple number pattern.

JOHNNY APPLESEED

> ## Grades 6–9
>
> Examples of data sets are commonplace in today's mathematics texts, but the numbers that are generated therein typically seem artificial. What mathematics teachers request more than any other activities are situations that generate real-world data and more graphing opportunities for their students. This activity addresses that need in a very straightforward and inexpensive fashion. This activity correlates to the following highlighted expectation for students:
>
> - **Formulate *questions* that can be asked with data and collect, organize, and display relevant data to answer them**
> - Select and use appropriate statistical *methods* to analyze data
> - Develop and evaluate inferences and *predictions* that are based on data
> - Understand and *apply* basic concepts of probability

Seeds of Learning

Each student needs the following materials:

- Paper towels
- A plastic spoon
- Seeds-Apples Table (see the appendix for a full-page blackline master)
- A 3 × 5-inch card
- One piece of precopied and specially drawn graph paper (the graph paper should be a grid with squares large enough so that students can draw Figures 5.5 and 5.6 without too much difficulty)
- A four-function calculator
- A sharp pencil
- One apple (you may want to have students bring one to school on the designated day, but make sure you have plenty of apples on hand, just in case)

The teacher needs the following materials:

- A sharp knife (never let students handle the knife)
- A bulletin board with *x*- and *y*-axes in an L-shape (see Figure 5.1)

Begin the activity by going from student to student and cutting their apples. Cut each apple with a plane sideways cut (across the apple, as opposed to an up-and-down cut through the stem). The result is a double-star pattern on the insides of both halves of the apple. Have students use the plastic spoon to dig out and separate (on the paper towels) all of the seeds.

The following is an example of a conversation that may take place with students. You might consider letting students eat their apples as long as their seeds remain intact.

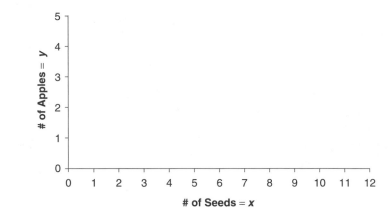

Figure 5.1

Teacher: Why do you think we are interested in the seeds?

Students: They grow trees that grow more apples.

Teacher: OK. So, how many apples do you think we have here in the room today? How could we figure out that number?

Students: We all have one apple. So, if we count ourselves, we also have the total number of apples. *(This is known as a one-to-one correspondence.)*

Teacher: That's correct. Now, are there *other* questions we could ask ourselves today?

Students: How many total *seeds* are there in the room?

Teacher: Fair enough, but that's much harder to figure out. If you got up all at once and started going around the room counting, the numbers would start getting big, you might forget to count someone's seeds, and it would get pretty noisy. Tell you what. Use your Seeds-Apples Table (see the appendix for a full-page blackline master), and let me start you on the road to a more efficient answer.

Who has the highest number of seeds? *(Students volunteer their answers, and it is decided that the one student with 12 has the most.)* Let's put 0 through 12 in the # of Seeds = *x* column (see Figure 5.2).

OK. With a show of hands, how many of you have no seeds? *(No one raises a hand.)*

Please put the number 0 in the second column across from the 0 in the first column. Now, how many of you have one seed? *(Continue through to twelve.)* (See Figure 5.3 for the class example.)

Students: What's the third column for?

Teacher: Before we get to that, note how the second column serves a checking purpose. (If you add up the second column [# of apples], that number should match the head count for how many students are in the room. The number of apples should match the number of students.)

Students: If we add the second column, we get the total number of apples (*21 for this example*).

Teacher: Let me repeat what was just said. If *adding* helps us find the total number of apples, then what *other* operation might help us determine the total number of seeds?

Students: Multiplication!

Teacher: That's right. Remember your work with **dimensional analysis,** and let's pick an example from your tables (see Figure 5.4):

5 seeds per apple means 5 seeds ÷ 1 apple

$$\frac{5 \text{ seeds}}{1 \text{ apple}} \cdot 3 \text{ apples} = 15 \text{ seeds}$$

(Multiply column 1 [# of seeds per apple] times column 2 [# of apples] to find the value for column 3.)

# of Seeds = x	# of Apples = y	
0		
1		
2		
3		
4		
5		
6		
7		
8		
9		
10		
11		
12		

Figure 5.2

# of Seeds = x	# of Apples = y	x • y =
0	0	
1	1	
2	1	
3	0	
4	1	
5	3	
6	1	
7	5	
8	2	
9	4	
10	2	
11	0	
12	1	
Totals	21	

Figure 5.3

# of Seeds = x	# of Apples = y	x • y =
0	0	0
1	1	1
2	1	2
3	0	0
4	1	4
5	3	15
6	1	6
7	5	35
8	2	16
9	4	36
10	2	20
11	0	0
12	1	12
Totals	21	147

Figure 5.4

Students: Should we add up the third column, too?

Teacher: Sure. That sum turns out to be what?

Students: 147 total seeds.

Teacher: So, how should we label that column?

Students: $x \cdot y$

Teacher: Let's now take our tables to the next stage. **Statistics** is the collection, organization, and analysis of data. Keep that definition in mind because the best statistics do *each* of those three things. We've done the collection part, so now let's organize them. *(The teacher makes reference to the bulletin board with x- and y-axes in an L-shape for this part of the lesson.)*

Write your name on your 3 × 5-inch card in big block letters. Now, let's have a volunteer put his or her card on the graph on the bulletin board. *(The teacher chooses a volunteer and guides him or her to make the proper placement.)*

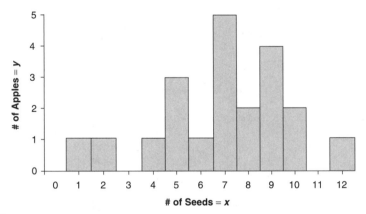

Figure 5.5

Now, how about someone else? *(Every student gets a turn. The teacher has students transcribe the graph in Figure 5.5 onto graph paper.)*

Now, what kind of graph is this? I'll give you a hint—this is not a **bar graph,** even though it obviously has bars.

Students: *(Students do not respond unless they have been introduced to histograms.)*

Teacher: It's a histogram.

Students: What's the difference?

Teacher: Well, a histogram is used for continuous data. The bars, as we have drawn them, touch. Bar graphs are used when doing separate categories, such as tuition paid by in-state versus out-of-state students at a particular university. In a true bar graph, the bars do not touch.

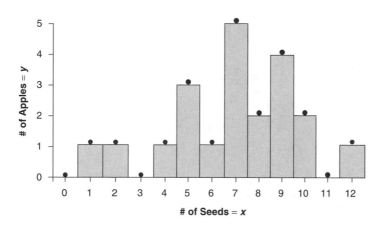

Figure 5.6

Students: Didn't we study other kinds of graphs before?

Teacher: You did. We could draw circle graphs if we were interested in various percentages. Since we aren't doing that here with our seeds, the next logical step for us would be to draw a line graph.

Students: Do we have to make a brand-new graph?

Teacher: No, just put a dot on top of each of the bars in your histogram and then connect the dots. If you don't have a bar, put the dot on the bottom (horizontal) axis. (See Figure 5.6.)

Students: OK, we're all done.

Teacher: Not so fast. Go back to the definition of statistics you just put in your notes, and *then* decide if we're done.

Students: We haven't *analyzed* yet. But how do you expect us to do that? Wait . . . what about **mean, median,** and **mode?**

Teacher: And do you remember what needs to be done *before* you start?

Students: Arrange the data from lowest to highest.

(The teacher writes 1, 2, 4, 5, 5, 5, 6, 7, 7, 7, 7, 7, 8, 8, 9, 9, 9, 9, 10, 10, 12.)

Teacher: Your tables will help you with calculating the mean. The median and the mode will both come from this data listing.

Students: The mean is $\frac{147}{21}$ = 7. The median is 7, and the mode is 7. They're all the same number!

Teacher: That coincidence indicates that something else might be happening here. Write down another definition in your notes: A **normal distribution** is a theoretical frequency distribution for a group of data, represented by a bell-shaped curve that is symmetrical to its mean.

First practice drawing a bell on the back of your graph paper. Then, try to draw one right on your graph (see Figure 5.7).

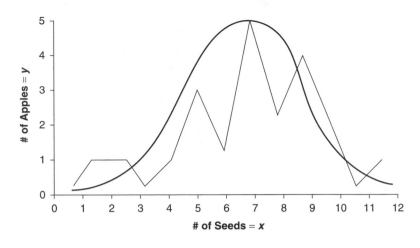

Figure 5.6

Let's take one more look back and make a list of all of the mathematical ideas we reviewed today:

- Frequency distribution (making a two-column [*x* and *y*] chart)
- Dimensional analysis (e.g., 7 seeds per apple times 5 apples = 35 seeds)
- The difference between a histogram and a bar graph
- How to make a histogram and a frequency polygon (line graph) from it
- Mean, median, and mode
- How to draw a bell curve

One Step Further

The following are ideas for further research:

Mathematics: standard deviation
Chebeshev's Theorem (to test for normalcy of data)

Science: oxidation (making apple-head dolls)
density and displacement (floating apples in water)

THE 100-YARD FIELD

Grades 6–9

A compact and efficient tool for comparing sets of data is the **five-number summary L-Q1-M-Q3-H** (L = the lowest term or minimum, Q1 = the first quartile, M = the median, Q3 = the third quartile, and H = the highest term or maximum). In this activity, students learn what each number means and compute each of the five numbers before they summarize and draw the graph of the five numbers. This activity correlates to the following highlighted expectation for students:

- Formulate *questions* that can be asked with data and collect, organize, and display relevant data to answer them
- **Select and use appropriate statistical *methods* to analyze data**
- Develop and evaluate inferences and *predictions* that are based on data
- Understand and *apply* basic concepts of probability

You may want to review some terms before proceeding:

A **percentile** is a number that corresponds to 1 of 100 equal divisions of the range of a group of data. A percentile characterizes a value contained in the data group therein but does not exceed the specified percentage of the data group. (For example, a score higher than 80% of all of those who took the same test is said to be at the 80th percentile.)

A **quartile** is the value of the boundary at the 25th percentile (first quartile), 50th percentile (second quartile or median), or 75th percentile (third quartile) of a group of data divided into four parts, each containing a quarter of the data.

Determining a percentile is simply a matter of using a formula and responding accordingly from one of two possible scenarios:

%-tile $P_k = \frac{n \bullet k}{100}$ (in which k = % desired and n = # of pieces of data)

Case 1: If the answer is a whole number, *add .5* to it.

Case 2: If the answer is a decimal, *round up* to the next whole number.

As an example, consider the arithmetic sequence of natural numbers from 1 to 10, inclusive (1, 2, 3, 4, 5, 6, 7, 8, 9, 10). A dividing line drawn right through the middle (the median in this example = 5.5) could, in football parlance, be the 50-yard line, which is the same as the 50th percentile. The half-field to the left with numbers less than 5.5 reads 1, 2, 3, 4, 5, and *its* median (the 25-yard line, which can be called either the 25th percentile or the first quartile) = 3. By the same argument, the half-field to the right with numbers greater than 5.5 reads 6, 7, 8, 9, 10, and *its* median (the *other* 25-yard line, which can be called either the 75th percentile or the third quartile) = 8.

Now, verify these yard line placements with the following formula:

$$\text{Median} = \text{50th \%-tile} = P_{50} = \frac{10 \cdot 50}{100} = \frac{500}{100} = 5 \text{ (add .5} \rightarrow \text{``5.5th'')}$$

(The median is the "5.5th" number [halfway between 5 and 6] = 5.5.)

$$Q1 = \text{25th \%-tile} = P_{25} = \frac{10 \cdot 25}{100} = \frac{250}{100} = 2.5 \text{ (round up to ``3rd'')}$$

(The first quartile is the number in the 3rd position = 3.)

$$Q3 = \text{75th \%-tile} = P_{75} = \frac{10 \cdot 75}{100} = \frac{750}{100} = 7.5 \text{ (round up to ``8th'')}$$

(The third quartile is the number in the 8th position = 8.)

The remainder of this section examines the data listing that was generated in the Johnny Appleseed activity (1, 2, 4, 5, 5, 5, 6, 7, 7, 7, 7, 7, 8, 8, 9, 9, 9, 9, 10, 10, 12). Visually, the median is the 11th number (= 7), but be cautious in helping students identify the two other quartiles. Any number *directly on* the 50-yard line (such as 7) counts for both halves of the field when computing quartiles.

For example, the first quartile would use the 11 numbers *left of and including* the median (1, 2, 4, 5, 5, 5, 6, 7, 7, 7, 7), with the 6th number being the 25-yard line (= 5), and the third quartile would use the 11 numbers *right of and including* the median (7, 7, 8, 8, 9, 9, 9, 9, 10, 10, 12), with the 6th number there, or 16th overall, being the other 25-yard line (= 9). To verify:

$$\text{Median} = \text{50th \%-tile} = P_{50} = \frac{21 \cdot 50}{100} = \frac{1,050}{100} = 10.5 \text{ (round up to ``11th'')}$$

(The median is the "11th" number = 7.)

$$Q1 = \text{25th \%-tile} = P_{25} = \frac{21 \cdot 25}{100} = \frac{525}{100} = 5.25 \text{ (round up to ``6th'')}$$

(The first quartile is the number in the 6th position = 5.)

$$Q3 = \text{75th \%-tile} = P_{75} = \frac{21 \cdot 75}{100} = \frac{1,575}{100} = 15.75 \text{ (round up to ``16th'')}$$

(The third quartile is the number in the 16th position = 9.)

CALCULATOR APPLICATION

Box-and-Whiskers Plot

Improvements built into the TI-73 include the ability to draw **circle graphs** (or pie charts) and bar graphs. Before we engage those, however, let's explore drawing a box-and-whiskers plot using the two-column frequency distribution (below) created in the previous unit.

Using the Application With Students

Seeds = $L1$	Apples = $L2$
1	1
2	1
4	1
5	3
6	1
7	5
8	2
9	4
10	2
12	1

Erase: **2nd PLOT 4 ENTER CLEAR**

Go to the **Y =** *screen*

(*and* **CLEAR** *all old lines*)

2nd MEM 6 ENTER CLEAR

Input: **LIST**

1 ENTER   2 ENTER . . .

2nd PLOT 1

Select: **On, B-and-W, 2nd STAT 1** (*for* **L1**),
2nd STAT 2 (*for* **L2**)

Output:

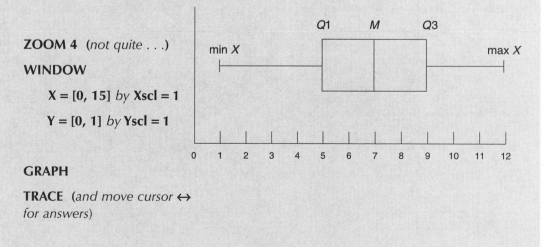

ZOOM 4 (*not quite . . .*)

WINDOW

    X = [0, 15] *by* **Xscl = 1**

    Y = [0, 1] *by* **Yscl = 1**

GRAPH

TRACE (*and move cursor* ↔
for answers)

(*Continued*)

(Continued)

The **circle graph** (or pie chart) uses categories instead of regular discrete data. So, looking back at the previous table, we may opt to sort our data into the number of students who found an odd number of seeds (13) and the number of students who found an even number of seeds (8).

The **LIST** function on the TI-73 reflects this new procedure. To create the table at the right, one must essentially begin with the last available list (the unnamed **L7**) for the odd and even categories and work backward to the **L6** list to input their respective data:

L6	TYPE
13	ODD
8	EVEN

Erase Steps (as performed previously)

Input: **LIST**

    (*Move cursor to heading of* **L7**)

    DEL (*to get the prompt* **Name=** *along the bottom of the screen*)

    2nd TEXT
    Click on: T ENTER
                Y ENTER
                P ENTER
                E ENTER
                "Done" ENTER
    ENTER

    (*Move cursor down underneath the heading to* **TYPE(1) =**)

    2nd TEXT
    Click on: " ENTER
                O ENTER
                D ENTER
                D ENTER
                " ENTER
                "Done" ENTER

ENTER

2nd TEXT

Click on: " **ENTER**

E **ENTER**

V **ENTER**

E **ENTER**

N **ENTER**

" **ENTER**

"Done" ENTER

ENTER

(*Move cursor left underneath the heading to* **L6(1) =**)

13 ENTER 8 ENTER

2nd PLOT 1

Select: **On, Circle, 2nd STAT 7** (*for* **TYPE**),

2nd STAT 6 (*for* **L6**), **Percent**

GRAPH

Output (picture at the right):

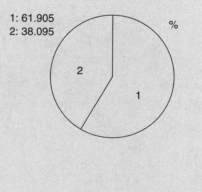

1: 61.905
2: 38.095
%

NOTE: If you select **Number** (instead of **Percent**),
the figure remains the same, but the upper left-hand
corner will read as follows:

1: 13

2: 8

(Continued)

(Continued)

The **bar graph** is another way to illustrate categories and discrete data (and should be differentiated in the students' minds from a **histogram,** which uses continuous data):

Return to: **2nd PLOT 1**

Select: **On, Bars, 2nd STAT 7** (*for* **TYPE),**

   2nd STAT 6 (*for* **L6), (***skip over* **DataLists 2 and 3), Vert, 1**

   GRAPH

   TRACE (*move the cursor ↔*)

Output (picture at the right):

NOTE: *If you select* **Hor** (*instead of* **Vert**)*, the bars will be displayed sideways.*

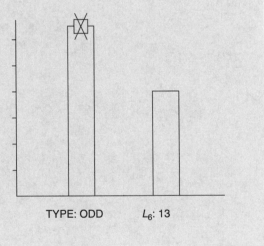

TYPE: ODD L_6: 13

MIND YOUR P's & C's

Grades 8–10

This activity explores the difference between permutations and combinations. There is even a technology component that illustrates nPr and nCr functions. This activity correlates to the following highlighted expectation for students:

- Formulate *questions* that can be asked with data and collect, organize, and display relevant data to answer them
- Select and use appropriate statistical *methods* to analyze data
- **Develop and evaluate inferences and *predictions* that are based on data**
- Understand and *apply* basic concepts of probability

A teacher once asked her class how many of them had access to combination locks, and every student raised his or her hand. When the teacher replied, "There is no such thing as a combination lock," the class became very confused. NOTE: The lock boxes used by realtors are considered combination locks. Realtors punch in four numbers in any order to open them. For this activity, the vast majority of students will be thinking of their lockers, bike locks, and so on.

Truth is, the teacher is correct under the strict definitions of the terms **permutation** (any arrangement of numbers in which order is also important) and **combination** (in which order does not matter). This activity will illustrate the difference.

Each student needs the following materials:

- A set of four different-colored tiles or blocks (e.g., blue, yellow, red, and green)
- Permutations-Combinations Table (see the appendix for a full-page blackline master)
- A ruler
- A sharp pencil

1. Ask students to arrange the tiles in ordered pairs without replacement. (In other words, there should be no repeating-color pairs: no blue-blue, yellow-yellow, red-red, or green-green.) The matrix in Figure 5.8 illustrates the 12 possible permutations.

2. Then ask students the following question: How does making such pairs, regardless of order (e.g., red-blue = blue-red), change the matrix?

   Draw a diagonal line through cells A1, B2, C3, and D4 to create a line of symmetry (see Figure 5.9). Direct students' focus to the top triangle (A2, A3, A4, B3, B4, and C4).

   There are six possible combinations (four items taken two at a time), which is half the number of the previous permutations.

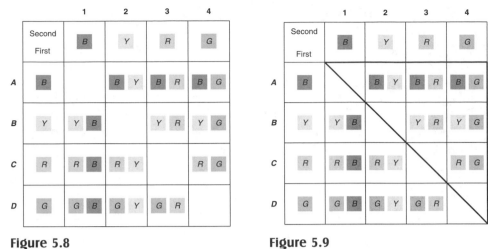

Figure 5.8   **Figure 5.9**

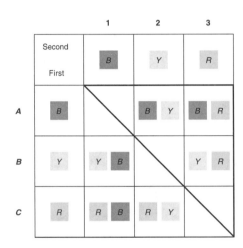

Figure 5.10

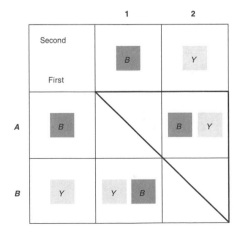

Figure 5.11

3. Instruct students to take away one of the colors (e.g., green) before repeating Steps 1 and 2 (see Figure 5.10). Students will see that the removal of green significantly affects the result matrix—row D and column 4 no longer exist. The number of permutations decreases to six, and the number of combinations shrinks to three (although that number is still half the number of permutations).

4. Now ask students the following question: What are the number of permutations and the number of combinations for only *two* colors (e.g., blue and yellow)?

   Because row C and column 3 no longer exist, there are two permutations (blue-yellow *and* yellow-blue) and $2 \div 2 = 1$ combination (blue-yellow *or* yellow-blue). Refer to Figure 5.11.

5. Then ask students the following question: Given "n" colored tiles or blocks, how many two-color permutations and combinations (again, without replacement) are possible?

   Have students organize their data using the Permutations-Combinations Table (see Figure 5.12; see the appendix for a full-page blackline master). Students will see that two patterns seem to emerge that lead to a couple of possible formulas.

6. Testing the formulas requires expanding the result matrix to include a fifth colored tile or block (e.g., white: row E and column 5) and seeing if the resulting data verify. However, to prove that the formulas are accurate, students may wish to construct appropriate finite difference equations (see Chapter 2).

A more direct proof possibility requires students to match suspected formulas from the Permutations-Combinations Table to results from the formulas for permutations and combinations, respectively:

$$_nP_r = \frac{n!}{(n-r)!} \quad \text{and} \quad _nC_r = \frac{n!}{r! \cdot (n-r)!}$$

Colors	Permutations	Combinations
2	$2 \times 1 = 2$	$2 \div 2 = 1$
3	$3 \times 2 = 6$	$6 \div 2 = 3$
4	$4 \times 3 = 12$	$12 \div 2 = 6$
n	$n(n-1)$	$\frac{n(n-1)}{2}$

Figure 5.12

For $r = 2$ (taking n items 2 at a time), students can confirm that

$$_nP_2 = \frac{n!}{(n-2)!} = n \cdot (n-1) \text{ (permutations)}$$

and

$$_nC_2 = \frac{n!}{2! \cdot (n-2)!} = \frac{n \cdot (n-1)}{2} \text{ (combinations)}$$

One Step Further

So, why are locks misnamed combination locks? As most people know, the prototypical lock requires that the operator remember not only three numbers but also their sequential order.

Pick any three numbers ($n = 3$), and consider the above formulas ($r = 3$ at a time). Which formula actually belongs to these locks?

$$_3P_3 = \frac{3!}{(3-3)!} = 3 \cdot 2 \cdot 1 = 6 \text{ (permutations)}$$

TI-83/84 Plus Calculator Steps for $_3P_3$: 3 MATH ← ("PRB") 2 3 ENTER

$$_3C_3 = \frac{3!}{3! \cdot (3-3)!} = \frac{3!}{3!} = 1 \quad \text{(combination)}$$

TI-83/84 Plus Calculator Steps for $_3C_3$: 3 MATH ← ("PRB") 3 3 ENTER

Therefore, if all you knew were the three numbers, any order would open the lock (one combination of three numbers). But, and much more accurately, if order matters (and it certainly does), then you need to know the numbers and their proper order (six permutations of three numbers) to open the lock.

Therefore, the teacher at the beginning of this unit was right—there is no such thing as a combination lock.

BAG OF BEADS

> ## Grades 6–9
>
> This activity allows students to discover for themselves how the sophisticated concept of limit can arise while working with probabilities. This activity correlates to the following highlighted expectation for students:
>
> - Formulate *questions* that can be asked with data and collect, organize, and display relevant data to answer them
> - Select and use appropriate statistical *methods* to analyze data
> - Develop and evaluate inferences and *predictions* that are based on data
> - **Understand and *apply* basic concepts of probability**

The **Law of Large Numbers** states that empirical (experimental) probability begins to approach the value of theoretical (predictive) probability the longer a particular experiment is repeated. NOTE: This activity is most successful when students work in pairs.

Students need the following materials:

- A small paper bag with 100 small beads of three different colors (make sure to put the same number of colored beads [e.g., 50 red, 30 white, and 20 green] into each bag)
- Group Tally Table (see the appendix for a full-page blackline master)
- Class Summary Table (see the appendix for a full-page blackline master)
- A four-function calculator
- A sharp pencil

Collection Phase

Without looking inside, one student should reach into his or her bag and pull out either exactly 10 beads or fewer than 10 (to which more may be added to get 10). NOTE: If students pull out more than 10, they must put all the beads back in the bag for a retrial (try again).

Have the other student record the results of each trial on the Group Tally Table (see Figure 5.13; see appendix for a full-page blackline master). Have students repeat this process 10 times. Make sure students return the beads to the bag after each selection. Instruct students to calculate the sum of each color and put it on the Group Tally Table.

Now give students these instructions for making a prediction: Given the information you have on your Group Tally Tables, and *before* dumping your beads out to be hand counted, predict how many of each color of beads there are in your bag.

Trial #	Red	White	Green
1			
2			
3			
4			
5			
6			
7			
8			
9			
10			
Totals			

Figure 5.13

Afterward, allow students to dump the beads on their desks to see how accurate their predictions were.

Prediction Phase

Assign a number to each group (e.g., 1, 2, 3, . . .) and canvass each group's results, putting the data onto the Class Summary Table (see Figure 5.14; see the appendix for a full-page blackline master). NOTE: Figure 5.14 was set up for a class of 20 students (10 pairs), but it can certainly be reconfigured for larger or smaller classes.

For this example class, students counted a total of 1,000 beads (10 groups selected 100 beads each). This makes the sums of each of the three colors fairly easy to write as fractions (and convert to decimals and percents). Those experimental decimals should round very closely to the respective values 0.50, 0.30, and 0.20, the theoretical values approached under the Law of Large Numbers (see Figure 5.15).

If students read the chart horizontally and compare the results obtained by each partnership, they would conclude that there is a great deal of variability in those results. However, using the percentages calculated in the last line of the chart after tabulating vertically, that last line (red 50%, white 30%, and green 20%) indicates that each individual bag should approach the following results: 50 red beads, 30 white beads, and 20 green beads. Should there exist any

Group #	Red	White	Green
1			
2			
3			
4			
5			
6			
7			
8			
9			
10			
Totals			
Probability %			

Figure 5.14

Group #	Red	White	Green
1	53	28	19
2	48	31	21
3	54	24	22
4	51	33	16
5	49	31	20
6	47	32	21
7	50	27	23
8	53	30	17
9	46	35	19
10	52	25	23
Totals	503	296	201
Probability %	= 50.3 or Approx. 50%	= 29.6 or Approx. 30%	= 20.1 or Approx. 20%

Figure 5.15

lingering doubts, have the class repeat the process, retabulate the results, and see that those percentages will, by the Law of Large Numbers and its built-in limiting concept, approach the 50-30-20 percentages more closely because rounding will have even less of an effect.

CALCULATOR APPLICATION

Random Number Generator

```
PROGRAM:NUMBAG
:Disp "TWO_SETS_OF"
:Disp "TEN_RANDOM_
NOS"
:Disp "_"
:1 → J
:Lbl 99
:If J ≤ 4
:Then
:Disp randInt(0, 99, 5)
:J + 1 → J
:Goto 99
:Else
:Pause
```

Both the TI-73 and TI-83/84 Plus graphing calculators have random number generators built into memory that can allow a programmer to use either model to create a simulation model for the Bag of Beads activity.

The original program in the sidebar ("**NUMBAG**") essentially picks two sets of 10 numbers at random from 00 through 99, inclusive, with every run of the program.

Students should be supplied with modified versions of the Group Tally and Class Summary Tables. For example, if the teacher wishes to get results similar to the original hands-on Bag of Beads activity, then column headings could be given as follows:

RED = numbers beginning with 0, 2, 4, 6, 8

WHITE = numbers beginning with 1, 3, or 9

GREEN = numbers beginning with 5 or 7

The theoretical percentages of 50%, 30%, and 20%, respectively, would thus be preserved.

Using the Application With Students

Your Input	Output
Press: **ON**	
PRGM	
(*Scroll down to* **NUMBAG**)	
ENTER	prgmNUMBAG
ENTER	TWO SETS OF
(*Remember that the output is random*)	TEN RANDOM NOS
	{43 1 52 11 81}
	{70 27 37 89 95}
	{78 86 92 57 89}
	{62 45 80 15 97}

(Continued)

(Continued)

Your Input	Output
ENTER	prgmNUMBAG Done
PRGM	
(*Scroll down to* **NUMBAG**)	prgmNUMBAG Done
ENTER	prgmNUMBAG
ENTER	TWO SETS OF
(*Two more random sets of numbers repeat as many times as you wish*)	TEN RANDOM NOS
	{49 2 33 61 11}
	{26 77 47 94 24}
	{46 9 0 52 80}
	{1 79 10 86 18}
ENTER	prgmNUMBAG Done
	prgmNUMBAG Done

THE 1–3–3–1 PATTERN

NOTE: This activity could easily fit in Chapter 9 (Connections), but it serves equally well as a provocative conclusion to the first half of this book, which addresses all five curriculum content standards.

The following 10 scenarios illustrate the 1–3–3–1 pattern. Decide which of these scenarios is worth exploring with your students. The fullest impact, as stated previously, is realized when two or more of these scenarios are used with the same students. Patterns—more than any other piece of mathematics—are the most easily accessible and reusable.

Scenario 1: Checkers

This scenario features a variation of a game of checkers. To begin, give each student a copy of the 1–3–3–1 Checkerboard (see Figure 5.16; see the appendix for a full-page blackline master). Have each student place a game piece on the arrow beneath "Enter Here" and progress diagonally to the various lettered squares (the same as they would in a game of checkers).

The purpose of this exercise is for a "player" (i.e., one student) to predict and verify that there is only one way for the checker to get from the arrow to Square J (from A to C to F to J).

Ask students: How many ways can you get from the arrow to *each* of the four squares along the last row (G, H, I, and J)?

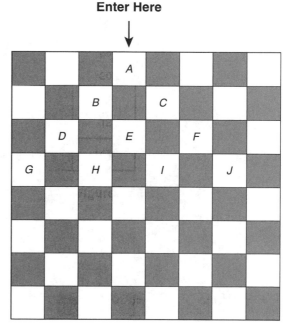

Enter Here

Figure 5.16

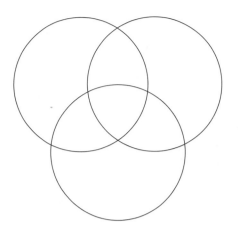

Figure 5.17

One way to G:	from A to B to D to G
Three ways to H:	from A to B to D to H from A to B to E to H from A to C to E to H
Three ways to I:	from A to B to E to I from A to C to E to I from A to C to F to I
One way to J:	from A to C to F to J

Have students place the number of paths from the arrow to G, H, I, and J in the respective squares. The 1–3–3–1 pattern emerges in the last lettered row (1–3–3–1 ways to get to G–H–I–J, respectively).

Scenario 2: Venn Diagram

Remind students that they can use a Venn diagram (see Figure 5.17) to sort three attributes of predetermined items (e.g., size, color, and shape).

Using the example from Sorting It All Out (see Chapter 4), the entire first circle (upper left) contains large items (size), the entire second circle (upper right) contains green items (color), and the entire third circle (bottom middle) contains triangles (shape). The rest of the 32 pre-cut items (e.g., the small blue diamond) would occupy the region outside of all three circles in the diagram. Refer to Figure 5.18.

In Figure 5.19, each of the labeled regions represents some combination of size, color, and/or shape:

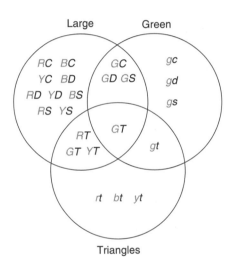

Figure 5.18

One region (V) has three attributes.

Three regions (II, IV, and VI) have two attributes.

Three regions (I, III, and VII) have one attribute.

One region (VIII) has no attributes

Scenario 3: Subsets

Ask students the following question: What subsets can be constructed from the given set $\{a, b, c\}$?

The formula for the number of subsets $y = 2^n$ (in which n is the number of elements in the given set) says that for a given set with three elements, the number of subsets $= 2^3 = 8$. Those subsets are as follows:

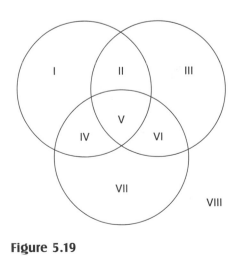

Figure 5.19

	{a} {b} {c}	{a, b} {a, c} {b, c}	
{ } 1	3	3	{a, b, c} 1

Scenario 4: Logic

In formal logic, the letters p, q, and r represent given statements (such as Today is Friday; It is raining; etc.) that are either true or false.

Figure 5.20 demonstrates that there are only eight possibilities for the truth or falsity of p, q, and r simultaneously. To prove this, have students reconfigure the formula from Scenario 3 so that n stands for the number of given statements and y stands for the number of possible true-false scenarios (again, $2^3 = 8$).

p	q	r
T	T	T
T	T	F
T	F	T
T	F	F
F	T	T
F	T	F
F	F	T
F	F	F

Figure 5.20

One row (1st) has all three statements true.

Three rows (2nd, 3rd, 5th) have two statements true and one false.

Three rows (4th, 6th, 7th) have one statement true and two false.

One row (8th) has no statements true (all false).

Scenario 5: Binomial Expansion

Expand $(x + y)^3$ and notice the coefficients in the answer:

$$(x + y)^3 = (x + y) \cdot (x + y) \cdot (x + y)$$
$$= (x + y) \cdot (x^2 + 2xy + y^2) = 1x^3 + 3x^2y + 3xy^2 + 1y^3$$

Scenario 6: Combinations

Ask students the following question: How many combinations of three given items are possible?

For n = the number of given items and r = how many of those items are being considered at any one time, use the formula

$$_nC_r = \frac{n!}{r! \cdot (n - r)!} :$$

$$_3C_0 = 1 \quad _3C_1 = 3 \quad _3C_2 = 3 \quad _3C_3 = 1$$

Scenario 7: Coin Flipping (Empirical)

Arrange students in pairs and have one student drop three coins (either real or cut out) at once while the other records the number of heads that result. Have students repeat this process 9 times and then switch roles and complete 10 more trials.

Bring students back together as a class, and have each partnership report how many times out of their 20 drops of coins there were 3 heads, 2 heads, 1 head, and no heads (all tails).

Then help the class construct a theoretical tree diagram and its accompanying sample space (the list of all possible outcomes of a given activity). Refer to Figure 5.21.

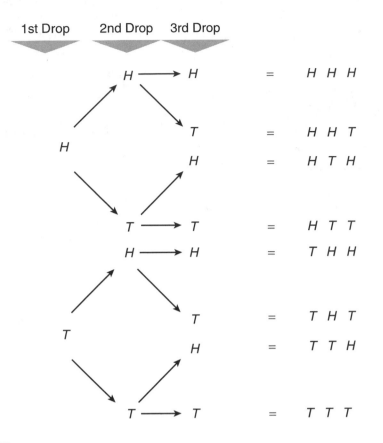

Figure 5.21

Students can evaluate the empirical probabilities (a class of 20 students would have made 200 total coin drops), and everyone can see how close (in decimal form) the entire class was to $\frac{1}{8} - \frac{3}{8} - \frac{3}{8} - \frac{1}{8}$ (which, when converted to nearest hundredth decimals, are $0.13 - 0.38 - 0.38 - 0.13$, respectively).

Compare the results of the tree diagram (see Figure 5.21) to the true-false table (see Scenario 4). Note the one-to-one correspondences between heads and true, tails and false, and the sample space.

Scenario 8: Coin Flipping (Theoretical)

Ask students the following question: What is the theoretical probability of flipping a coin three times and getting exactly two heads?

Students can solve this question for any number of heads using any of the previous three scenarios:

Scenario 5: Set $x = y = \frac{1}{2}$ and plug those values into the second term of the expansion $\left(= \frac{3}{8} \right)$.

Scenario 6: Take the $_3C_2 = 3$ term and divide it by the total number of combinations (8) to get $\frac{3}{8}$.

Scenario 7: Count the number of entries in the sample space (Figure 5.21) that have two Hs (3) and divide by the total (8) to get $\frac{3}{8}$.

Scenario 9: Pascal's Triangle

The last row of Figure 5.22 shows the coefficients of the binomial expansion from Scenario 7. Note the interesting configuration of numbers—a perfect match to those that students uncovered in Scenario 1.

$(x + y)^0 =$				1		
$(x + y)^1 =$			1		1	
$(x + y)^2 =$		1		2		1
$(x + y)^3 =$	1		3		3		1

Figure 5.22

To generate the triangle-pattern numbers without the help of the checkerboard, the numbers along the two borders are always 1 (there is only one way for the checker to get to any of those squares). Students can form the numbers in the middle by adding the two entries directly above it; for example, the 2 (in Square E) results from adding the 1s in Squares B and C. Therefore, the bottom of the triangle would then read 1–3–3–1.

One Step Further

Ask students to predict the coefficients for $(x + y)^4$ in Pascal's Triangle.

Since the numbers on the outsides are always 1s, the only part left is to add the pairs of numbers in the preceding row: $1 + 3 = 4$, $3 + 3 = 6$, and $3 + 1 = 4$. The next row of numbers after 1–3–3–1 would read 1–4–6–4–1.

Scenario 10: Bell Curve

Have students review Scenario 3 and note that the subset answers are stacked in such a way as to replicate the relative heights of the bars in the frequency histogram (see Figure 5.23).

If students place a point atop each bar, they can connect the dots to form a symmetric, bimodal frequency distribution (i.e., a bell-shaped curve). The further one progresses completing rows in Pascal's Triangle, the closer the subsequent histogram or curve comes to being a true normal distribution.

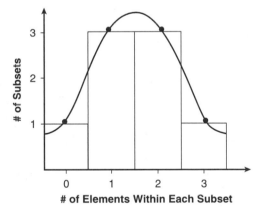

Figure 5.23

CALCULATOR APPLICATION

Baseball

```
PROGRAM:PASCROW
:Input "OBJECTS_=_,"N
:Disp "_"
:Disp "PROBABILITIES"
:For (R,0,N,1)
:Disp ((N_nC_r R) / (2^N)) F ↔ D
:Pause
:End
```

If you noticed your students having trouble back in Scenario 3 with either the empty set or the notion that every set is a subset of itself, consider a real-life application using one of my favorite pastimes—the great American game of baseball—as a backdrop (Scenario 11, if you will).

Excluding home plate, the three remaining bases on a baseball diamond can be occupied during the course of a game in only one of eight different ways: bases empty; a runner on first, a runner on second, or a runner on third; runners on first and second, runners on first and third, or runners on second and third; or bases loaded. Now, revisit Scenario 3 in context with the combination formula from Scenario 6:

Bases Empty = $_3C_0$ = 1 (out of 8) (*the empty set*)

One Runner on Base = $_3C_1$ = 3 (out of 8)

Two Runners on Base = $_3C_2$ = 3 (out of 8)

Bases Loaded = $_3C_3$ = 1 (out of 8) (*every set is a subset of itself*)

NOTE: It should also be clear as to why these eight possibilities are, in fact, combinations and not permutations. Having runners on first and second, for example, is the *same* offensive configuration as having runners on second and first.

The probabilities themselves come to life with a short original program for the graphing calculator (see the sidebar). Titled "PASCROW" in honor of Pascal's Triangle, it works on either the TI-73 or the TI-83/84 Plus model (but assumes that all eight base-occupation possibilities are equally likely, which in real baseball is hardly the case):

Using the Application With Students

Your Input	Output

Press: **ON**

PRGM

(*Scroll down to* **PASCROW**)

ENTER

ENTER

3 (*selected for this example*)

ENTER

ENTER

ENTER

ENTER

prgmPASCROW	
OBJECTS =	
PROBABILITIES	
	1/8
	3/8
	3/8
	1/8
prgmPASCROW	
	Done

Part II

Thematic Organizing Standards

Problem Solving 6

According to the standards listed in *Principles and Standards for School Mathematics* (National Council of Teachers of Mathematics [NCTM], 2000), all students in Grades 6 through 12 should be able to do the following:

Whatever obstacles you encounter in life, in school, or in the work environment, your ability to engage, adapt, and overcome obstacles generally depends on knowing what to do when you do not immediately know what to do. When studying mathematics, falling back on what you know and using a variety of thinking strategies to make the adjustments necessary for success lies at the very heart of this Problem-Solving Standard.

The first activity, Absolute Value Inequality, presents the idea of graphing as a visual solution strategy and introduces an accompanying mnemonic, or memory device, for students searching for an alternative to the common and more tedious algebraic approach. The Less Is More activity demonstrates how two nontraditional mathematical topics (nonbase-10 numbers and modular, or clock, arithmetic) are not only visually related to each other but also related by strategies used both for adding mixed numbers and solving time problems. The Maximizing Opportunity activity features another example of a *good problem*— it brings together a host of solution strategies seen in the upper high school grades.

Number properties that produce some offbeat results accompanied by some interesting formulas are the focus of the final activity, Without a Calculator (and are presented exactly as the title implies).

ABSOLUTE VALUE INEQUALITY

Grades 11–12

Solving problems can become a much more satisfying activity if the solver can interpret or actually listen to what the question is asking. This activity correlates to the following highlighted expectation for students:

- **Build new mathematical *knowledge* through problem solving**
- Solve *problems* that arise in mathematics and other contexts
- Apply and adapt a *variety* of appropriate strategies to solve problems
- Monitor and reflect on the *process* of mathematical problem solving

Solving the Absolute Value Inequality $|2x - 3| < 7$ for x

Ask students to solve the absolute value inequality $|2x - 3| < 7$ for x.

The preferred method of solution in most textbooks involves a two-case algebraic process requiring students to recognize and apply a previously stated rule. However, borrowing a labeling method from the TI-83/84 Plus, consider each side of the inequality as separate functions (First y and Second y) and then interpret the two on the same set of axes.

Beginning with the left-hand side of the equation ($|2x - 3|$), instruct students to take the linear function $y = 2x - 3$ (see Figure 6.1) and reflect the portion of that line beneath the x-axis *over* that same axis to graph the absolute value function $y = |2x - 3|$ (see Figure 6.2).

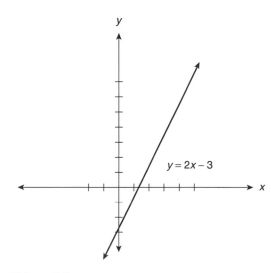

Figure 6.1

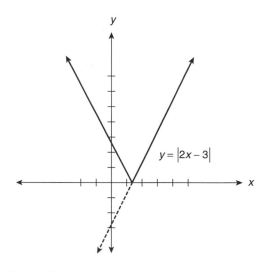

Figure 6.2

Then have students draw the right-hand side of the inequality (< 7), which is the constant function $y = 7$. Have students put both functions on the same set of axes, which will result in a kind of isosceles triangle (see Figure 6.3).

What does $|2x - 3| < 7$ "say" graphically? This equation is actually asking the following: What part of $Y1$ (First y) is less than—or *below*—$Y2$ (Second y)? The visual answer to that question is highlighted (darkened) in Figure 6.4.

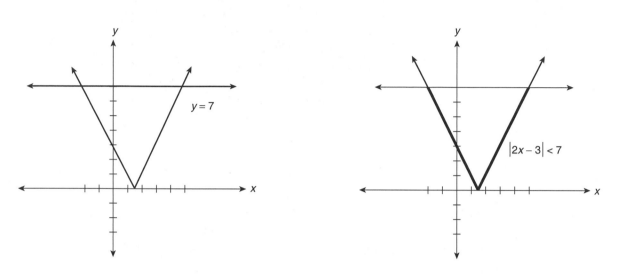

Figure 6.3   **Figure 6.4**

The critical values in this problem are the points of intersection between $Y1$ and $Y2$ (circled in Figure 6.5). Keep in mind that students are interested in only the x-coordinates at those points because they are solving the original inequality for x.

The points highlighted in this fashion are $(-2, 7)$ and $(5, 7)$ (see Figure 6.6).

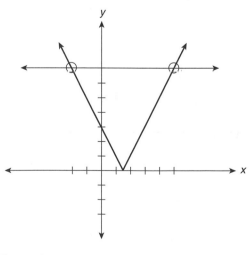
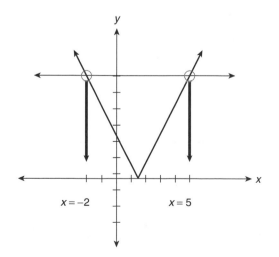

Figure 6.5   **Figure 6.6**

Have students translate those points down to the *x*-axis and drop the *y*-coordinates to yield the critical values *x* = −2 and *x* = 5 (see Figure 6.7).

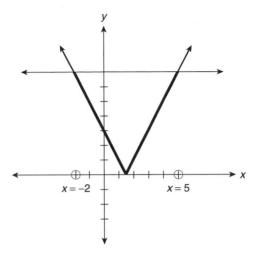

Figure 6.7

Then have students complete the solution with the darkened portion of the graph by "straightening" it, "telescoping" it, and "pasting" it onto the *x*-axis between −2 and 5. The results are the number-line and set-builder notation solutions shown in Figure 6.8.

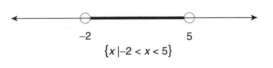

Figure 6.8

Solving the Absolute Value Inequality |2x − 3| > 7 for x

Now ask students to solve the absolute value inequality $|2x - 3| > 7$ for *x*.

Have students draw the *Y*1 and *Y*2 graphs as they did for the first problem. Point out that *this* time, they are interested in the part of the first graph that is *above* the second graph (see Figure 6.9).

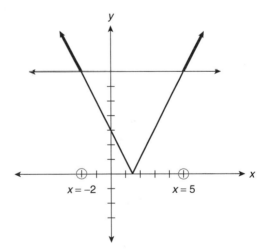

Figure 6.9

When students "straighten," "telescope," and "paste" the two arrows from *Y*1, which are above the line *y* = 7 (*Y*2), the results are the number-line and set-builder notation solutions in Figure 6.10.

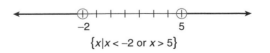

Figure 6.10

Interesting Math Fact

<u>G</u>ood <u>T</u>omatoes <u>D</u>on't <u>L</u>ose <u>T</u>heir <u>C</u>olor

What this mnemonic does is alert the solver that the process for solving a given absolute value inequality (whether algebraically or graphically) will eventually yield a number-line solution.

Note that the solution strategy for the second problem, solving the absolute value inequality $|2x - 3| > 7$ for x (a given *greater-than* absolute value inequality), produced a diverging number-line solution and that the solution strategy for the first problem, solving the absolute value inequality $|2x - 3| < 7$ for x (a given *less-than* absolute value inequality), produced a converging number-line solution. Therefore, if <u>G</u>reater <u>T</u>han <u>D</u>iverges, <u>L</u>ess <u>T</u>han <u>C</u>onverges (GTDLTC) or <u>G</u>ood <u>T</u>omatoes <u>D</u>on't <u>L</u>ose <u>T</u>heir <u>C</u>olor.

One Step Further

Students seem to appreciate different approaches to traditional lessons, especially when multiple steps are involved.

After introducing the idea of an isosceles triangle in the first problem (solving the absolute value inequality $|2x - 3| < 7$ for x), symmetry becomes clearer when students add the perpendicular bisector $x = \frac{3}{2}$. Note how $\frac{3}{2}$ acts as the midpoint along the x-axis between the two critical values 5 and –2 (see Figure 6.11).

Have students work through the resulting algorithm:

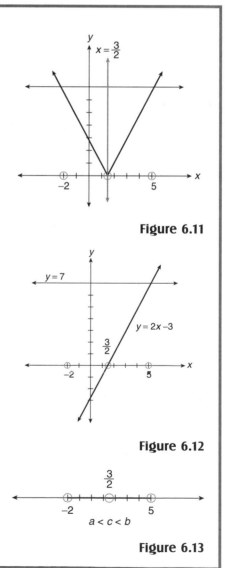

Figure 6.11

1. Locate the right endpoint (b) by simply dropping the absolute value and solving the equation $2x - 3 = 7$ ($x = b = 5$).

2. Locate the midpoint (c) by determining the x-intercept (set $y = 0$) of the linear equation $y = 2x - 3$ ($x = c = \frac{3}{2}$). Refer to Figure 6.12.

3. By symmetry, the distance from b to c is the same as the distance from c to the left endpoint (a). Refer to Figure 6.13.

If $b - c = c - a$, then $a = 2c - b$:

$$a = 2\left(\frac{3}{2}\right) - 5 = 3 - 5 = -2$$

$$-2 < c < 5$$

Figure 6.12

Figure 6.13

LESS IS MORE

A student may very well be exposed to essentially the same cognitive process given in three different contexts; unfortunately, should that same student be taught by three separate text-bound teachers, one algorithm that may be applied to three forms of the same problem is often overtaught and misinterpreted as three disconnected sets of rules. To illustrate, consider this nonbase-10 addition problem:

$$240_{(six)} + 150_{(six)}$$

Typically, a textbook would use the standard strategy (Pólya heuristic) of translating those numbers to equivalent base-10 numbers, evaluating the sum, and then untranslating the sum from base-10 back to base-6:

$$= [(2 \bullet 6^2) + (4 \bullet 6^1) + (0 \bullet 6^0)] + [(1 \bullet 6^2) + (5 \bullet 6^1) + (0 \bullet 6^0)]$$

$$= 96 + 66 = 162_{(ten)} = [(4 \bullet 6^2) + (3 \bullet 6^1) + (0 \bullet 6^0)] = 430_{(six)}$$

But addition problems similar in appearance and solution strategy to this one from number theory may have been done by students twice before in earlier mathematics classes—as a time question and as a mixed-number question:

1. 2 hours 40 minutes
   + 1 hour 50 minutes

2. $2\frac{2}{3}$
   $+1\frac{5}{6}$

Each of the preceding problems uses the same translate, combine, and untranslate strategy to solve the problems:

1. Since 2:40 = 160 minutes and 1:50 = 110 minutes, then

$$160 + 110 = 270 \text{ minutes} = 4 \text{ hours } 30 \text{ minutes} = 4\frac{1}{2} \text{ hours}$$

2. Since $2\frac{2}{3} = 2\frac{4}{6} = \frac{16}{6}$, and $1\frac{5}{6} = \frac{11}{6}$, then

$$\frac{16}{6} + \frac{11}{6} = \frac{27}{6} = 4\frac{3}{6} = 4\frac{1}{2}$$

An alternative (and widely seen) heuristic that students could also apply here is give-and-take:

1. [2 hours 40 minutes (−10 minutes)] + [1 hour 50 minutes (+10 minutes)]
    = [2 hours 30 minutes] + [1 hour 60 minutes = 2 hours] = $2\frac{1}{2} + 2 = 4\frac{1}{2}$ hours

2. $\left[2\frac{2}{3} + 1\frac{5}{6}\right] = \left[2\frac{4}{6} + 1\frac{5}{6}\right] = \left[2\frac{4}{6}\left(+\frac{2}{6}\right)\right] + \left[1\frac{5}{6}\left(-\frac{2}{6}\right)\right]$

$$= 2\frac{6}{6} + 1\frac{3}{6} = 3 + 1\frac{1}{2} = 4\frac{1}{2}$$

You also have the option of having students use a graphing calculator to add the two mixed numbers. Directions are on the following page.

CALCULATOR APPLICATION

Adding Mixed Numbers

To add the two mixed numbers on the TI-73 graphing calculator, use the following steps:

ON 2 UNIT 2 (ArrowDown) 3 (ArrowRight)

+ 1 UNIT 5 (ArrowDown) 6 (ArrowRight) ENTER

Now, push the white $A\dfrac{b}{c} \leftrightarrow \dfrac{d}{e}$ button and **ENTER** to make $\dfrac{9}{2}$ into $4\dfrac{1}{2}$.

Nevertheless, where the graphing calculator gives a correct solution, true understanding for a student is revealed through the rigor of the mathematical process in pursuit of the solution (the classic "How?-vs.-Why?" debate).

One Step Further

The following is the derivation of the formula for factoring the difference of two cubes. Note the use of the give-and-take strategy.

$$
\begin{aligned}
x^3 - y^3 &= x^3 - x^2y + x^2y - y^3 \\
&= x^2(x - y) + y(x^2 - y^2) \\
&= x^2(x - y) + y(x + y)(x - y) \\
&= (x - y)[x^2 + y(x + y)] \\
&= (x - y)[x^2 + xy + y^2]
\end{aligned}
$$

So far, the student has seen the translate, combine, and untranslate strategy (with the base-6, time, and mixed-number problems) and the give-and-take strategy (with the time and mixed-number problems, as well as the derivation of the difference of the Two-Cubes Formula). The following revisits the base-6 problem, only this time using modular, or clock, arithmetic.

A **module** is a part of a mathematical construction used as the standard to which the rest is proportioned. Given that definition, it would follow that the concept of base-6 numbers is akin to a fraction wheel divided into sixths (see Figure 6.14). Starting at 0 and progressing clockwise, it makes sense that going all the way around back to $0 = \dfrac{6}{6} = 1$ whole module.

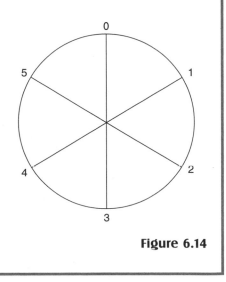

Figure 6.14

(Continued)

(Continued)

For this example, a module is nothing more than a unit (= 1) along the circumference of an equally-partitioned circle or wheel. Spinning around the circle is the same as adding, and passing the 0 on the way around is the same as borrowing. For example, picture a circle such as seen in Figure 6.14, only with 10 radii and the digit 0 (at the top) clockwise to 1, 2, 3, and so forth, around to the last digit 9 before reaching the top 0 again. These are the traditional base-10 numbers. Now, let's suppose you add 8 and 7 using this base-10 wheel. Start at 0, count off eight numbers, and stop (at the digit 8). Now, from there, count seven more numbers clockwise (you would tick off the next seven digits on the wheel as 9, 0, 1, 2, 3, 4, and 5) and stop at the digit 5. Since you passed the 0 once on the way around, you would add that 1 (borrowed) to the tens' digit in your final answer (15).

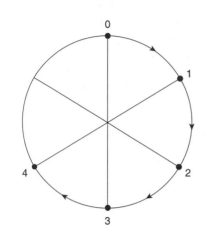

Figure 6.15

Reevaluating $240_{(six)}$ + $150_{(six)}$ vertically and computing right to left, the first nonzero sum of 4 and 5 tells the student to begin at 0, travel clockwise and stop at 4 (see Figure 6.15), and then continue five more units clockwise (see Figure 6.16) before stopping at what used to be 3.

The fact is, when the student passed 0 on the way around a second time, he or she had gone a full module (which carries left to the next sum of 2 and 1 = 1 + 2 + 1 = 4) before going another 3 out of 6 (or halfway to a second full module):

$$
\begin{array}{r}
1 \\
2\ 4\ 0 \\
+\ 1\ 5\ 0 \\
\hline
4\ 3\ 0 \\
\end{array}
= 4 \text{ hours } 30 \text{ minutes}
$$

$$= 4\frac{1}{2} \text{ hours}$$

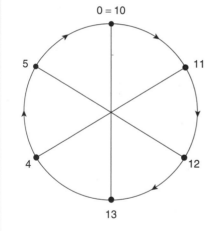

Figure 6.16

This base-6 strategy is actually the visual equivalent of the two other base-6-type problems solved earlier:

1. Adding 2 hours 40 minutes and 1 hour 50 minutes (in which 1 hour = 60 minutes = 6 numbers on the modular wheel each representing $\frac{1}{6}$ of an hour)

2. Adding $2\frac{4}{6}$ and $1\frac{3}{6}$ (in which the whole number $1 = \frac{6}{6} = 6$ numbers on the modular wheel each representing $\frac{1}{6}$ of the whole)

So what might seem different to students can actually be presented as "an old friend."

MAXIMIZING OPPORTUNITY

Grades 11–12

The following algebraic fallacy is an oldie but a goodie, especially if your students have never seen it before. It explores different approaches that develop insight into a problem. This activity correlates to the following highlighted expectation for students:

- Build new mathematical *knowledge* through problem solving
- Solve *problems* that arise in mathematics and other contexts
- **Apply and adapt a *variety* of appropriate strategies to solve problems**
- Monitor and reflect on the *process* of mathematical problem solving

Challenge students to find the one step that makes the entire argument fall apart (which is dividing by $[a - b]$; since $a = b$, the quantity $[a - b]$ must $= 0$, and division by 0 is undefined).

What went wrong here?

Let	a	$=$	b
(multiply both sides by a)	a^2	$=$	ab
(subtract b^2 from both sides)	$a^2 - b^2$	$=$	$ab - b^2$
(factor both sides)	$(a + b)(a - b)$	$=$	$b(a - b)$
(divide both sides by $(a - b)$)	$a + b$	$=$	b
(substitute b for a from "Let")	$b + b$	$=$	b
(combine like terms)	$2b$	$=$	b
(divide both sides by b)	2	$=$	1?

The more students are exposed to mathematics, the more opportunities they should have to work through good mathematical problems. The emphasis here is on *good*. Good problems force students to think back to their past mathematical experiences for ideas, help teachers to identify learning preferences (visual, mechanical, etc.) more clearly, and give students more opportunities to hear and see their peers' insights and solution strategies. You can find some excellent problems in mathematics competitions, which you can offer to students on a regular basis as a Problem of the Week or a Weekend Challenge.

The following mathematical problem is from a past New York City Interscholastic Math League meet. There are five different ways that students can solve this problem—one of the attributes of a *good problem*.

Given $x^2 + y^2 = 1$, maximize $(x + y)^2$

Method 1: Euclidean Geometry

To maximize $(x + y)^2$ means to draw a triangle of greatest possible area—namely, a right isosceles (or 45°-45°-90°) triangle. If hypotenuse = 1, then

$$b = h = \frac{\sqrt{2}}{2}, \text{ and } (x + y)^2 = (b + h)^2 = \left(\sqrt{2}\right)^2 = 2.$$

Method 2: Analytic Geometry

The equation $x^2 + y^2 = 1$ represents the unit circle in Figure 6.17. Note that its intersection in Quadrant I with the line $y = x$ visually confirms the solution to Method 1.

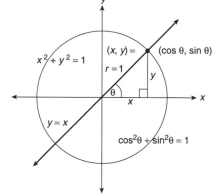

Method 3: Trigonometry

By letting $x = \cos\theta$ and $y = \sin\theta$, maximize $f(\theta) = (\cos\theta + \sin\theta)^2 = \cos^2\theta + 2\sin\theta\cos\theta + \sin^2\theta = 1 + \sin 2\theta$. The amplitude at either 45° or 225° = maximum of 2.

Method 4: Differential Calculus

Since $y = \pm\sqrt{1 - x^2}$, restate the problem as maximizing

$$f(x) = \left(\pm\sqrt{1 - x^2}\right)^2. \text{ For the upper semicircle (positive } \sqrt{\ }),$$

$$f'(x) = 2\left(x + \sqrt{1 - x^2}\right)\left(1 - \frac{x}{\sqrt{1 - x^2}}\right) = 0$$

$$\text{yields } x = \frac{\sqrt{2}}{2} \text{ and } f\left(\frac{\sqrt{2}}{2}\right) = 2.$$

Figure 6.17

Method 5: Trig Derivatives

$$f(\theta) = (\cos\theta + \sin\theta)^2$$
$$f'(\theta) = 2(\cos\theta + \sin\theta)(-\sin\theta + \cos\theta)$$
$$= 2(\cos^2\theta - \sin^2\theta) = 2\cos 2\theta$$

Maximum value when $f'(\theta) = 0$: $\theta = [180° \cdot (2k + 1)]/4$, in which k is an integer = 45° or 225° (return to solution Method 3).

CALCULATOR APPLICATION

Trig Derivatives

An excellent means of providing students with more insight into the solution for Method 5 is possible with the TI-83/84 Plus graphing calculator:

Using the Application With Students

Erase: **2nd STAT PLOT 4 ENTER CLEAR**

Go to the **Y** = *screen*

(*and* **CLEAR** *all old lines*)

Input: **Y1 = (cos (X) + sin (X))^2**

Y2 = MATH 8

VARS   (**ArrowRight** *to* **Y-VARS**)

ENTER ENTER

, X , X)

(*Press* **ArrowUp** *twice and* **ArrowLeft** *once to get the cursor on top of the equal sign next to* **Y1**)

ENTER   (*to turn off the* **Y1** *graph*)

MODE   (*Select* **RADIAN**)

Output: **ZOOM 7**   (*which shows the graph of* **y = 2 cos 2X**)

WINDOW (*Change X min to 0*)

GRAPH

Students should be able to identify **Y2** (a cosine graph with an amplitude of 2 and a frequency of 1) and other selected visual examples so as to extend their thinking *inductively* toward the formalization of rules for trig derivatives.

WITHOUT A CALCULATOR

Grades 6–11

This activity contains four arithmetic problems with a different algebraic rationale behind the solution for each one. It is dedicated to the student whose first instinct is creative thinking and to the teacher who expects more from herself and her class on a daily basis . . . without resorting to button pushing! This activity correlates to the following highlighted expectation for students:

- Build new mathematical *knowledge* through problem solving
- Solve *problems* that arise in mathematics and other contexts
- Apply and adapt a *variety* of appropriate strategies to solve problems
- **Monitor and reflect on the *process* of mathematical problem solving**

Problem 1: Compute 65^2

First, students express *any* two-digit number ending in 5 as $10t + 5$. This means that $t5^2 = (10t + 5) \cdot (10t + 5) = 100t^2 + 100t + 25 = [100 \cdot t \cdot (t + 1)] + 25$.

So, $65^2 = 65 \cdot 65 = [100 \cdot 6 \cdot (6 + 1)] + 25 = [100 \cdot 6 \cdot 7] + 25 = 4,225$.

However, computing sideways (horizontally) is not as dramatic an approach as computing up and down (vertically). Therefore, challenge students to solve the same problem vertically.

$[100 \cdot 6 \cdot (6 + 1)]$ means that, Instead of multiplying $6 \cdot 6$, multiply $6 \cdot \underline{7}$. The "100" allows the solver to think of 42 as 4,200 minus the double zeroes.

$$\begin{array}{r} 6\,|\,5 \\ \times 6\,|\,5 \\ \hline 42\,|\,25 \end{array}$$ And, remember to tack on 25.

As a follow-up, ask students for a show of hands (amassing fairly quickly once the algorithm is understood) for computing 85^2:

$85^2 = not\ 8 \cdot 8$ but $8 \cdot \underline{9} = 72$, put in front of a "25" $= 7,225$.

Problem 2: How Many Total Squares Are There on a Standard (8-by-8) Checkerboard?

This activity illustrates two of Pólya's (1951) heuristics (solving with a smaller problem *and* finding a pattern). Rather than work exclusively with the

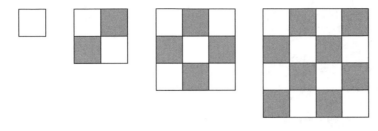

Figure 6.18

regular 8-by-8 checkerboard (see the appendix for a full-page blackline master), begin a discussion around some smaller prepared versions (perhaps cut out for illustration on the overhead projector). Refer to Figure 6.18.

The challenge for students then becomes not so much recognizing the sum of an increasing sequence of perfect squares but taking the time to arrange their data in such a manner that a more subtle "periscoping" of numbers can be fully appreciated.

As per the Checkerboard Chart (see Figure 6.19; see the appendix for a full-page blackline master), the 2-by-2 checkerboard contains an identity square (2-by-2) and four squares from the previous dimension (1-by-1); the 3-by-3 checkerboard contains an identity square (3-by-3), four squares from the previous dimension (2-by-2), and nine squares from the dimension before that (1-by-1); and so forth. Extending the pattern to the standard 8-by-8 checkerboard, then, the total number of squares is as follows:

$$1^2 + 2^2 + 3^2 + 4^2 + 5^2 + 6^2 + 7^2 + 8^2 = 204$$

	Number of These Squares Within			
Size of Checkerboard	1-by-1	2-by-2	3-by-3	4-by-4
1-by-1	1			
2-by-2	4	1		
3-by-3	9	4	1	
4-by-4	16	9	4	1

Figure 6.19

As a follow-up, ask students the following: How many total squares are there on an "*n*-by-*n*" checkerboard?

What is required to meet this challenge is a reorganization of the Checkerboard Chart (see Figure 6.19) and a review of the finite difference equations process (see Chapter 2) for finding algebraic relationships.

# of Squares Along One Side	1	2	3	4	5	6	7	8
Total # of Squares on Board	1	5	14	30	55	91	140	204
1st Differences:		4	9	16	25	36	49	64
2nd Differences:			5	7	9	11	13	15
3rd Differences:				2	2	2	2	2

Figure 6.20

First, ask students to use the bottom half of the Checkerboard Chart (see the appendix). If x = # of squares along one side of a given checkerboard and y = total # of squares on that particular board, then the fact that the third differences of the y data are constant suggests that there is a third-degree relationship between x and y (i.e., $y = ax^3 + bx^2 + cx + d$). Refer to Figure 6.20.

Since students are seeking four parameters (a, b, c, and d), they need to construct four simultaneous equations. (See Chapter 9 for a solution that uses matrices as an alternative to lengthy algebra.) Students can factor the result, $y = (2x^3 + 3x^2 + x)/6$, so that this formula for finding the total number of squares on *any* "*n*-by-*n*" checkerboard can be used and proven (by mathematical induction):

$$1^2 + 2^2 + 3^2 + \ldots + n^2 = \frac{n \cdot (n+1) \cdot (2n+1)}{6}$$

Note that the 8-by-8 checkerboard still has $\dfrac{8 \cdot 9 \cdot 17}{6} = 204$ squares.

Problem 3: Compute $\sqrt{31 \cdot 30 \cdot 29 \cdot 28 + 1}$

This question comes from an American Invitational Mathematics Examination (AIME) for the brightest high school mathematics problem solvers. All answers on the AIME are expressible as whole numbers from 000 to 999, inclusive, and the use of calculators is not allowed.

Have students consider the products of the extremes (the two outside numbers) and the means (the two middle numbers) of any four consecutive whole numbers, symbolized here by the polynomials a, $(a + 1)$, $(a + 2)$, and $(a + 3)$. Note that the product of the extremes is $[a(a + 3)] = a^2 + 3a$ and that the product of the means is $[(a + 1) \cdot (a + 2)] = a^2 + 3a + 2$. Students can conclude from these results that the product of the extremes is 2 less than the product of the means.

So, in the given problem, students let the product of the means $30 \cdot 29 = 870 = N$ and the product of the extremes $31 \cdot 28 = 868 = N - 2$. Students rewrite and solve the following:

$$\sqrt{N(N-2)+1} = \sqrt{N^2 - 2N + 1} = \sqrt{(N-1)^2} = |N - 1| = |870 - 1| = 869$$

Problem 4: Validate the Thinking Behind the Game of Mathematical Hopscotch

This problem is a quick test to determine the divisibility of a given whole number by 11.

Question 1: Is the Number 5,874 Divisible by 11?

Divisibility Test A. Working from right to left, find the two sums of the given number's alternating digits.

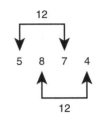

Conclusion. Since the two sums are the same (12 = 12), the number 5,874 *is* divisible by 11. (A long-division arithmetic check will confirm it.)

This is one of the two hopscotch scenarios. If the two sums of the alternate digits (taking every other digit, hence the term *hopscotch*) of a given number match, then that given number is divisible by 11.

Beginnings of an Inductive Proof for Test A (for mature audiences only)

1. Given a two-digit whole number $(10t + u)$, test its divisibility by 11; that is, is $(10t + u) \div 11$ also a whole number?

    If $u = t$ by hopscotch, then $(10t + u) \div 11 = (10t + t) \div 11 = 11t \div 11 = t$ (a whole number).

2. Given a three-digit whole number $(100h + 10t + u)$, test its divisibility by 11; that is, is $(100h + 10t + u) \div 11$ also a whole number?

    If $u + h = t$ by hopscotch, then $u = t - h$ and $[100h + 10t + (t - h)] \div 11 = (99h + 11t) \div 11 = 9h + t$ (a whole number).

3. Given a four-digit whole number $(1{,}000T + 100h + 10t + u)$, test its divisibility by 11; that is, is $(1{,}000T + 100h + 10t + u) \div 11$ also a whole number?

    If $u + h = t + T$ by hopscotch, then $u = t + T - h$ and $[1{,}000T + 100h + 10t + (t + T - h)] \div 11 = (1{,}001T + 99h + 11t) \div 11 = 91T + 9h + t$ (a whole number).

Question 2: Is the Number 946 Divisible by 11?

Divisibility Test B. Working from right to left, find the two sums of the given number's alternating digits.

Conclusion. Since the difference of the two sums is 11, the number 946 *is* divisible by 11. (A long-division arithmetic check will confirm it.)

This is the second part of the hopscotch divisibility-by-11 rule. Note how the difference between 15 and 4 is 11, and since 11 is divisible by 11, that means the given number (946) is also divisible by 11. Calculators will confirm that both 5,874 and 946 are divisible by 11 (no decimal remainders on the display).

Beginnings of an Inductive Proof for Test B (for mature audiences only)

In the type of three-digit number like 946, if $h + u = t + 11$ by hopscotch, then $u = t + 11 - h$:

$$(100h + 10t + u) \div 11 = (100h + 10t + (t + 11 - h) \div 11)$$
$$= (99h + 11t + 11) \div 11 = 9h + t + 1 \text{ (a whole number).}$$

As a follow-up, write the following information about each digit's coefficients generated back in Test A:

$$t = 10 - 9 = 1$$
$$h = 100 - 91 = 9$$
$$T = 1{,}000 - 909 = 91$$

Students then discover patterns and help perpetuate the Test A example further with a five-digit number $(10{,}000T^* + 1{,}000T + 100h + 10t + u)$ in a similar process to Test A's to help them predict what the coefficients are for the million's digit, given a seven-digit number that successfully plays hopscotch.

Reasoning and Proof 7

According to the standards listed in *Principles and Standards for School Mathematics* (National Council of Teachers of Mathematics [NCTM], 2000), all students in Grades 6 through 12 should be able to do the following:

Of the four steps in Pólya's (1951) problem-solving sequence (understand, plan, execute, look back), the look-back step is invaluable—if for no other reason than simply allowing the problem solver a chance to consider whether a stated answer makes any sense. When it does, that answer speaks more to the precision of the first three steps of the sequence—an affirmation that the process undertaken was indeed a correct one. As stated before, teaching students to ask *why* more often will help them become more confident, independent thinkers as opposed to a room full of individuals who just want to memorize the *hows*.

Sometimes, the best way to work through a problem is to develop a proof—ignoring the extraneous, eliminating the erroneous, and putting together a step-by-step rationale. The first activity for the Reasoning and Proof

155

Standard is Areas and Quadratics. In the activity, students develop reasoning that combines areas with a parabolic function as preludes to using a derivative test to verify the solution. The second activity, Area of a Circle, is a conjecture of the well-known formula (see Easy as Pi in Chapter 4) in which gradually increasing the number of sides of an inscribed polygon will create an unexpected result through limits.

The third activity, Visual Thinking, enables students to reevaluate (with much more visual insight) the proofs of three separate formulas with heretofore long-winded and tedious derivations. Finally, Double Triangle takes that visual mind-set one step further in trigonometry by introducing the students to the Law of Cotangents as a natural extension and one-step alternative to the traditional Law of Sines.

Whether the reasoning is algebraic, geometric, graphic, or statistical, the student with experience in all of these arenas develops some important thinking skills in real-life situations.

AREAS AND QUADRATICS

> ### Grades 10–12
>
> This activity is an exploration into maximizing the area of rectangles. This activity correlates to the following highlighted expectation for students:
>
> - **Recognize** *reasoning and proof* **as fundamental aspects of mathematics**
> - Make and investigate mathematical *conjectures*
> - Develop and evaluate mathematical *arguments and proof*
> - Select and use *various types* of reasoning and methods of proof

Any list of common attributes shared by effective teachers and successful students of mathematics includes, but is not limited to, the following:

- A willingness to engage mathematically (i.e., *do* math)
- An ability to access past experiences in order to apply and compare them to current learning situations

Consider the following question, which serves as the focus of this activity: Given 40 feet of fencing, what would the dimensions of a four-sided enclosure have to be for the area within to be *maximized?*

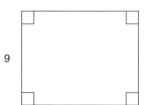

There are a variety of skills that teachers and students would have to know and be able to recall to solve this problem:

1. Computing perimeters and areas
2. Drawing parabolas on a coordinate grid
3. Completing the square and writing in function notation
4. Taking and evaluating derivatives

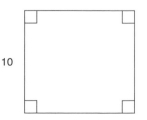

The following steps illustrate to students how they can combine different mathematical concepts and strategies to help solve a problem. The ability to do so helps students become good problem solvers.

Computing Perimeters and Areas

An opening confidence builder for students is looking for a pattern, as evidenced by the widths of the four rectangles in Figure 7.1 (each with a given perimeter of 40). Since $P = 2l + 2w$, students should be able to make substitutions and perform the mental calculations necessary to determine the length of each rectangle (reading down): 13, 12, 11, and 10.

Have students organize the data to determine the resulting areas of each rectangle and to discover a more significant pattern (see Figure 7.2). You may want to demonstrate the first row (for width

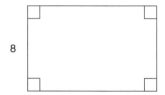

Figure 7.1

w	20 − w = l	l • w = A
7	13	91
8	12	96
9	11	99
10	10	100
11	9	99
12	8	96
13	7	91

Figure 7.2

$w = 7$, the length $l = 20 − 7 = 13$, making the area of the rectangle $13 • 7 = 91$) and then let students fill in the rest. Note how the greatest possible area (100) belongs to the equilateral rectangle better known as a 10-by-10 square.

Drawing Parabolas on a Coordinate Grid

Next, have students use graph paper to plot the points in the form (w, A), in which the widths are along the horizontal axis and the areas are along the vertical axis (see Figure 7.3). Remind students that they are looking to maximize area, which means they should look for the highest point plotted on the parabola.

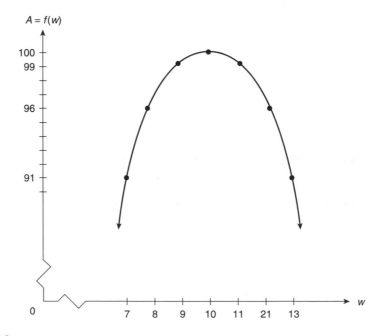

Figure 7.3

CALCULATOR APPLICATION

Graphing Parabolas

Back in Chapter 2, we "strung the beads" with the TI-73 while following steps in the Straw Balances unit. Let's do something similar here with the TI-83/84 Plus, using the data from this unit to duplicate the paper-and-pencil graph and extend our work with some additional technological features:

Using the Application With Students

1. "String the Beads"

Erase: **2nd STAT PLOT 4 ENTER CLEAR**

          Go to the **Y=** *screen*

             (*and* **CLEAR** *all old lines*)

          2nd MEM 4 ENTER CLEAR

Input: **STAT ENTER** (**ArrowLeft** *to position cursor*)

          7 ENTER 8 ENTER . . .

L1	L2
7	91
8	96
9	99
10	100
11	99
12	96
13	91

          2nd STAT PLOT 1

             (*Select:* **On, Scatterplot, L1, L2, Bead**)

          WINDOW

             (*Set* **X = [0, 20]** *by* **Xscl = 5**)

             (*Set* **Y = [80, 110]** *by* **Yscl = 5**)

          GRAPH

          Y1 = –X² + 20X

             GRAPH

2. Drawing the Axis of Symmetry

Input: **2nd QUIT**

          2nd DRAW 4 10 (*because* $x = -b \div 2a = 10$)

          ENTER

3. Finding the Maximum Value

Input: **2nd STAT PLOT 4**

          ENTER

          CLEAR

          2nd CALC 4

             (*Press* **ArrowLeft** *four times*)

          ENTER

             (*Press* **ArrowRight** *eight times*)

          ENTER

          ENTER

(Continued)

(Continued)

(*Answer is shown along the bottom of the screen:* **X = 10, Y = 100**)

4. The Slope of the Tangent Line, dy/dx (at any point on the curve)

Input: **2nd CALC 6**

              10 (*from the Maximum Value Answer above*)

              ENTER

(*Answer is shown along the bottom of the screen:* **dy/dx = 0**)

(*Return to* **Y = SCREEN** *and input* **Y₂ = 100**)

              GRAPH

Completing the Square and Writing in Function Notation

Even though the data and the parabola seem to indicate that the 10-by-10 square is the sought-after four-sided figure of greatest area, students must still verify the results. Writing the area as a function of the width and completing the square can accomplish this task for a noncalculus student:

$$2l + 2w = 40 \rightarrow l + w = 20 \rightarrow l = 20 - w (\text{substitute})$$

$$A = l \bullet w = (20 - w) \bullet w = 20w - w^2 = -w^2 + 20w = f(w)$$

$$f(w) = -w^2 + 20w = -[w^2 - 20w + \_\_] + \_\_ = -[w^2 - 20w + 100] + 100$$

$$= -[(w - 10) \bullet (w - 10)] + 100 = -[(w - 10)^2] + 100$$

$$A = f(w) = 100 - (w - 10)^2$$

Encourage students to think about the final statement. If the width w = 10, then the area (located along the vertical axis of the graph) = 100. If the width is any other number besides 10, then the area takes on a value that is less than 100. Therefore, the maximum area is found when the width = 10, which makes the length = 10 and makes the rectangle a square (length = width).

Taking and Evaluating Derivatives

The preceding clarifies reasoning but uses calculus to provide a proof:

$$f(w) = -w^2 + 20w \rightarrow f'(w) = -2w + 20$$

$$\text{Set } -2w + 20 = 0 \rightarrow w = 10 \text{ and } A = f(10) = 100$$

The second-derivative test, $f''(w) = -2$, proves mathematically that $A = f(10) = 100$ is the maximum area.

AREA OF A CIRCLE

Grades 10–12

This activity presents a conjecture that uses both visualization and the idea behind a **limit** (the value of a dependent variable [function] approached while its independent variable is approaching some other value). This activity correlates to the following highlighted expectation for students:

- Recognize *reasoning and proof* as fundamental aspects of mathematics
- **Make and investigate mathematical *conjectures***
- Develop and evaluate mathematical *arguments and proof*
- Select and use *various types* of reasoning and methods of proof

What follows is a series of circles, each of which includes an inscribed regular polygon with a progressively increasing number of sides. The formula is one of geometry's most flexible (as shown by Figures 7.4–7.8) but least recognized formulas for finding the area of a regular polygon. You may want to walk through the equilateral triangle example with students. After that, let students work their way through the sequence of the other regular polygons drawn inside the same circle—from square to regular hexagon to regular octagon and, finally, to regular dodecagon (12-sided polygon).

Legend

A = area

P = perimeter of polygon

s = side of polygon

r = radius of circle

a = **apothem** (the perpendicular distance from the center of the polygon to any one of its sides)

Equilateral Triangle

$[s = \left(\frac{1}{3}\right) P]$. Refer to Figure 7.4.

$$A = 3 \cdot \left[\left(\frac{1}{2}\right) \cdot b \cdot h\right]$$
$$= 3 \cdot \left[\left(\frac{1}{2}\right) \cdot s \cdot a\right]$$
$$= 3 \cdot \left[\left(\frac{1}{2}\right) \cdot \left(\frac{1}{3}\right) P \cdot a\right]$$
$$= \left(\frac{1}{2}\right) \cdot a \cdot P$$

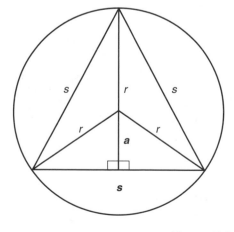

Figure 7.4

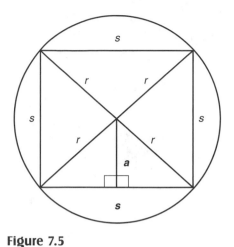

Figure 7.5

Square

$[s = \left(\dfrac{1}{4}\right) P]$. Refer to Figure 7.5.

$$A = 4 \cdot \left[\left(\dfrac{1}{2}\right) \cdot b \cdot h\right]$$

$$= 4 \cdot \left[\left(\dfrac{1}{2}\right) \cdot s \cdot a\right]$$

$$= 4 \cdot \left[\left(\dfrac{1}{2}\right) \cdot \left(\dfrac{1}{4}\right) P \cdot a\right]$$

$$= \left(\dfrac{1}{2}\right) \cdot a \cdot P$$

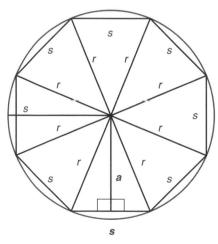

Figure 7.6

Regular Hexagon

$[s = \left(\dfrac{1}{6}\right) P]$. Refer to Figure 7.6.

$$A = 6 \cdot \left[\left(\dfrac{1}{2}\right) \cdot b \cdot h\right]$$

$$= 6 \cdot \left[\left(\dfrac{1}{2}\right) \cdot s \cdot a\right]$$

$$= 6 \cdot \left[\left(\dfrac{1}{2}\right) \cdot \left(\dfrac{1}{6}\right) P \cdot a\right]$$

$$= \left(\dfrac{1}{2}\right) \cdot a \cdot P$$

Figure 7.7

Regular Octagon

$[s = \left(\dfrac{1}{8}\right) P]$. Refer to Figure 7.7.

$$A = 8 \cdot \left[\left(\dfrac{1}{2}\right) \cdot b \cdot h\right]$$

$$= 8 \cdot \left[\left(\dfrac{1}{2}\right) \cdot s \cdot a\right]$$

$$= 8 \cdot \left[\left(\dfrac{1}{2}\right) \cdot \left(\dfrac{1}{8}\right) P \cdot a\right]$$

$$= \left(\dfrac{1}{2}\right) \cdot a \cdot P$$

Regular Dodecagon

$[s = \left(\frac{1}{12}\right) P]$. Refer to Figure 7.8.

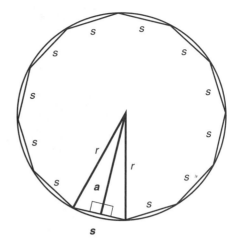

Figure 7.8

Having established $A = \left(\frac{1}{2}\right) \cdot a \cdot P$ as the formula for the area of a regular polygon, students should now recognize two visual clues as the number of sides of the preceding polygons progressively increases:

1. As seen with the regular dodecagon (see Figure 7.8), the apothem has grown to be almost the same length as the radius (i.e., $a \to r$, or "a approaches r").

2. The perimeter is now almost the same as the circumference C ($P \to C$).

$$A = \left(\frac{1}{2}\right) \cdot a \cdot P \approx \left(\frac{1}{2}\right) \cdot r \cdot C$$

$$= \left(\frac{1}{2}\right) \cdot r \cdot (2\pi r) = \pi r^2$$

VISUAL THINKING

Grades 9–12

The effect of a well-conceived proof on an aficionado of mathematics is directly proportional to its degree of elegance—the simpler its execution, the more profound its impact. The easiest way to open the door to all students—but especially to those who are not natural mathematical learners—is to prove formulas visually. The finest collection of exercises in visual thinking is *Proofs Without Words* (Nelson, 1993). This activity visually illustrates how four formulas are derived in a thought-provoking manner. This activity correlates to the following highlighted expectation for students:

- Recognize *reasoning and proof* as fundamental aspects of mathematics
- Make and investigate mathematical *conjectures*
- **Develop and evaluate mathematical *arguments and proof***
- Select and use *various types* of reasoning and methods of proof

The Area of a Square Expressed as an Arithmetic Series

B	R	B	R	B
B	R	B	R	R
B	R	B	B	B
B	R	R	R	R
B	B	B	B	B

Figure 7.9

Provide students with a two-color supply of counting tiles (e.g., red and blue). Instruct students to take one blue tile and build an even larger square around it with an increasing sequence of alternate-colored (red, blue, red, blue, etc.) *L*s. Refer to Figure 7.9.

Point out to students (or let them discover) that the first-used blue tile and each of the subsequent *L*s are all odd numbers and that the area of the built-up square is by definition a perfect square:

$$1 = 1^2$$
$$1 + 3 = 2^2$$
$$1 + 3 + 5 = 3^2$$
$$1 + 3 + 5 + 7 = 4^2, \text{ etc.}$$

If the first turn starts with $(2 \cdot 1 - 1)$ blue tiles, and the second turn adds $(2 \cdot 2 - 1)$ red tiles, and the third turn adds $(2 \cdot 3 - 1)$ blue tiles, and so on, then the nth term adds $(2 \cdot n - 1)$ tiles to make a square with an area of n^2:

$$1 + 3 + 5 + 7 + \ldots + (2n - 1) = n^2$$

Two Transformed Trigonometry Formulas

Provide students with a scalene triangle *BCA* (ΔBCA) circumscribed by circle O (see Figure 7.10).

Instruct students to slide (translate) point A counterclockwise along the circle until it stops at the point (A'), which creates diameter $A'B$. By Ptolemy's Theorem, $\triangle A'CB$ is a right triangle with its hypotenuse $= d$ (diameter $A'B$).

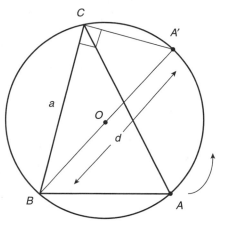

The measures of inscribed angles A and A' are congruent because they subtend (cut off) the same arc ($\overset{\frown}{CB}$). Thus $\sin A' = \sin A = \frac{a}{d}$.

Many intermediate algebra and/or trigonometry textbooks include an alternative formula for the area of a triangle:

$$A = \left(\frac{1}{2}\right) b \cdot c \cdot \sin A$$

Figure 7.10

By substitution for $\sin A$,

$$A = \left(\frac{1}{2}\right) b \cdot c \cdot \left(\frac{a}{d}\right). \text{ But since } d = 2r, \ A = \frac{abc}{2d} : A = \frac{abc}{4r}$$

The area of a triangle is the product of its three sides, divided by four times the radius of its circumcircle.

In circle O (refer back to Figure 7.10), note that $\sin A = \frac{a}{d}$ implies that $d = \frac{a}{\sin A}$. In addition, either point B or point C could have been chosen (the other two points remaining stationary) to slide along the circle. Therefore, if it were possible for $d = \frac{b}{\sin B}$ or for $d = \frac{c}{\sin C}$, then by substitution,

$$\frac{a}{\sin A} = \frac{b}{\sin B} = \frac{c}{\sin C} \text{ (the Law of Sines)}$$

Distance From a Point to a Line

NOTE: This is adapted from "Mathematics Doesn't Have to Be Maddening," from an article by A. S. Gazdar, in *Japan Times Tokyo*, Tokyo, Japan.

The formula for the perpendicular distance from a point to a line is as follows:

$$d = \frac{|Ax_0 + By_0 + C|}{A^2 + B^2}$$

Given the point $P(x_0, y_0)$ and the line $Ax + By + C = 0$ anywhere on the coordinate plane, have students extend from P to the line horizontal distance $s = PT$ and vertical distance $t = PS$ to make right triangle SPT (see Figure 7.11).

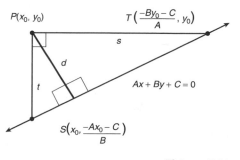

Note how point P shares the same x-coordinate (x_0) with point S and the same y-coordinate (y_0) with point T.

Have students substitute x_0 for x in the linear equation $Ax + By + C = 0$ to find the y-coordinate at point S, and substitute y_0 for y in the same linear equation to find the x-coordinate at point T.

Figure 7.11

Students can find the area of $\triangle SPT$ *two* ways:

1. $\dfrac{1}{2} b \cdot h = \dfrac{1}{2} s \cdot t$

2. Since $ST = \sqrt{s^2 + t^2}: \dfrac{1}{2} d \cdot ST = \dfrac{1}{2} d \sqrt{s^2 + t^2}$

Equating (1) and (2) and then solving for d,

$$\frac{1}{2} s \cdot t = \frac{1}{2} d \sqrt{s^2 + t^2} \;\rightarrow\; d = \frac{st}{\sqrt{s^2 + t^2}}$$

Refer students back to Figure 7.11. Let $Ax_0 + By_0 + C =$ some constant value (call it N), and write expressions for s and for t using the standard Point-to-Point Distance Formula:

$$s = \left| \frac{N}{A} \right| \text{ and } t = \left| \frac{N}{B} \right| \text{ (some student assembly required)}$$

Now, have students substitute these new expressions for s and for t back into the formula for d:

$$d = \frac{st}{\sqrt{s^2 + t^2}} = \frac{\left| \dfrac{N^2}{AB} \right|}{\sqrt{\left(\dfrac{N^2}{A} \right) + \left(\dfrac{N^2}{B} \right)}} = \frac{|N|}{\sqrt{A^2 + B^2}} \;\rightarrow\; d = \frac{|Ax_0 + By_0 + C|}{\sqrt{A^2 + B^2}}$$

Note that the distance d runs from the point P to the line $Ax + By + C = 0$. As the figure indicates, that distance is an altitude, and altitudes by definition are perpendicular, making d the shortest distance possible from the point to the line.

DOUBLE TRIANGLE

In the state of Florida, two spotters (*A* and *B*) for the National Aeronautics and Space Administration (NASA) program are at locations that lie in a straight line directly west of Cape Canaveral. At the 30,000-foot altitude point during a recent launch of the space shuttle *Discovery*, spotter *A* indicated a 28° angle of elevation from her vantage point and spotter *B* a 55° angle of elevation from his (see Figure 7.12).

How far apart (to the nearest tenth of a mile) are the two spotters?

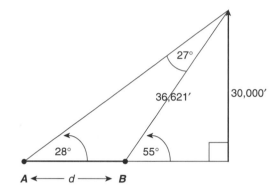

Figure 7.12

Solution 1

Most textbooks recommend that students think of the large triangle as being divided into a *double* triangle by the interior line segment drawn up from *B* (a cevian). Working from right to left, students should perform the following three steps:

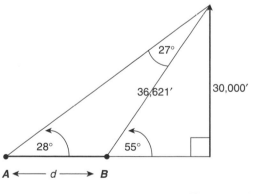

Figure 7.13

1. Evaluate the length of the cevian, the hypotenuse of the right-hand right triangle (sin 55° = 30,000 ÷ cevian *c*, or *c* ≈ 36,621' as per Figure 7.13).

2. Subtract 28° from 55° (an exterior angle to the left-hand obtuse triangle) to find the missing remote interior angle (27°) in the second diagram.

3. Use the Law of Sines in the obtuse triangle to get *d* ≈ 35,412' and then divide by 5,280' (= 1 mile) to determine that spotters *A* and *B* are 6.7 miles apart.

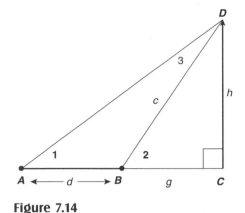

Figure 7.14

NOTE: From this point forward, this activity takes an alternative path. In Solution 2, students notice how quickly they can evaluate a solution (in one step, as opposed to the three steps in Solution 1). However, to get to this more efficient (and nontraditional) process, students need to make some changes to the Law of Sines. Formula 1 is a step in the right direction, but it still contains the sine values for three angles. Formula 2, on the other hand, is more efficient than Formula 1 in that it contains the cotangent values for only two angles: the two angles from the spotters in the space shuttle question. Formula 2 is hereafter referred to as the Law of Cotangents and is proven easily and elegantly in the proof of Formula 2.

Formula 1: A Better Double-Triangle Formula

Hard as it may seem for students, mathematics—like any other body of knowledge—has evolved over time and continues to do so. Formulas have generally resulted from attempts to bring order to chaos and brevity to tedium, but the true payoff in learning mathematics lies not in the formula itself but in appreciation for those journeys of logical thought known as proofs.

As an example, consider the following, as per Figure 7.14:

$$\sin(\text{angle } 2) = \frac{h}{c} \rightarrow c = \frac{h}{\sin(\text{angle } 2)} \text{ (substitute)}$$

$$\frac{d}{\sin(\text{angle } 3)} = \frac{c}{\sin(\text{angle } 1)} \rightarrow d = \frac{c \cdot \sin(\text{angle } 3)}{\sin(\text{angle } 1)}$$

$$\rightarrow d = \frac{h \cdot \sin(\text{angle } 3)}{\sin(\text{angle } 2) \cdot \sin(\text{angle } 1)}$$

Formula 2: The Law of Cotangents

This formula uses one less angle and uses only the side lengths (the height of the shuttle $= h$ and the distance between the two spotters $= d$) specific to the original space shuttle question.

Since angle 3 = angle 2 – angle 1, improve on the above:

$$\frac{d}{h} = \frac{\sin(\text{angle } 2 - \text{angle } 1)}{\sin(\text{angle } 2) \cdot \sin(\text{angle } 1)}$$

$$= \frac{\sin(\text{angle } 2) \cdot \cos(\text{angle } 1) - \cos(\text{angle } 2) \cdot \sin(\text{angle } 1)}{\sin(\text{angle } 2) \cdot \sin(\text{angle } 1)}$$

$$= \frac{\cos(\text{angle } 1)}{\sin(\text{angle } 1)} - \frac{\cos(\text{angle } 2)}{\sin(\text{angle } 2)}$$

$$= \cot(\text{angle } 1) - \cot(\text{angle } 2) = \cot A - \cot B$$

Solution 2

Substitute into the Law of Cotangents the following: $h = 30,000$, angle $A = 28°$, angle $B = 55°$.

$$\frac{d}{30,000} = \cot 28° - \cot 55° = \frac{1}{\tan 28°} - \frac{1}{\tan 55°}$$

$$= 1.8807 - 0.7002 = 1.1805 \rightarrow d = (30,000 \cdot 1.1805) \div 5,280 \approx 6.7 \text{ miles}$$

Proof of Formula 2: The Law of Cotangents

$$\cot A = \frac{d+g}{h} = \frac{d}{h} + \frac{g}{h} \text{ and } \cot B = \frac{g}{h}$$

Therefore, $\cot A - \cot B = \left(\dfrac{d}{h} + \dfrac{g}{h}\right) - \left(\dfrac{g}{h}\right) = \dfrac{d}{h}$

Communication 8

A classroom in which teachers encourage students to share their insights (to explain, inquire, and strive for understanding) is a classroom led by a teacher-as-artist who knows content and engenders trust. This chapter examines the Communication Standard from a mathematics perspective—as language for students who have to translate symbols and words into action.

Engaging Exponents opens the chapter with an activity that helps students cope with the ups and downs of negative exponents. The next activity, the

Sound of Mathic, explores the connections harmonic sequences and series have with making beautiful sounds in music. In the Three Amigos activity, students use three of the most interesting numbers (the integers −1, 0, and +1) to guide them as they draw each of the reciprocal functions from three given and basic graphs. Finally, the Sign Language activity borrows ideas from number patterns, symmetry, and transformations to create three bet-you-didn't-knows to help students gain a deeper appreciation for the quadratic function (parabola).

ENGAGING EXPONENTS

Grades 8–10

This activity asks three questions: Where is the decimal point going? What happens after the decimal point jumps the fence? Do exponents also have their ups and downs? It provides a useful model to deal with positive and negative exponents. This activity correlates to the following highlighted expectation for students:

- **Organize and *consolidate* mathematical thinking through communication**
- *Communicate* mathematical thinking coherently and clearly to peers, teachers, and others
- *Analyze* and evaluate the mathematical thinking and strategies of others
- Use the language of mathematics to *express* mathematical ideas precisely

---

Where Is the Decimal Point Going?

Powers of 10 provide a good starting point for any discussion around positive, zero, and negative exponents. Begin with $10^3 = 10 \cdot 10 \cdot 10 = 1,000$ and look for a pattern as the exponent decreases by one integral value at a time.

To help generate a pattern, think of 10^3 as 1. and then move that decimal point the same number of places (3) as the exponent says. So, students write "1." and then move the decimal point three positive places or three places to the right: $1\_\_\_. = 1,000$.

$10^3 = 1,000$. 10^3 is "1 and 3 jumps right." (Fill in jumped spaces with zeros = 1,000.)

$10^2 = 100$. 10^2 is "1 and 2 jumps right" (= 100).

$10^1 = 10$. 10^1 is "1 and 1 jump right" (= 10).

$10^0 = $ _____ (*Hint:* What is 1 point and *no* jumps right or left?) Any base raised to a zero exponent = 1.

The leftward movement of the decimal point as students read down the right-hand column above provides a built-in progression, but the following illustrates what the true meaning behind the zero exponent is:

$$\frac{x^a}{x^b} = x^{a-b} \rightarrow \frac{x^3}{x^3} = x^{3-3} = x^0 = 1$$

As seen previously in this book, a specifics-then-generality (inductive) teaching model is recommended over the reverse (formula-then-examples or deductive approach) to stimulate student curiosity.

Notice in the next section how closely related zero exponents are to negative exponents by just extending the opening pattern on the previous page.

What Happens After the Decimal Point Jumps the Fence?

The pattern being displayed by the decimal point in this list is the same as before: continuous movement to the left by one place value every time the exponent decreases by one. However, notice that when the decimal point "jumps the fence" (goes over to the left-hand side of 1), the exponent becomes negative.

$10^3 = 1,000.$

$10^2 = 100.$

$10^1 = 10.$

$10^0 = 1.$

$10^{-1} =$ _____ (*Hint:* What is "1 point, and 1 jump left?" Or what is another way to express .1?)

What is happening here?

$$10^{-1} = .1 = 1 \div 10 = 1 \div 10^1$$
$$10^{-2} = .01 = 1 \div 100 = 1 \div 10^2$$
$$10^{-3} = .001 = 1 \div 1,000 = 1 \div 10^3 \ldots$$
$$10^{-x} = 1 \div 10^x$$

Students will recognize once more the natural connection between decimals and fractions. Encourage them to check the accuracy of that base-10 list above by means of a scientific or graphing calculator.

$$\frac{10^{-x}}{1} = \frac{1}{10^x} \rightarrow 10^x \cdot 10^{-x} = 1 \rightarrow 10^{[x + (-x)]} = 10^0 = 1$$

By proportionality and because $x^a \cdot x^b = x^{a+b}$, the rule for negative exponents is just an extension of that for the zero exponent. But this connection is not limited to base-10 numbers alone, as illustrated here:

$$\frac{x^a}{x^b} = x^{a-b} \rightarrow \frac{x^3}{x^5} = x^{3-5} = x^{-2} = \frac{1}{x^2}$$

Do Exponents Also Have Their Ups and Downs?

If x^{-2} is the same as $\frac{x^{-2}}{1}$, and if $\frac{x^{-2}}{1}$ is the same as $\frac{1}{x^2}$, then consider what happened to the position of the x-term in the above rational expression. It is as if x had a negative exponent *upstairs* (in the numerator) and then was allowed

175

to shift itself *downstairs* (into the denominator) when it changed the sign of its exponent (negative to positive). Any *vacated floor* is given a 1.

Consider how playing this elevator game affords students the flexibility to move terms quickly and legally. It also serves to confirm this mathematical suspicion: Is a rational base raised to a negative power equivalent to the reciprocal of that base raised to the positive of that power?

$$\left(\frac{x}{y}\right)^{\frac{-a}{b}} = \frac{x^{-\frac{a}{b}}}{y^{-\frac{a}{b}}} = \frac{\frac{1}{x^{\frac{a}{b}}}}{\frac{1}{y^{\frac{a}{b}}}} = \frac{1}{x^{\frac{a}{b}}} \cdot \frac{y^{\frac{a}{b}}}{1} = \frac{y^{\frac{a}{b}}}{x^{\frac{a}{b}}} = \left(\frac{y}{x}\right)^{\frac{a}{b}}$$

THE SOUND OF MATHIC

Grades 11–12

The following is a wonderful essay on the connections between mathematics and harmonics. It is reprinted from the student mathematics journal the *Math Mirror* (Donovan, Lucarelli, Sun Park, & Rogers, 1992), written and produced by students at Manhasset High School, Manhasset, New York. Their faculty adviser, Curt Boddie, empowered his precalculus students through their publication to experience success in their own creations and to use available media to communicate their accomplishments. This activity correlates to the following highlighted expectation for students:

- Organize and *consolidate* mathematical thinking through communication
- ***Communicate* mathematical thinking coherently and clearly to peers, teachers, and others**
- *Analyze* and evaluate the mathematical thinking and strategies of others
- Use the language of mathematics to *express* mathematical ideas precisely

NOTE: The following is adapted and reprinted by permission of Curt Boddie (ret.), formerly of Manhasset High School, Manhasset, New York.

In our teacher's dreams, the halls are alive with the sound of mathic, a harmony only he can sense. Transcendental functions and irrational numbers such as π, e, and $\sqrt{2}$ send him into ecstasy, the kind of heightened feeling others get when they view an exquisite painting or observe the faultless architecture of a cathedral. They are, we repeat, mathic to his ears. His is a well-ordered life, everything flowing, it seems, in proper sequence.

Sequence. Now there's a word we heard much about this year. Take a gander at the sequence 5, 9, 13, 17, . . . If we told you that the immediate successor of each term in the sequence exceeded it by 4, then you would call this an arithmetic sequence or progression. Can you determine, without continuing the list, what the 100th term would be? Let's see:

$$5 = 5$$

$$9 = 5 + 4 = 5 + 1\,(4)$$

$$13 = 9 + 4 = (5 + 4) + 4 = 5 + 4 + 4 = 5 + 2\,(4)$$

$$17 = 13 + 4 = (9 + 4) + 4 = (5 + 4 + 4) + 4 = 5 + 3\,(4)$$

So, it would seem that in an arithmetic progression, all you need to know to find any term, say, a_n, is the first term, a_1, and the common difference, d. These quantities are related by the formula

$$a_n = a_1 + (n - 1)\,d$$

Therefore, the 100th term,

$$a_{100} = 5 + (100 - 1)(4)$$
$$= 5 + (99)(4)$$
$$= 5 + 396$$
$$= 401$$

The sequence $\frac{1}{5}, \frac{1}{9}, \frac{1}{13}, \frac{1}{17}, \ldots$ is another kind of sequence, known as harmonic. Notice that the reciprocals of the terms of this sequence form the above-mentioned arithmetic sequence. This is true of any harmonic sequence.

Moreover, the sequence $1, \frac{1}{2}, \frac{1}{3}, \frac{1}{4}, \ldots, \frac{1}{n}$ is called *the harmonic sequence.* The name, as you might have suspected, has something to do with music. In music, the word *harmonic* means a fainter and higher tone heard along with the main tone. The fundamental tone of a musical string comes from vibrating the string. You can get the first harmonic by gently touching the midpoint $\left(\frac{1}{2}\right)$ of the string, the second harmonic by touching it $\frac{1}{3}$ of the way down, and so on. In general, the $(n-1)$th harmonic is obtained by touching the vibrating string at a point that is $\left(\frac{1}{n}\right)$ of the way down.

Although there is no general formula for the sum of a harmonic sequence (i.e., a harmonic series), it is known that three given quantities (a, b, and c) are in harmonic progression if the proportion $\frac{a}{c} = \frac{a-b}{b-c}$ is true. Problems involving such a sequence are usually solved by inverting its terms (getting their reciprocals) and using the properties of the corresponding arithmetic progression. For example, given the sequence $-6, 3, \frac{6}{5}, \frac{3}{4}, \ldots$

1. Show that the numbers form a harmonic progression.

2. Write the next two terms of the progression.

    a. For $a = -6$, $b = 3$, and $c = \frac{6}{5} = 1.2$:

    $$\frac{a}{c} = \frac{a-b}{b-c} \rightarrow \frac{-6}{1.2} = \frac{-6-3}{3-1.2} \rightarrow -5 = -5$$

    b. The arithmetic progression translated from the given harmonic one is $-\frac{1}{6}, \frac{1}{3}, \frac{5}{6}, \frac{4}{3},$ ____, ____. Using the least common denominator (6), rewrite the arithmetic progression as $-\frac{1}{6}, \frac{2}{6}, \frac{5}{6}, \frac{8}{6},$ ____, ____. One should note the common difference d as $\frac{3}{6}\left(=\frac{1}{2}\right)$, making the next two terms $\frac{11}{6}$ and $\frac{14}{6}\left(=\frac{7}{3}\right)$.

Therefore, untranslating back to the original harmonic progression makes its next two terms $\frac{6}{11}$ and $\frac{3}{7}$.

We shall now try to *find the harmonic mean between* $\frac{3}{5}$ *and* $\frac{1}{3}$. The easiest way, of course, would be to find the average (*arithmetic mean*) between $\frac{5}{3}$ and 3, which is $\frac{7}{3}$ and then state its reciprocal, $\frac{3}{7}$ as our answer. Or, we could use the formula, given above, to show that when three quantities, a, b, and c, are in harmonic progression, then

$$\frac{\frac{3}{5}}{\frac{1}{3}} = \frac{\frac{3}{5} - b}{b - \frac{1}{3}} \rightarrow b = \frac{3}{7}.$$

Next, let's *insert four harmonic means between* $\frac{4}{3}$ *and* $\frac{2}{9}$. Solution: The corresponding arithmetic progression would be $\frac{3}{4}$, _____, _____, _____, _____, $\frac{9}{2}$, with $\frac{3}{4}$ being the first term, a_1, and $\frac{9}{2}$ its sixth term, a_6.

$$a_6 = a_1 + (6-1)\,d \rightarrow \frac{9}{2} = \frac{3}{4} + 5d \ \textit{(multiply by 4)} \rightarrow$$

$$18 = 3 + 20d \rightarrow \frac{3}{4} = d$$

The four *arithmetic means* are $\frac{6}{4}$, $\frac{9}{4}$, $\frac{12}{4}$, and $\frac{15}{4}$, which simplify to $\frac{3}{2}$, $\frac{9}{4}$, 3, and $\frac{15}{4}$. Consequently, our four harmonic means are $\frac{2}{3}$, $\frac{4}{9}$, $\frac{1}{3}$, and $\frac{4}{15}$.

During this past semester, our course content introduced and exposed us primarily to arithmetic and geometric sequences and their series. Our teacher deliberately reserved the topic of harmonic sequences for us to research. He also informed us that some of us might encounter "unnamed" types of sequences in further math studies. We feel we have explored the topic in some depth so that they will not pose so overwhelming a problem.

We also think we can live rather harmoniously with all kinds of sequences. Can you?

THE THREE AMIGOS

Grades 11–12

This activity deals with graphing pairs of reciprocal functions on the same set of coordinate axes. Graphing functions become standard at the late stages of a high school student's career. What is different here is the use of three much easier graphs and the Three Amigos to make the total graphing experience more meaningful. This activity correlates to the following highlighted expectation for students:

- Organize and *consolidate* mathematical thinking through communication
- *Communicate* mathematical thinking coherently and clearly to peers, teachers, and others
- ***Analyze* and evaluate the mathematical thinking and strategies of others**
- Use the language of mathematics to *express* mathematical ideas precisely

Fortunately, because the reciprocal of 1 is itself 1 and, in a similar fashion, the reciprocal of −1 is −1, such pairs of graphs share any and all points in which the y-coordinate is either 1 or −1.

At the same time, since the reciprocal of 0 is $\frac{1}{0}$, or undefined, any graph with points in which the value of $y = 0$ forces its codrawn reciprocal partner to have **vertical asymptotes** through those same points. The numbers 1, −1, and 0, then, constitute a powerful triumvirate of numbers—a student's trio of guiding friends, or Three Amigos—when it comes to graphing reciprocal functions.

The following asks students to graph three reciprocal functions ($\frac{1}{x}$, $\frac{1}{x^2}$, and the trig function $y = \csc x$). The alternative graphing strategy using the Three Amigos helps students see any reciprocal graph as two related graphs instead of a single one.

Graph $y = \frac{1}{x}$

To draw this equilateral hyperbola (see Figure 8.1), start by drawing the line $y = x$ and then plot the shared points (−1, −1) and (1, 1). Note that $y = x$ goes through the origin; therefore, $y = \frac{1}{x}$ uses the y-axis as a vertical asymptote (approaching negative infinity from the left and positive infinity from the right). The chart (see Figure 8.2) confirms how the values of the reciprocal pair (line and hyperbola) flip-flop in the four intervals around the Three Amigos.

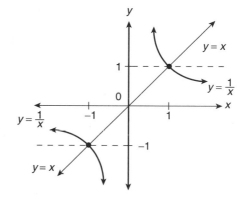

Figure 8.1

x	$y = x$	$y = \frac{1}{x}$
$x < -1$	$y < -1$	$-1 < y < 0$
$= -1$	-1	-1
$-1 < x < 0$	$-1 < y < 0$	$y < -1$
$= 0$	0	$- \infty$ $+ \infty$
$0 < x < 1$	$0 < y < 1$	$y > 1$
$= 1$	1	1
$x > 1$	$y > 1$	$0 < y < 1$

Figure 8.2

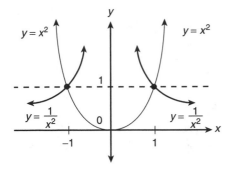

Figure 8.3

x	$y = x^2$	$y = \frac{1}{x^2}$
$x < -1$	$y > 1$	$0 < y < 1$
$= -1$	1	1
$-1 < x < 0$	$0 < y < 1$	$y > 1$
$= 0$	0	$+ \infty$ \ $+ \infty$
$0 < x < 1$	$0 < y < 1$	$y > 1$
$= 1$	1	1
$x > 1$	$y > 1$	$0 < y < 1$

Figure 8.4

Graph $y = \frac{1}{x^2}$

For this diagram (see Figure 8.3), start by drawing parabola $y = x^2$ and then plot the shared points $(-1, -1)$ and $(1, 1)$. Note, as before, that $y = x^2$ goes through the origin; therefore, $y = \frac{1}{x^2}$ once again uses the y-axis as a vertical asymptote (this time approaching positive infinity from *both* the left and the right). And again the chart (see Figure 8.4) confirms how the values of the reciprocal pair flip-flop in the four intervals around the Three Amigos.

NOTE: The whole point of the first two graphing examples is that the x-values of -1, 0, and $+1$ (the Three Amigos) break up the set of all x-values into four groups (the first column of either chart: the numbers to the left of -1, the numbers between -1 and 0, the numbers between 0 and $+1$, and the numbers to the right of $+1$). See how, no matter if one is graphing $y = x$ or $y = \frac{1}{x}$ in the first case, for either $x = -1$ or for $x = +1$, the values of the $y = x$ and $y = \frac{1}{x}$ columns are both the same: They both $= -1$ for $x = -1$, and they both $= +1$ for $x = +1$. For $x = 0$, the line $y = x$ has no problem (y also $= 0$), but for $y = \frac{1}{x}$, the value of $x = 0$ makes $y = \frac{1}{0}$, which is undefined (division by zero is impossible). For the four in-between zones around the Three Amigos, the two graphs $y = x$ and $y = \frac{1}{x}$ take opposite paths from each other. (For example, if one has a y-value greater than 1, the other has a y-value *between* 0 and 1.)

First Set of Challenge Questions

After illustrating the Three Amigos concept, challenge students to answer the following questions:

1. Describe in words (without referring to Figure 8.2) the relationship between the line $y = x$ and the equilateral hyperbola $y = \frac{1}{x}$ around the Three Amigos (i.e., in the $x < -1$ region, the $-1 < x < 0$ region, the $0 < x < 1$ region, and the $x > 1$ region).

2. Categorize the exponents (as either even or odd), and connect your answer to the symmetry that *both* the line $y = x$ and the equilateral hyperbola $y = \frac{1}{x}$ have in common.

3. Reconsider the first two questions for the reciprocal pair drawn in Figure 8.3. Why are both graphs drawn almost completely *above* the x-axis?

Graph $y = \csc x$

For this diagram (Figure 8.5), start by drawing the function $y = \sin x$ and then plot the shared points $(90°, 1)$ and $(270°, -1)$. Note how $y = \sin x$ goes through the x-axis at $x = 0°$, 180°, and 360°; therefore, $y = \csc x$ has vertical asymptotes for those three values of x. And the chart (see Figure 8.6) confirms how the values of the reciprocal pair flip-flop in the intervals between $y = -1$, 0, and 1.

NOTE: Of the six trigonometry ratios that students study (sine, cosine, tangent, cotangent, secant, and cosecant), students spend 95% of the time with just the first three, and the first one (sine) is done ad infinitum. What makes Figure 8.5 so interesting is the dual presence of sine (seen all the time) and its reciprocal function cosecant (abbreviated csc x and seen about as often as the Loch Ness Monster). The reason the cosecant graph receives poor treatment in most trigonometry textbooks is its strange appearance, which is exactly why the Three Amigos have come to the rescue. In Figure 8.6, note how the Three Amigos are listed in the y-columns (x contains the various angle measures from 0° to 360°). The same rationale applies as before, only this time with the other variable.

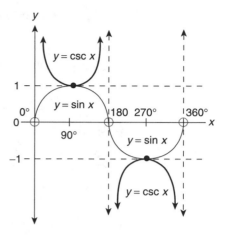

Figure 8.5

Second Set of Challenge Questions

Now challenge students to answer the following questions.

1. If the range of $y = \sin x$ is $-1 \le y \le 1$, then what is the range for its reciprocal partner $y = \csc x$?

2. Describe in words the symmetry demonstrated by Figure 8.5.

3. Group the remaining four trigonometric functions into their reciprocal pairs (cos and sec, tan and cot), and create two more sketches similar to Figure 8.5.

4. After determining symmetries for both sketches, use a graphing calculator to check all of your work. (How would you input reciprocal trigonometric functions?)

x	$y = \sin x$	$y = \csc x$
0°	0	$+\infty$
$0° < x < 90°$	$0 < y < 1$	$y > 1$
90°	>1	1
$90° < x < 180°$	$0 < y < 1$	$y > 1$
180°	0	$+\infty$ / $-\infty$
$180° < x < 270°$	$-1 < y < 0$	$y < -1$
270°	-1	-1
$270° < x < 360°$	$-1 < y < 0$	$y < -1$
360°	0	$-\infty$

Figure 8.6

SIGN LANGUAGE

> ### Grades 10–12
>
> This activity provides three nontraditional insights into the subtle language of parabolas. These three insights involve bringing number patterns, symmetry, and transformational geometry to quadratic functions (graphs of parabolas) to add greater insight and deeper understanding of the various important features already built into graphs of parabolas. This activity correlates to the following highlighted expectation for students:
>
> - Organize and *consolidate* mathematical thinking through communication
> - *Communicate* mathematical thinking coherently and clearly to peers, teachers, and others
> - *Analyze* and evaluate the mathematical thinking and strategies of others
> - **Use the language of mathematics to *express* mathematical ideas precisely**

Typically, drawing a parabola graph is accomplished through a series of steps:

- Evaluating its axis of symmetry
- Locating its vertex (or turning point)
- Determining its shape (upward "smile" or downward "frown")
- Filling out an *x*-*y* chart
- Plotting and connecting points on a coordinate grid

Use the following three insights to supplement your routine teaching or reviewing of parabolic graphs. Then have students practice graphing parabolas with questions built into the class discussion or with worksheets that include these insights wherever possible or prudent.

Uncovering Number Patterns

For $y = x^2 - 4x - 5$ (see Figure 8.7), consider how the *y*-values of the points around the vertex $(2, -9)$ evolve. With the vertex as the origin (and because there is the unit coefficient $a = 1$ for the x^2-term), the subsequent pattern points for plotting this parabola are as follows:

$$(2 \pm 1, -9 + 1)$$
$$(2 \pm 2, -8 + 3)$$
$$(2 \pm 3, -5 + 5), \text{ etc.}$$

Suppose the coefficient of the x^2-term is changed to $a = 2$, as would be the case for $y = 2x^2 - 8x$. The pattern points around its vertex $(2, -8)$ are as follows:

$(2 \pm 1, -8 + \mathbf{2})$

$(2 \pm 2, -6 + \mathbf{6})$

$(2 \pm 3, 0 + \mathbf{10})$, etc.

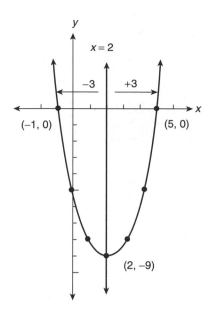

Figure 8.7

in which the new boldface numbers are just twice the size of the first set. Thus, *the y-values around the vertex of a parabola appear to be separated by an increasing sequence of odd numbers times the coefficient (a) of the* x²-*term.*

Analyzing Symmetry

Rewrite the Quadratic Formula $x = \frac{-b \pm \sqrt{b^2 - 4ac}}{2a}$ as two separate fractions: $x = \frac{-b}{2a} \pm \frac{\sqrt{b^2 - 4ac}}{2a}$. The first fraction, of course, becomes the Axis of Symmetry Formula $x = \frac{-b}{2a}$; for $y = x^2 - 4x - 5$, it yields $x = 2$, upon which the y-value for the vertex $(2, -9)$ can be determined.

Information about the second fraction, $x = \frac{\pm\sqrt{b^2 - 4ac}}{2a}$, is relatively more difficult to locate in traditional textbooks. But a revisit of Figure 8.7 shows how the calculated value $x = \pm 3$ here constitutes the distance from the axis of symmetry $x = 2$ to the two x-intercepts of the parabola.

Noteworthy here is that the x-values of those intercepts are the two roots (solutions) of the quadratic equation $x^2 - 4x - 5 = 0$. It is a known fact that the intersection of any parabola $y = ax^2 + bx + c$ with the x-axis yields the real root(s) of the equation $ax^2 + bx + c = 0$; however, the visual learner would find the relationship between the parabola and the Quadratic Formula a much more engaging approach to the nature of its roots and the discriminant $b^2 - 4ac$.

Using Transformations

Complete the following square: $y = x^2 - 4x - 5 \rightarrow y + 5 + \underline{\quad} = x^2 - 4x + \underline{\quad}$ (take the coefficient (b) of the x-term, divide it by 2, and square the result) $\rightarrow$ $y + 5 + 4 = x^2 - 4x + 4 \rightarrow y + 9 = (x - 2)^2 \rightarrow y = (x - 2)^2 - 9$.

Now, translate the parabola verbally while "think-sketching" its graph:

1. Start with the basic parabola through the origin: $y = x^2$.

2. "Slide" it right 2 units (*opposite* the included sign): $y = (x - 2)^2$.

3. From the point $(2, 0)$, "shift" it down 9 units: $y = (x - 2)^2 - 9$.

The vertex $(2, -9)$ can thus be "read" from this alternative equation.

(NOTE: A positive number N in front of the parentheses either "pinches" the parabola $(N > 1)$ or "fans" it $(0 < N < 1)$. A negative number N would "flip" it over the x-axis.)

CALCULATOR APPLICATION

x-Intercepts

So, it would make sense that if the student knew the vertex and the two x-intercepts, then she or he would have a very good idea as to the shape of the corresponding parabola prior to drawing its pencil-and-paper representation.

Using the Application With Students

The original program at the right, titled **"QUADINTS"** (which works for both the TI-73 and the TI-83/84 Plus graphing calculators), tells the student where to place the two x-intercepts:

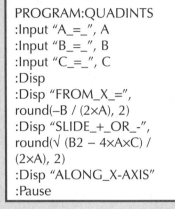

```
PROGRAM:QUADINTS
:Input "A_=_", A
:Input "B_=_", B
:Input "C_=_", C
:Disp
:Disp "FROM_X_=",
round(–B / (2×A), 2)
:Disp "SLIDE_+_OR_-",
round(√ (B2 – 4×A×C) /
(2×A), 2)
:Disp "ALONG_X-AXIS"
:Pause
```

Your Input (Example)	**Output**
Press: **ON**	
PRGM	
(*Scroll down to* **QUADINTS**)	
ENTER	**prgmQUADINTS**
(*Remember that the quadratic equation $x^2 - 4x - 5 = 0$ is represented by the quadratic function, or parabola, $y = x^2 - 4x - 5$.*)	

ENTER
  1 ENTER
  –4 ENTER
  –5 ENTER
	A = 1
	B = –4
	C = –5

Your Input (Example)	Output

ENTER	FROM X =
	          2
	 SLIDE + OR –
	          3
	 ALONG X-AXIS

ENTER	prgmQUADINTS Done

The results   The **axis of symmetry is** $x = 2$.

The **vertex** is found by substituting $x = 2$ into the quadratic ($y = -9$), which yields **the point (2, –9).**

The **x-intercepts** are 2 ± 3, which is equivalent to **(–1, 0) and (5, 0).**

CALCULATOR APPLICATION

Solving the Quadratic

Coincidentally, there are others who would prefer simply finding the *x*-intercepts algebraically—that is, solve the quadratic. It is strongly recommended that the teacher insist that the student use the following program ("SOLVQUAD") in a checking capacity only . . . and preferably after engaging with drawing the parabola and its accompanying "QUADINTS" program beforehand.

```
PROGRAM:SOLVQUAD                       :Disp "_"
:ClrHome                               :Input "C_=_",C
:Disp "SOLVE_EQUATIONS"                :Pause
:Disp "OF_THE_FORM"                    :ClrHome
:Disp "_"                              :((-B+√(B²-4*A*C)) / (2*A)) → P
:Disp "AX²_+_BX_+_C_=_0"               :((-B-√(B²-4*A*C)) / (2*A)) → Q
:Pause                                 :Disp "THE_ROOTS_ARE:"
:ClrHome                               :Disp "_"
:Disp "INPUT_A,_B,_C:"                 :Disp P → Frac
:Disp "_"                              :Disp " and "
:Input "A_=_",A                        :Disp Q → Frac
:Disp "_"                              :Disp "_"
:Input "B_=_",B
```

Input	**Output**

Press: **ON**

PRGM

(*Scroll down to* **QUADINTS**)

	PrgmSOLVQUAD

ENTER

	SOLVE EQUATIONS OF THE FORM AX² + BX + C = 0

ENTER
1 ENTER
–4 ENTER
–5

	INPUT A, B, C: A = 1 B = –4 C = –5

ENTER
ENTER

	THE ROOTS ARE: 5 and –1

	Done

Connections 9

According to the standards listed in *Principles and Standards for School Mathematics* (National Council of Teachers of Mathematics [NCTM], 2000), all students in Grades 6 through 12 should be able to do the following:

- Recognize and use connections among mathematical ideas

- Understand how mathematical ideas interconnect and build on one another to produce a coherent whole

- Recognize and apply mathematics in contexts outside of mathematics

Whether it is the energy generated when different branches of mathematics come together, the unveiling of the meaning of a real-world situation, or even the feeling of achievement shared by both teacher and student when they unravel and solve a problem, understanding mathematics is achieved when a student can create and sustain a connected framework of ideas. When you employ lessons and activities stressing any or all of these kinds of connections, students begin to appreciate not only the subject matter but also its utility as an active and dynamic body of knowledge.

The first activity for the Connections Standards, Slope of Angle Bisector, takes a problem situation and looks at four different methods of solution to demonstrate just how powerful those seemingly disjointed connections really are. Perhaps the most connected of those methods is spotlighted in the second activity, More Vector Rotations, which explains in more detail a method of determining the angle of point rotation. The final activity, Matrix Products, offers students three real-world applications of this most flexible, yet underpublicized, set of algorithms from the realm of discrete mathematics.

SLOPE OF ANGLE BISECTOR

NOTE: This activity works best as a teacher demonstration lesson.

Grades 10–12

Expanding on a point made in Flexible Arithmetic (see Chapter 1), Pedersen and Pólya (1984) state that the teacher who consistently augments the final look-back step of problem solving by challenging students to derive their results differently begins to develop students' deeper appreciation of mathematics. Such a multiple-solution mind-set affords students opportunities for a little inventiveness in "discovering" connectivity among various branches of mathematics. "Each problem encountered automatically becomes an unfinished exercise . . . a distinct improvement over the attitude that many students have of just 'finishing the exercise' and putting aside the ideas" (Pedersen & Pólya, 1984, p. 228).

 Thus, one well-chosen problem that students can solve in a variety of ways has the potential of providing a much richer learning experience than several disconnected, less stimulating exercises from a textbook. This activity demonstrates ideas from algebra, geometry, and trigonometry for students who are attempting to find the slope of the angle bisector in Quadrant I between the lines $y = x$ and $y = 7x$. This activity correlates to the following highlighted expectation for students:

- **Recognize and use connections among mathematical ideas**
- Understand how mathematical ideas interconnect and build on one another to produce a coherent whole
- Recognize and apply mathematics in contexts outside of mathematics

---

Method 1: Using Compass and Straightedge (Grade 10)

Find the slope of the angle bisector in Quadrant I between the lines $y = x$ and $y = 7x$.

NOTE: This method is fairly routine for a current geometry student in Grade 10 but may need a quick review (how to construct an angle bisector with a compass and a straightedge) for students in Grade 11 or 12.

 In a kind of visual hybrid approach, have students take a piece of graph paper and very carefully draw (with the help of a straightedge) the lines y_1 and y_2. Then, have them take a compass and perform the standard construction of the bisector of the angle between those two given lines.

 If this construction is accurately drawn on the graph paper, the straightedge result (on close inspection of its slope) should be the line $y = 2x$. Hence, the slope of the angle bisector = the slope of the line = 2.

Method 2: Tangent of the Difference of Two Angles (Grade 11)

Find the slope of the angle bisector in Quadrant I between the lines $y = x$ and $y = 7x$.

Refer to Figure 9.1: $S = Q + R \rightarrow Q = S - R \rightarrow$

$$\tan Q = \tan (S - R) = \frac{\tan S - \tan R}{1 + \tan S \tan R}.$$

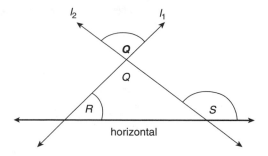

Figure 9.1

Define both angles R and S as angles of inclination (angles that their respective lines make with the horizontal). Thus,

$$m_1 = \tan R \text{ and } m_2 = \tan S \rightarrow \tan Q = \frac{m_2 - m_1}{1 + m_2 m_1}$$

Extend that formula for the tangent of the angle between two lines into an algebraic equation that takes into account what an angle bisector does.

Consider the bold line as the angle bisector in Figure 9.2.

$$R = S \rightarrow \tan R = \tan S \rightarrow \frac{7 - m}{1 + 7m} = \frac{m - 1}{1 + m}$$

$$\rightarrow 2m^2 - 3m - 2 = 0 \rightarrow m = \left\{ 2, -\frac{1}{2} \right\}$$

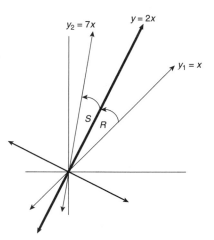

Figure 9.2

Reject $-\frac{1}{2}$ (the slope of the angle bisectors in Quadrants II and IV) $\rightarrow m = 2$

Method 3: Perpendicular Point-to-Line Distances (Grades 11–12)

Find the slope of the angle bisector in Quadrant I between the lines $y = x$ and $y = 7x$.

Present Figure 9.3 to students. Have students pick a point (x, y) on the bold angle bisector in which the perpendicular distances to lines y_1 and y_2 (labeled d_1 and d_2, respectively) are equal:

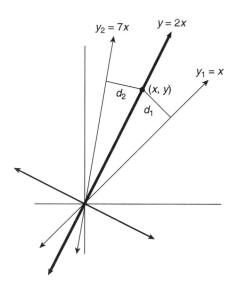

Figure 9.3

$$\frac{|1(x) - 1(y) + 0|}{2} = \frac{|7(x) - 1(y) + 0|}{52} \rightarrow$$

$$5|x - y| = |7x - y|$$

Because $|a| = |b| \rightarrow a = \pm b$, $5(x - y) = 7x - y \rightarrow y = \left(-\frac{1}{2}\right) \cdot$ (reject)

or $5(x - y) = -7x + y \rightarrow y = 2x$ (slope $= 2$)

Method 4: Using a Degree-Rotator Vector (Grade 12)

Find the slope of the angle bisector in Quadrant I between the lines $y = x$ and $y = 7x$.

To prepare, consider the following four-step process that rotates either a point or a line about the origin, using a sketch and some well-chosen multiplication:

1. Draw an arrow (a **position vector**) from the origin to a given point.

2. Label that and every vector as a complex number in the form $a \pm bi$.

3. Multiply that first vector by a second one, a **degree-rotator vector** (see More Vector Rotations for a more detailed explanation on how to multiply vectors).

4. Draw a resulting third vector representing the product of the first two (the tip of the third vector represents the answer).

NOTE: If you have trouble deciphering this method, refer to the next activity, More Vector Rotations, and then come back to this method of solution.

Now examine the fourth and final method of solution. Using an 8½ × 11-inch piece of paper and a piece of graph paper with the complex (*a-b*) axes drawn thereupon, follow the vectors in this explanation:

1. Identify the degree-rotator vector $a + bi$ that sweeps vector $1 + i$ (the line $y = \frac{1}{1}x$) over to and on top of vector $1 + 7i$ (the line $y = \frac{7}{1}x$):

$$(1 + i) \cdot (a + bi) = (1 + 7i)$$

$$\rightarrow a + bi = \frac{1 + 7i}{1 + i} \cdot \frac{1 - i}{1 - i}$$

$$= 4 + 3i$$

2. Translate the vector representing that sweep angle (call it Q) into an acute triangle in the coordinate plane with the same Q as its **reference angle** (see Figure 9.4):

$$\text{Since } \|4 + 3i\| = \sqrt{4^2 + 3^2} = 5, \ \cos Q = \frac{4}{5}$$

3. Use the Half-Angle Formula for tangent (keep in mind that angle Q is being bisected).

NOTE: If angle Q represents the angle between the two lines, then the bisected angle (cut in half) would be half of Q, or $\frac{Q}{2}$.

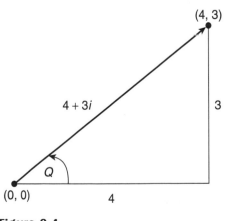

Figure 9.4

$$\tan \frac{Q}{2} = \sqrt{\frac{1 - \cos Q}{1 + \cos Q}}$$

$$= \sqrt{\frac{1 - \frac{4}{5}}{1 + \frac{4}{5}}}$$

$$= \sqrt{\frac{1}{9}}$$

$$= \frac{1}{3}$$

4. Construct a second triangle with $\frac{Q}{2}$ as the reference angle and the numbers 1 (the opposite side) and 3 (the adjacent side). The hypotenuse can be "untranslated" into the vector $3 + 1i$ (see Figure 9.5).

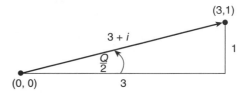

Figure 9.5

5. This vector $3 + i$ now acts as the degree-rotator vector for $\frac{Q}{2}$. That is, multiplying the first vector $(1 + i)$ by $(3 + i)$ has the same effect as sweeping the line $y = x$ to the angle bisector's (halfway) position between $y = x$ and $y = 7x$:

$$(1 + i) \bullet (3 + i) = (a + bi) = 2 + 4i$$

6. Note that the tip of the vector $2 + 4i$ on the complex plane can be translated to the point $(2, 4)$ on the coordinate plane. The line that runs from the origin through the point $(2, 4)$ is the line $y = 2x$, and its slope $= 2$.

MORE VECTOR ROTATIONS

> ### Grades 11–12
>
> A closer inspection of Method 4 from Slope of Angle Bisector reveals a four-step process that combines skills from algebra, geometry, and trigonometry within a transformation (rotation) framework. This activity investigates the effects of using vectors to perform transformations. This activity correlates to the following highlighted expectation for students:
>
> - Recognize and use connections among mathematical ideas
> - **Understand how mathematical ideas interconnect and build on one another to produce a coherent whole**
> - Recognize and apply mathematics in contexts outside of mathematics

To gain a deeper understanding of the degree-rotator vector, consider the Pólya (1951) heuristic of solving a simpler problem. Take the unit vector 1 (which represents the complex number $1 + 0i$) and apply some selected degree-rotator vectors emanating from either the a- or b-axis (which represent quadrantal angles).

For example:

$$i \bullet (1 + 0i) = i + 0 = 0 + 1i \text{ (multiplying by } i \text{ rotates the unit vector } 90°)$$

$$i^2 \bullet (1 + 0i) = i^2 + 0 = -1 + 0i \text{ (multiplying by } i^2 \text{ rotates the unit vector } 180°)$$

NOTE: Because positive angles in trigonometry rotate *counter*clockwise from Quadrant I, this rotation might explain why Quadrants II, III, and IV are also labeled in a *counter*clockwise sequence.

Now consider degree-rotator vectors connected to the two special right triangles, 30°-60°-90° and 45°-45°-90°. To rotate the unit vector 30° (the corresponding triangle in which the hypotenuse = 1), adjacent side $a = \frac{\sqrt{3}}{2}$ and opposite side $b = \frac{1}{2}$, which makes the 30° rotator $= \frac{\sqrt{3}}{2} + \frac{1}{2} i$. To rotate the unit vector 45°, adjacent side $a =$ opposite side $b = \frac{\sqrt{2}}{2}$, which makes the 45° rotator $= \frac{\sqrt{2}}{2} + \frac{\sqrt{2}}{2} i$, and so on.

Each student needs the following materials:

- One piece of large-square graph paper
- A ruler
- A sharp pencil

Question 1

Challenge students to find the coordinates (the nearest tenth) of point C such that, along with given points A(2, 5) and B(6, 1), the three points combine to form the vertices of an equilateral triangle in Quadrant I.

NOTE: Point C must rest on the perpendicular bisector of side AB.

Setup

To begin, have students translate side AB into side A′B′ under the rule $T(x, y) \rightarrow (x - 2, y - 5)$. Note how point A′ is positioned at the origin (see Figure 9.6).

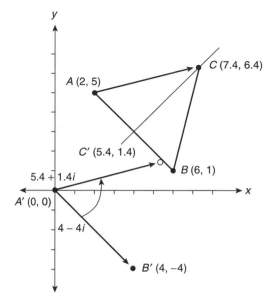

Figure 9.6

Steps 1 and 2

Because the same translation puts point B′ at (4, –4), instruct students to draw the vector $4 - 4i$.

Step 3

Next, have students multiply $4 - 4i$ by the 60° rotator, which would be $\frac{1}{2} + \frac{\sqrt{3}}{2}i$. The resulting vector, A′C′, is roughly $5.4 + 1.4i$, meaning that C′ is positioned at the point (5.4, 1.4).

For a quick verification of student work, the TI-83/84 Plus has some nice imaginary-number operations features. In this case, input the following:

MODE

(Move the arrow down to the second line and over to the number "2.")

ENTER

(NOTE: This allows for your answers to be rounded to the nearest hundredth.)

2nd QUIT

(4 – 4 2nd *i*) ((1 ÷ 2) + ((2nd √3) ÷ 2) 2nd *i*)

ENTER

Step 4

Finally, have students untranslate vector A′C′ (by reversing the Setup step) to create vector AC, which in turn can be used to draw side AC of triangle ABC. The tip of vector AC, then, identifies the coordinates of desired point C at about (7.4, 6.4).

NOTE: To check, perform the standard compass-and-straightedge construction of the perpendicular bisector of a line segment (in this case, side AB) to verify that point C is properly positioned.

Question 2

Challenge students to discover how many degrees are "swept" from Quadrant I to Quadrant II by rotating the line $y = 4x$ about the origin onto the line $y = -\dfrac{5}{3}x$.

If slope is defined on the **Cartesian plane** (x- and y-axes) as change in y divided by change in x, then it follows for the complex number plane (a- and b-axes) that any position vector in the form $a \pm bi$ would have to have the same slope as the line drawn right on top of it (i.e., change in b divided by change in a).

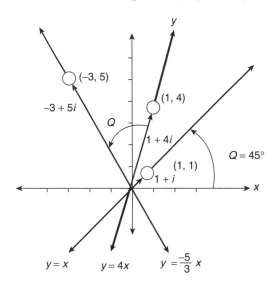

Figure 9.7

As per Figure 9.7, have students represent the first line as position vector $(1 + 4i)$, the second line as position vector $(-3 + 5i)$, and the unknown degree-rotator vector as the usual $(a + bi)$. Restate the question as follows:

Solve for a and b in $(1 + 4i) \cdot (a + bi) = (-3 + 5i)$.

The following methods of solution both involve algebra and illustrate for students why they should learn how to solve a system of simultaneous equations (in the first method) and how to rationalize a complex number denominator (in the second method).

F.O.I.L. and Pair Off

$$(1 + 4i)(a + bi) = -3 + 5i$$
$$a + 4ai + bi - 4b = -3 + 5i$$
$$(a - 4b) + (4a + b)i = -3 + 5i$$

Solve for a and b:

$$a - 4b = -3$$
$$4a + b = 5$$
$$\{a = 1, b = 1\} \rightarrow a + bi = 1 + 1i$$

or Divide and Rationalize

$$(1 + 4i) \cdot (a + bi) = (-3 + 5i) \rightarrow (a + bi) = \frac{-3 + 5i}{1 + 4i}$$
$$= \frac{-3 + 5i}{1 + 4i} \cdot \frac{1 - 4i}{1 - 4i}$$
$$= \frac{17 + 17i}{17} = 1 + 1i$$

Conclusion

Since the tip of the vector $(1 + 1i)$ is the point $(1, 1)$ on the line $y = x$, the sweep angle $Q = 45°$.

MATRIX PRODUCTS

Grades 9–12

The entire branch of discrete mathematics, which includes the concept of matrices, has been receiving more attention from curriculum writers due to its timeliness and relevance. Discrete mathematics is a more contemporary branch of mathematics and includes (among other things) networking, efficient routing, task scheduling, game theory, election theory, and decision making, as well as matrices. Units are not necessarily connected to branches of traditional mathematics (e.g., algebra, geometry); therefore, they are considered discrete.

One interesting offshoot is the notion of graphing in a nontraditional sense; graphs are drawn as geometric figures connecting points (vertices) by line segments (edges). When those segments are drawn as vectors, they assume direction, and examples of such **directed graphs** abound—from water lines to work schedules to networks.

This activity illustrates three applications of multiplying matrices: routing networks, conducting magnetic resonance imaging (MRI) scans, and devising military strategy (which also uses the graphing calculator). A **matrix** is a rectangular array of numerical or algebraic quantities in an *m*-by-*n* format that is treated as an algebraic entity (*m* = # of rows [or "across" lines] of elements; *n* = # of columns [or "up-and-down" lines] of elements). This activity correlates to the following highlighted expectation for students:

- Recognize and use connections among mathematical ideas
- Understand how mathematical ideas interconnect and build on one another to produce a coherent whole
- **Recognize and apply mathematics in contexts outside of mathematics**

Before getting down to specifics, you may want to review the basics of matrix multiplication.

Basics of Matrix Multiplication

$$A = \begin{vmatrix} -3 & 5 & 8 \\ 4 & -2 & -6 \end{vmatrix}$$

Figure 9.8

Introduce Figures 9.8 and 9.9 to students:

- Matrix *A* is in a 2-by-3 array (two rows across, three columns up and down), its numbers perhaps representing a tracking of the stock prices of two companies.
- Matrix *B* is in a 3-by-2 array (three rows, two columns), its numbers perhaps representing a week's win-loss records for three baseball teams.

$$B = \begin{vmatrix} 5 & -1 \\ 3 & -2 \\ 2 & -4 \end{vmatrix}$$

Figure 9.9

Now, have students position the two array descriptors side by side:

$$(2 \bullet 3) \bullet (3 \bullet 2)$$

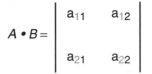

$$A \bullet B = \begin{vmatrix} a_{11} & a_{12} \\ \\ a_{21} & a_{22} \end{vmatrix}$$

Figure 9.10

Because the two means (the middle 3s) match, students can multiply matrices A and B. In fact, their resulting product is a 2-by-2 matrix, as shown in Figure 9.10 (the remaining extreme numbers of the product of the array descriptors).

The numbers that constitute this new matrix are sums of the products of matched elements from the two gray rows of matrix A and the two black columns of matrix B (see Figure 9.11).

$$A \bullet B = \begin{vmatrix} (-3)\,(5) + & (5)\,(3) + & (8)\,(2) & (-3)\,(-1) + & (5)\,(-2) + & (8)\,(-4) \\ (4)\,(5) + (-2)\,(3) + (-6)\,(2) & & (4)\,(-1) + (-2)\,(-2) + (-6)\,(-4) \end{vmatrix}$$

Figure 9.11

$$A \bullet B = \begin{vmatrix} 16 & -39 \\ \\ 2 & 24 \end{vmatrix}$$

Figure 9.12

By performing the indicated operations, students create the desired 2-by-2 matrix in Figure 9.12. (This is strictly an academic exercise—one would be hard-pressed to justify the logic behind multiplying company stocks and baseball standings matrices together!)

Routing Networks

Present the following scenario to students:

Figure 9.13

Suppose you own a small package service with branch offices in three cities (see Figure 9.13). The arrows indicate daily one-leg flights, but since cutting costs is always a major concern, you want to know how many two-leg flights you could create from this pattern.

		TO		
		Chi	Buf	NYC
	Chi	0	0	2
FROM	Buf	1	0	1
	NYC	1	1	0

Figure 9.14

1. Instruct students to unscramble the diagram into a table of one-leg flights, which will (without all the labels) become matrix L (see Figure 9.14).

2. Present the following theorem to students: If matrix L represents the number of one-leg routes between the vertices of a directed graph, then matrix L^n represents the number of n-leg routes between those same vertices. Refer to Figure 9.15.

Therefore, to determine the number of two-leg routes for the shipping company, students simply need to multiply matrix L times itself; that is, find L^2 (see Figure 9.16).

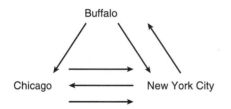

$$L = \begin{vmatrix} 0 & 0 & 2 \\ 1 & 0 & 1 \\ 1 & 1 & 0 \end{vmatrix}$$

Figure 9.15

3. Have students refit matrix L^2 with the appropriate labels to create a table of possible two-leg flight routes (see Figure 9.17).

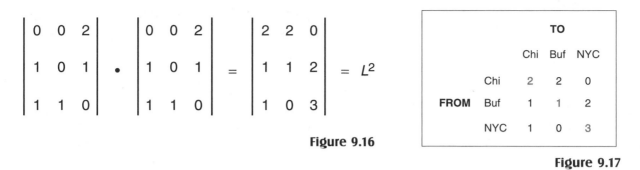

$$\begin{vmatrix} 0 & 0 & 2 \\ 1 & 0 & 1 \\ 1 & 1 & 0 \end{vmatrix} \cdot \begin{vmatrix} 0 & 0 & 2 \\ 1 & 0 & 1 \\ 1 & 1 & 0 \end{vmatrix} = \begin{vmatrix} 2 & 2 & 0 \\ 1 & 1 & 2 \\ 1 & 0 & 3 \end{vmatrix} = L^2$$

Figure 9.16

		TO		
		Chi	Buf	NYC
	Chi	2	2	0
FROM	Buf	1	1	2
	NYC	1	0	3

Figure 9.17

Point out the following to students:

> Note how the main diagonal now has numbers (in gray), whereas matrix L did not. This information allows your company to plot a more profitable business strategy—you can schedule planes to travel from and return to their points of origin in one day.

Conducting MRI Scans

Have students consider the following scenario:

> You are conducting an MRI scan on a patient who damaged her knee while skiing. Starting at the top of the knee and working vertically, you send two different-colored laser beams through the affected area and move about to find the intersection points of "false return," which will help determine locations and degrees of damage.

> For example, suppose at a depth of 2 inches, the MRI sends the line $2x - 3y = 7$ (colored light blue) through a suspected region simultaneously with the line $x + 4y = -2$ (bright yellow). The on-computer-screen return shows a very dark green, almost black, hue (rather than the preferred light green) at the point of intersection, indicating severe internal damage at that particular point. With the kneecap itself as the on-screen origin, find the point of intersection.

Have students write the problem as a system of simultaneous equations (see Figure 9.18). Rather than having them perform any standard algorithms, instruct them to follow three matrix-based steps.

$$2x - 3y = 7$$
$$x + 4y = -2$$

Figure 9.18

1. Remove all variables and equal signs, and reconfigure the six numbers that remain into a 2-by-3 matrix. Then, match those numbers with another (general) 2-by-3 matrix (see Figure 9.19).

$$\begin{vmatrix} 2 & -3 & 7 \\ 1 & 4 & -2 \end{vmatrix} = \begin{vmatrix} a & c & e \\ b & d & f \end{vmatrix}$$

Figure 9.19

2. Use a hybrid of **Cramer's Rule** (see Figure 9.20) to solve for y (notice where each gray-colored term goes). Refer to Figure 9.21.

$$y = \frac{a \cdot f - b \cdot e}{a \cdot d - b \cdot c}$$

Figure 9.20

$$y = \frac{a \cdot f - b \cdot e}{a \cdot d - b \cdot c} = \frac{(2)\,(-2) - (1)\,(7)}{(2)\,(4) - (1)\,(-3)} = \frac{-11}{11} = -1$$

Figure 9.21

3. Return to the original system of equations. Substitute $y = -1$ into the first equation to solve for x:

$$2x - 3\,(-1) = 7 \rightarrow 2x + 3 = 7 \rightarrow 2x = 4 \rightarrow x = 2$$

Then, use the second equation to check to see if both answers are correct:

$$(2) + 4\,(-1) = -2 \rightarrow 2 - 4 = -2 \rightarrow -2 = -2$$

The doctor now knows that the area of severest damage is, for the sake of this example, two units to the right of and one unit below the kneecap. Any resulting surgery or other treatment options or therapies become much more precise, thus removing the need for major reconstructive knee surgery and its accompanying costs.

CALCULATOR APPLICATION

Two Simultaneous Equations

Let's now extend the MRI Scan application for solving two simultaneous equations with matrices into a program titled "**TWOEQS**," which will work on either the TI-73 or TI-83/84 Plus model of graphing calculator:

PROGRAM:TWOEQS	:Input "C_=_", C
:Disp "GIVEN_2_SIMUL."	:Input "D_=_", D
:Disp "GENERAL_EQS."	:Input "E_=_", E
:Disp "_"	:Input "F_=_", F
:Disp "AX_+_BY_=_C"	:Pause
:Disp "DX_+_EY_=_F"	:ClrScreen
:Disp "_"	:(C × E − B × F) → P
:Disp "SOLVE_FOR_(X,Y)"	:(A × F − C × D) → Q
:Pause	:(A × E − B × D) → R
:Disp "_"	:Disp "X_=", P / R
:Input "A_=_", A	:Disp "Y_=", Q / R
:Input "B_=_", B	:Pause

Using the Application With Students

Your Input (Example)	Output
Press: **ON**	
PRGM	
(*Scroll down to* **TWOEQS**)	
ENTER	**prgmTWOEQS**
ENTER	**GIVEN 2 SIMUL.** **GENERAL EQS.**
	AX + BY = C **DX + EY = F** **SOLVE FOR (X,Y)**

(Continued)

(Continued)

Your Input (Example)	Output
ENTER	A = 2
(Solve for x *and* y *from **Figure 4.18:*** $2x - 3y = 7$	B = –3
$x + 4y = -2)$	C = 7
	D = 1
2 ENTER	E = 4
–3 ENTER . . .	F = –2
ENTER	X =
	2
	Y =
	–1
ENTER	prgmPERFSQRS Done

Now, return to page 50 and solve this system for *a* and *b*:

$$-4a + b = 13$$
$$-2a + b = 9$$

Devising Military Strategy

Present the following scenario to students:

Your assignment is to simplify the lengthy process it takes to locate an enemy plane over water. To guide a missile to the target (i.e., the enemy plane), a spotter submarine projects a point underwater through which a missile launched from point *A* (the submarine's position) will travel underwater in a parabolic arc, pass through projected imaginary point *B*, and hit point *C* (the plane). Information obtained by a U.S. destroyer at *A* (–2, 6) in the Persian Gulf is used to send a missile to be guided through *B* (3, –9) and timed so that it strikes the enemy plane just as it is passing through *C* (5, 13). Find the equation of the parabola that would pass through all three points.

The more complex the problem, the more important understanding matrix products becomes. For example, demonstrate for students the efficient solution of this unrelated three-equation–three-variable system of simultaneous equations, especially the original equations being first rewritten as a single matrix equation (see Figure 9.22).

$$
\begin{aligned}
-x + 2y - 3z &= 1 \\
2x \qquad + z &= 0 \\
3x - 4y + 4z &= 2
\end{aligned}
\quad\leftrightarrow\quad
\begin{vmatrix} -1 & 2 & -3 \\ 2 & 0 & 1 \\ 3 & -4 & 4 \end{vmatrix}
\cdot
\begin{vmatrix} x \\ y \\ z \end{vmatrix}
=
\begin{vmatrix} 1 \\ 0 \\ 2 \end{vmatrix}
$$

Arrays: $(3 \cdot 3) \cdot (3 \cdot 1) = (3 \cdot 1)$

Figure 9.22

Observe how the product of the rows of the 3-by-3 matrix and the column of the 3-by-1 matrix must be a 3-by-1 matrix. By multiplying both sides of a matrix equation by the inverse of the 3-by-3 matrix present, one isolates the 3-by-1 matrix of variables on one side of the equation and a 3-by-1 matrix of numeric solutions on the other.

What follows are the two remaining steps to determine the solutions for x, y, and z and directions for using a graphing calculator.

Whatever the inverse of A actually looks like (designated by A^{-1} in Figure 9.23 and determinable by using other rules from the study of matrix mathematics), consider the double impact of A^{-1}:

$$\begin{vmatrix} - & - & - \\ - & - & - \\ - & - & - \end{vmatrix} \bullet \begin{vmatrix} -1 & 2 & -3 \\ 2 & 0 & 1 \\ 3 & -4 & 4 \end{vmatrix} \bullet \begin{vmatrix} x \\ y \\ z \end{vmatrix} = \begin{vmatrix} - & - & - \\ - & - & - \\ - & - & - \end{vmatrix} \bullet \begin{vmatrix} 1 \\ 0 \\ 2 \end{vmatrix}$$

$$A^{-1} \quad \bullet \quad A \quad \bullet \quad V \quad = \quad A^{-1} \quad \bullet \quad B$$

Figure 9.23

Left side: The product of A^{-1} and A is the 3-by-3 **identity matrix I_3**, which has the equivalent value (**determinant**) of 1.

Right side: A^{-1} cannot be placed on the end of the equation because $B \times A^{-1}$ would be incompatible $(3 \bullet \underline{1}) \bullet (\underline{3} \bullet 3)$, the two mean numbers failing to match. (*Observation:* Matrix multiplication is not commutative.)

Find: $A^{-1} \bullet B$

Figure 9.24

Thus, we may now see the final matrix equation (see Figure 9.24) and the following TI-83/84 Plus calculator process for identifying x, y, and z.

Erase Phase:

2nd MEM 2 5 DEL . . . (*repeat* **DEL** *to clear all old matrices*)

2nd QUIT

Input Phase:

2nd MATRIX $\rightarrow \rightarrow$ ("Edit")

ENTER 3 ENTER 3 ENTER

    (*Read across and input elements of* **[A],** *always followed by* **ENTER**)

(Continued)

(Continued)

2nd QUIT

2nd MATRIX → → ("Edit") ↓

ENTER 3 ENTER 1 ENTER

  (*Read down and input elements of* **[B]**, *always followed by* **ENTER**)

2nd QUIT

2nd MATRIX ENTER [press x^{-1} and "times" keys]

2nd MATRIX [press ArrowDown key]

ENTER ENTER

Output: (*answers:* **0.8, –1.5, –1.6**)

MATH ENTER ENTER

  (*answers now given as fractions:* $x = \dfrac{4}{5}$, $y = \dfrac{-3}{2}$, $z = \dfrac{-8}{5}$)

Returning to the military operation problem, should it be stipulated that the solution be a quadratic function, then *any* parabola passing through three given points must be of the form $y = ax^2 + bx + c$. The goal here is to find the values of a, b, and c, but three given points allows for three substitutions for x and y and the creation of another three-equation–three-variable system of equations. (Note how $y = ax^2 + bx + c$ is being treated as $ax^2 + bx + c = y$.) Refer to Figure 9.25.

$$(-2, 6):\ 4a - 2b + c = 6$$
$$(3, -9):\ 9a + 3b + c = -9 \quad \leftrightarrow \quad \begin{vmatrix} 4 & -2 & 1 \\ 9 & 3 & 1 \\ 25 & 5 & 1 \end{vmatrix} \cdot \begin{vmatrix} a \\ b \\ c \end{vmatrix} = \begin{vmatrix} 6 \\ -9 \\ 13 \end{vmatrix}$$
$$(5, 13):\ 25a + 5b + c = 13$$

Figure 9.25

Multiplying both sides of the matrix equation by A^{-1} and following the process for the graphing calculator reveals the missing values for a, b, and c (see Figure 9.26).

$$A^{-1} \cdot B = \begin{vmatrix} - & - & - \\ - & - & - \\ - & - & - \end{vmatrix} \cdot \begin{vmatrix} 6 \\ -9 \\ 13 \end{vmatrix} = \begin{vmatrix} 2 \\ -5 \\ 12 \end{vmatrix} = \begin{vmatrix} a \\ b \\ c \end{vmatrix}$$

Figure 9.26

Thus, the equation of the parabola is $y = 2x^2 - 5x - 12$.

In real life, checking and rechecking can make the difference between a smart decision (and an accompanying plan of attack) and a fatal one—a failed business, a botched operation, or a misguided missile.

To check that this is the correct quadratic function, one may substitute the coordinates for the points A, B, and C *or* plot the function on the graphing calculator and input 2nd CALC 1 to locate those points on the parabola.

Referring back to the original scenario, students can now program the on-board guidance system with the correct information, and the enemy plane would be hit by an unseen missile launched hundreds of miles away.

CALCULATOR APPLICATION

Three Simultaneous Equations

PROGRAM:TWOEQS	:Input "J_=_", J
:Disp "GIVEN_3_SIMUL."	:Input "K_=_", K
:Disp "GENERAL_EQS."	:Input "L_=_", L
:Disp "_"	:Pause
:Disp "AX+BY+CZ_=_D"	:ClrScreen
:Disp "EX+FY+GZ_=_H"	:D × (F × K − G × J)
:Disp "IX+JY+KZ_=_L"	+ H × (C × J − B × K)
:Pause	+ L × (B × G − C × F) → P
:ClrScreen	:D × (G × I − E × K)
:Disp "FIND_(X,Y,Z)"	+ H × (A × K − C × I)
:Disp "_"	+ L × (C × E − A × G) → Q
:Pause	:D × (E × J − F × I)
:Input "A_=_", A	+ H × (B × I − A × J)
:Input "B_=_", B	+ L × (A × F − B × E) → R
:Input "C_=_", C	:A × (F × K − G × J)
:Input "D_=_", D	+ B × (G × I − E × K)
:Input "E_=_", E	+ C × (E × J − F × I) → T
:Input "F_=_", F	:Disp "X_=", P / T
:Input "G_=_", G	:Disp "Y_=", Q / T
:Input "H_=_", H	:Disp "Z_=", R / T
:Input "I_=_", I	:Pause

NOTE: Should the teacher feel the learning curve too steep, it is possible to remain consistent and introduce a new program ("**THREEEQS**") that produces answers for x, y, and z in much the same way the program **TWOEQS** did previously (and that also works on both the TI-73 and TI-83/84 Plus graphing calculators):

NOTE: If you are not linking calculators to share programs, you must really take your time (for obvious reasons) inputting the last of these four "alphabet soup" commands in this program.

(Continued)

(Continued)

Your Input (Example)	**Output**
Press: **ON**	
PRGM	
(*Scroll down to* **THREEEQS**)	

ENTER

> prgmTHREEEQS

ENTER

> GIVEN 3 SIMUL.
> GENERAL EQS.
>
> AX+BY+CZ = D
> EX+FY+GZ = H
> IX+JY+KZ = L

ENTER
(*Solve for* x *,* y*, and* z *from* **Figure 9.22**:
$-x + 2y - 3z = 1$
$2x \quad + \quad z = 0$
$3x - 4y + 4z = 2$)

-1 **ENTER**

2 **ENTER** . . .

> FIND (X,Y,Z)]
>
> A = −1
> B = 2
> C = −3
> D= 1
> E = 2
> F = 0
> G= 1
> H= 0
> I = 3
> J = −4
> K = 4
> L = 2

ENTER

> X =
> .8
> Y =
> −1.5
> Z =
> −1.6

ENTER

> prgmTHREEEQS   Done

Now return to page 51 and solve this system for *a*, *b*, and *c*:

$$4a + 2b + c = 3$$

$$16a + 4b + c = 5$$

$$36a + 6b + c = 3$$

Representation 10

According to the standards listed in *Principles and Standards for School Mathematics* (National Council of Teachers of Mathematics [NCTM], 2000), all students in Grades 6 through 12 should be able to do the following:

The Representation Standard extends the notion that students take advantage of the multiple ways (numerical, algebraic, geometric, statistical, visual, or graphic) they can solve and communicate mathematical problems and ideas. For example, the fact that increasing sequences of odd numbers appeared several times in this book in topics as diffuse as constructing a table of perfect square numbers, adding "n" odd numbers to get the area of a geometric square n^2, and gaining insight into how to graph a parabola implies that they all belong to the same class of functions ($f(x) = ax^2$) and are actually the same idea reapplied under different circumstances.

The first activity, A Radical Departure, takes a step-by-step approach not only to construct a working chart of common trigonometry values but also to evaluate those same trigonometric values as a natural extension of some basic geometric principles. The next activity, Close Cevians, proves a little-known formula growing out of the Law of Cosines and then applies it to the solutions of various line segments identified in three given geometry contest problems. Finally, the last activity, Linear Reactions, comprises a full repertoire of transformations (reflections, translations, and rotations) to guide students as they look for clues before making the proper linear reactions in their sketching of straight lines and using the graphing calculator as their final check.

A RADICAL DEPARTURE

> **Grades 11–12**
>
> This activity illustrates a quick and easy way to generate and organize the sine and cosine values of the angles most commonly used in trigonometry problems and to check understanding of the underlying triangle relationships. This type of activity appears in many textbooks, although perhaps not exactly in this way. This activity correlates to the following highlighted expectation for students:
>
> - **Create and use representations to *organize*, record, and communicate mathematical ideas**
> - Select, apply, and *translate* among mathematical representations to solve problems
> - Use representations to model and *interpret* physical, social, and mathematical phenomena

To begin, show students the Radical Departure Chart (see Figure 10.1; see the appendix for a full-page blackline master), noting the radicands 1-2-3 (the number under the radical sign) in the first row and 3-2-1 in the second row.

Of course, the patterns of those **radicands** have no meaning unless you can verify their existence mathematically.

To derive the numbers reading down the middle 45° column of the Radical Departure Chart, create a **unit square** (each side = 1), such as the one in Figure 10.2.

Draw a diagonal inside and employ the Pythagorean Theorem to find its length (see Figure 10.3).

$$1^2 + 1^2 = d^2 \rightarrow d = \sqrt{2}$$

		30°	45°	60°	
sin		$\frac{\sqrt{1}}{2}$	$\frac{\sqrt{2}}{2}$	$\frac{\sqrt{3}}{2}$	
cos		$\frac{\sqrt{3}}{2}$	$\frac{\sqrt{2}}{2}$	$\frac{\sqrt{1}}{2}$	

Figure 10.1

Select either 45° angle as the reference angle, label the sides (hypotenuse, opposite side, adjacent side), and then apply the definitions of sine, cosine,

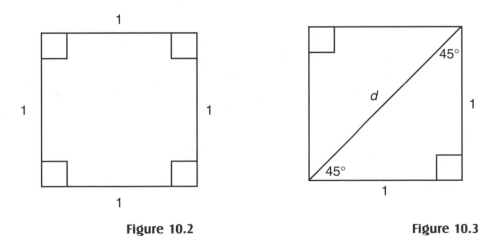

Figure 10.2   **Figure 10.3**

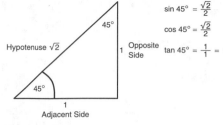

$\sin 45° = \frac{\sqrt{2}}{2}$

$\cos 45° = \frac{\sqrt{2}}{2}$

$\tan 45° = \frac{1}{1} = 1$

Figure 10.4

and tangent (recalled in the popular SOH-CAH-TOA acronym; see below). Refer to Figure 10.4, and use the Radical Departure Chart (see Figure 10.1) to verify sin 45° and cos 45°.

NOTE: SOH-CAH-TOA stands for the following three definitions:

the **S**ine of an angle = **O**pposite side ÷ **H**ypotenuse

the **C**osine of an angle = **A**djacent side ÷ **H**ypotenuse

the **T**angent of an angle = **O**pposite side ÷ **A**djacent side

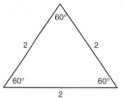

Figure 10.5

To derive the numbers reading down both the 30° and 60° columns in the Radical Departure Chart (see Figure 10.1), create an equilateral triangle of side = 2 (see Figure 10.5).

Draw a perpendicular bisector and employ the Pythagorean Theorem to find its length (see Figure 10.6).

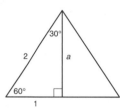

Figure 10.6

$$a^2 + 1^2 = 2^2 \rightarrow a = \sqrt{3}$$

Perform the same steps as before with 30° and 60° alternating as the reference angle: Label the sides (hypotenuse, opposite side, adjacent side), and then apply the definitions of sine, cosine, and **tangent** (see Figures 10.7 and 10.8). Use the Radical Departure Chart (see Figure 10.1) to verify sin 30°, cos 30°, sin 60°, and cos 60°.

What has been neglected thus far in chart form are the values of tan 30°, tan 45°, and tan 60°. The fact is that students can derive those values from the respective sine and cosine values already listed on the Radical Departure Chart (see Figure 10.1).

Given Quadrant I of the unit circle (radius = 1) at the right, it should be noted that a sine is *defined* as a semichord. Because the value of sine in

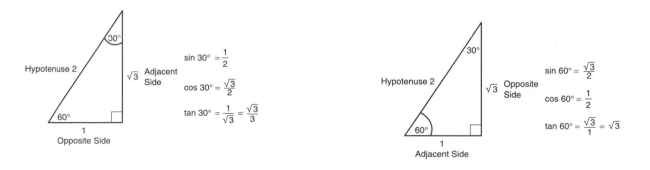

$\sin 30° = \frac{1}{2}$

$\cos 30° = \frac{\sqrt{3}}{2}$

$\tan 30° = \frac{1}{\sqrt{3}} = \frac{\sqrt{3}}{3}$

Figure 10.7

$\sin 60° = \frac{\sqrt{3}}{2}$

$\cos 60° = \frac{1}{2}$

$\tan 60° = \frac{\sqrt{3}}{1} = \sqrt{3}$

Figure 10.8

a right triangle is the opposite side divided by the hypotenuse (which = 1), sin Q is simply the semichord of the bold right triangle (see Figure 10.9).

The word *cosine* is the semichord (opposite side) of the complementary angle, and cos Q (or the adjacent side divided by hypotenuse = 1) assumes that role in the gray right triangle. The dotted right triangle in Figure 10.10 (with the tangent line to the unit circle in place) is similar to the gray right triangle by the Angle-Angle Postulate:

$$\frac{\sin Q}{\cos Q} = \frac{\tan Q}{1}$$

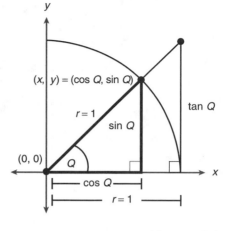

Figure 10.9

Returning to the Radical Departure Chart, students may read down, construct, and ultimately solve any of three complex fractions to get tangent values; for example, since

$\sin 45° = \cos 45° = \dfrac{\sqrt{2}}{2}$, $\tan 45° = \dfrac{\sqrt{2}}{2} \div \dfrac{\sqrt{2}}{2} = 1$. Refer to Figure 10.11.

Taking this "patterns-in-the-chart" approach one step further, it follows that adding 0° and 90° either side of the 30°-45°-60° trio already in place should extend the sine row's 1-2-3 radicand pattern to read 0-1-2-3-4 and the cosine row's 3-2-1 radicand pattern to read 4-3-2-1-0. In fact, a close examination of Figure 10.10 confirms those patterns:

For 0° (radius resting on the x-axis): sin 0° = 0 and cos 0° = the radius = 1.

For 90° (radius resting on the y-axis): sin 90° = the radius = 1 and cos 90° = 0.

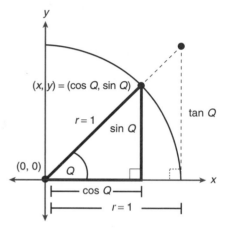

Figure 10.10

After constructing respective complex fractions, students can now solve for tan 0° and tan 90° (see Figure 10.12).

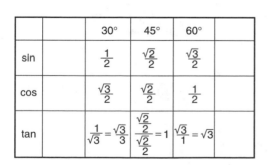

		30°	45°	60°	
sin		$\dfrac{1}{2}$	$\dfrac{\sqrt{2}}{2}$	$\dfrac{\sqrt{3}}{2}$	
cos		$\dfrac{\sqrt{3}}{2}$	$\dfrac{\sqrt{2}}{2}$	$\dfrac{1}{2}$	
tan		$\dfrac{1}{\sqrt{3}} = \dfrac{\sqrt{3}}{3}$	$\dfrac{\frac{\sqrt{2}}{2}}{\frac{\sqrt{2}}{2}} = 1$	$\dfrac{\sqrt{3}}{1} = \sqrt{3}$	

Figure 10.11

	0°	30°	45°	60°	90°
sin	$\dfrac{\sqrt{0}}{2} = 0$	$\dfrac{\sqrt{1}}{2} = \dfrac{1}{2}$	$\dfrac{\sqrt{2}}{2}$	$\dfrac{\sqrt{3}}{2}$	$\dfrac{\sqrt{4}}{2} = 1$
cos	$\dfrac{\sqrt{4}}{2} = 1$	$\dfrac{\sqrt{3}}{2}$	$\dfrac{\sqrt{2}}{2}$	$\dfrac{\sqrt{1}}{2} = \dfrac{1}{2}$	$\dfrac{\sqrt{0}}{2} = 0$
tan	$\dfrac{0}{1} = 0$	$\dfrac{1}{\sqrt{3}} = \dfrac{\sqrt{3}}{0}$	$\dfrac{\frac{\sqrt{2}}{2}}{\frac{\sqrt{2}}{2}} = 1$	$\dfrac{\sqrt{3}}{1} = \sqrt{3}$	$\dfrac{1}{0} =$ undefined

Figure 10.12

CLOSE CEVIANS

> ### Grades 10–12
>
> This activity presents three cevian problems from past American High School Mathematics Examinations, each accompanied by two methods of solution. A **cevian** (pronounced "SHAY-vee-en") is a segment inside of a triangle that connects a vertex with any point on the opposite side. Mathematical textbooks generally treat the entire family of cevians (medians, altitudes, and bisectors) as separate entities. This activity puts all three under one common term. Students use two obscure theorems, in addition to Stewart's Theorem, to solve the three selected problems. This activity correlates to the following highlighted expectation for students:
>
> - Create and use representations to *organize*, record, and communicate mathematical ideas
> - **Select, apply, and *translate* among mathematical representations to solve problems**
> - Use representations to model and *interpret* physical, social, and mathematical phenomena

To begin, work through the following step-by-step proof of Stewart's Theorem. This will allow students to solve the select geometry problems that involve cevians.

In Figure 10.13, cevian CD divides triangle ACB ($\triangle ACB$) into two smaller triangles: $\triangle ACD$ and $\triangle DCB$.

1. By the Law of Cosines:

$$b^2 = z^2 + x^2 - 2zx \cos R \text{ (in } \triangle ACD)$$
$$a^2 = z^2 + y^2 - 2zy \cos S \text{ (in } \triangle DCB)$$

Solving both for their cosine values:

$$\cos R - \frac{z^2 + x^2 - b^2}{2zx}$$
$$\cos S = \frac{z^2 + y^2 - a^2}{2zy}$$

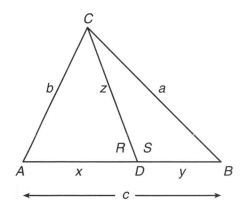

Figure 10.13

Angles R and S are supplementary $\rightarrow \cos R = -\cos S$ (see Reflections on Trig in Chapter 4).

$$\rightarrow \frac{z^2 + x^2 - b^2}{2zx} = -\frac{z^2 + y^2 - a^2}{2zy}$$
$$\rightarrow z^2y + x^2y - b^2y = -z^2x - y^2x + a^2x \rightarrow z^2(x + y) = a^2x + b^2y - xy(x + y)$$

But, since $c = (x + y) \rightarrow z^2 c = a^2 x + b^2 y - xyc \rightarrow$

Stewart's Theorem: $c(z^2 + xy) = a^2 x + b^2 y$

Cevian as Median

Have students consider the impact on Stewart's Theorem when the cevian represents a median. That is, given Figure 10.13, what happens to the formula when $x = y$ (both $= \frac{1}{2}c$)?

$$c(z^2 + xy) = a^2 x + b^2 y$$

$$\rightarrow c\left[z^2 + \left[\frac{1}{2}c\right] \cdot \left[\frac{1}{2}c\right]\right] = a^2 \left[\frac{1}{2}c\right] + b^2 \left[\frac{1}{2}c\right]$$

$$\rightarrow z^2 + \left[\frac{1}{4}c^2\right] = \frac{1}{2}a^2 + \frac{1}{2}b^2 \rightarrow z^2 = \frac{1}{2}(a^2 + b^2) - \left[\frac{1}{4}c^2\right]$$

Challenge students to solve the following problem: $\triangle ABC$ is such that $AC = b = 4$ and $CB = a = 8$. If M is the midpoint of side AB, and if $CM = z = 3$, what is the length of side AB ($= c$)?

The following are two possible solutions students could create.

Solution 1: Traditional

Refer to Figure 10.14.

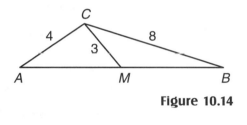

$$3^2 = \frac{1}{2}(4^2 + 8^2) - \frac{1}{4}c^2$$

$$9 = \frac{1}{2}(80) - \frac{1}{4}c^2$$

$$\frac{1}{4}c^2 = 31 \rightarrow c = 2\sqrt{31}$$

Figure 10.14

Students from other countries have a much different view of problems such as this. To them, a simple rotation around midpoint M would create a parallelogram with two diagonals: a length of 6 (double $CM = 3$) and AB (the final answer). The lengths of the two adjacent sides of the parallelogram (as per the following theorem) are already given.

Theorem: The sum of the squares of the lengths of the diagonals of a parallelogram equals twice the sum of the squares of any two adjacent sides.

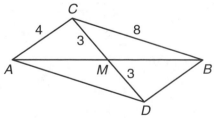

Rotate $\triangle ACB$ 180° around M, and label the image of point C as point D. Thus, parallelogram $ACBD$ is created (see Figure 10.15).

Figure 10.15

Rewrite Stewart's Theorem as

$$CM^2 = \frac{1}{2}(AC^2 + CB^2) - \frac{1}{4}AB^2 \text{ and multiply by } 4 \rightarrow$$

$$4CM^2 = 2[AC^2 + CB^2] - AB^2 \rightarrow 4CM^2 + AB^2 = 2[AC^2 + CB^2]$$

$$\rightarrow (2CM)^2 + AB^2 = 2\,[AC^2 + CB^2]$$

But, since $2CM = CD, \rightarrow CD^2 + AB^2 = 2\,[AC^2 + CB^2]$

Solution 2: Transformational

Refer to Figure 10.15.

$$6^2 + AB^2 = 2[4^2 + 8^2]$$

$$AB^2 = 2[80] - 36$$

$$AB^2 = 124 \rightarrow AB = 2\sqrt{31}$$

Cevian as Angle Bisector

Before students can solve the next problem, state and prove a theorem around a cevian that cuts angles in half.

> *Theorem: A cevian that acts as an angle bisector divides the side opposite the bisected angle into segments whose lengths are proportional to the other two sides.*

NOTE: The angle being bisected is at the top vertex of Figure 10.16. Angle ACD now has the same measure as angle DCB, but since the cevian CD is acting as an angle bisector here, the proportionality of segment $\div$ adjacent side = segment $\div$ adjacent side, or $\frac{x}{b} = \frac{y}{a}$.

Use the Law of Sines for the two triangles formed by cevian CD:

$$\frac{x}{\sin ACD} = \frac{b}{\sin R}$$

$$\frac{y}{\sin DCB} = \frac{a}{\sin S}$$

Rewrite, isolating sides and angles:

$$\frac{x}{b} = \frac{\sin ACD}{\sin R}$$

$$\frac{y}{a} = \frac{\sin DCB}{\sin S}$$

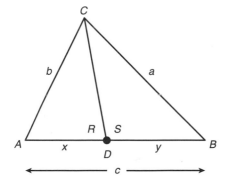

Figure 10.16

But, $\sin ACD = \sin DCB$ (equal halves of a bisected angle) *and* $\sin R = \sin S$. (See Reflections on Trig in Chapter 4—sines of supplementary angles are equal.)

$$\frac{\sin ACD}{\sin R} = \frac{\sin DCB}{\sin S} \rightarrow = \frac{x}{b} = \frac{y}{a}$$

Challenge students to solve the following problem: Point D is on side CB of $\triangle ACB$. If $AC = b = 3$, $CB = a = 6$, and the measure of angle ACD = angle DCB = 60°, find the length of CD ($= z$).

The following solutions both involve solving a different system of equations, but both use that great proportion $\left(\frac{x}{b} = \frac{y}{a}\right)$ proven above.

In preparation for both upcoming solutions, have students plug the given numeric values for the sides into the following proportion:

$$\frac{AD}{AC} = \frac{DB}{CB} \text{ (by the proportion theorem above)}$$

$$\frac{AD}{3} = \frac{DB}{6} \text{ (substitution)}$$

$DB = 2AD$ (solve for one missing segment in terms of the other)

If $AD = x$, then DB $= 2x$, and thus AB (the entire base of the triangle) $= 3x$.

Solution 1: Stewart's Theorem

Refer to Figure 10.17. By the original Stewart's Theorem:

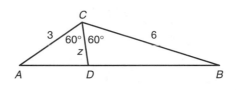

$$AB[z^2 + (AD)(DB)] = CB^2 \bullet AD + AC^2 \bullet (DB) \rightarrow$$
$$3x[z^2 + (x)(2x)] = 6^2 \bullet (x) + 3^2 \bullet (2x) \rightarrow$$
$$z^2 + 2x^2 = 18$$

Figure 10.17

Use the Law of Cosines to find x, then substitute to find $CD = z$:

$$AB^2 = AC^2 + CB^2 - 2(AC)(CB)[\cos 120°] \rightarrow$$

$$(3x)^2 = 3^2 + 6^2 - 2(3)(6)\left[-\frac{1}{2}\right] \rightarrow x = \sqrt{7} \rightarrow$$

$$z = CD = 2$$

Solution 2: Non-Stewart's Theorem

Notice that the cevian CD ($= z$) divides the one large triangle ($\triangle ACB$) into two smaller ones ($\triangle ACD$ and $\triangle DCB$) that can both be solved by the Law of Cosines and that will eventually combine into a new two-equation system:

For $\triangle ACD$: $x^2 = z^2 + 3^2 - 2(3)(z)(\cos 60°)$

For $\triangle DCB$: $(2x)^2 = z^2 + 6^2 - 2(6)(z)(\cos 60°)$

Since $\cos 60° = \dfrac{1}{2}$, substituting into both equations yields the following:

For $\triangle ACD$: $x^2 = z^2 + 9 - 3z$

For $\triangle DCB$: $4x^2 = z^2 + 36 - 6z$

If we multiply the first equation by 4, the first term $(4x^2)$ would then be common to both equations and, hence, could be the transitional piece to connect them.

For $\triangle ACD$: $4x^2 = 4z^2 + 36 - 12z$

For $\triangle DCB$: $4x^2 = z^2 + 36 - 6z$

Therefore: $4z^2 + 36 - 12z = z^2 + 36 - 6z$

which implies: $4z^2 - 12z = z^2 - 6z \rightarrow 3z^2 - 6z = 0 \rightarrow$

$z = CD = 2$

($z = 0$, of course, is extraneous)

Cevian as Angle Trisector

This cevian divides an angle of a triangle into two unequal parts, one of which is one third of the entire angle. This is a unique opportunity for students to test their problem-solving skills. The first solution method is the non–Stewart's Theorem solution, and the second *is* the Stewart's Theorem solution. Similar to the two previous problems, the name of the game is different representations, which in turn require different solution strategies.

Challenge students to solve the following problem: In $\triangle ACB$, the measure of angle ACB is three times that of angle A. If $CB = a = 27$ and $AB = c = 48$, find the length of AC (= b). Refer to Figure 10.18.

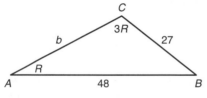

Figure 10.18

Solution 1: Non–Stewart's Theorem

Apply the Law of Sines twice (and some trigonometry):

First time:

$$\frac{CB}{\sin A} = \frac{AB}{\sin C}$$

$$\rightarrow \frac{27}{\sin A} = \frac{48}{\sin 3A} \rightarrow \frac{48}{27} = \frac{\sin 3A}{\sin A}$$

Know that

$\sin 3A = 3\sin A - 4\sin^3 A$ (worth deriving with an eager class)

$$\rightarrow \frac{16}{9} = \frac{3\sin A - 4\sin^3 A}{\sin A} \rightarrow \frac{16}{9} = 3 - 4\sin^2 A$$

$$\rightarrow \sin A = \frac{\sqrt{11}}{6} \text{ and } \cos A = \frac{5}{6} \text{ (assuming angle } A \text{ is acute)}$$

Second time:

$$\frac{AC}{\sin B} = \frac{CB}{\sin A}$$

$$\rightarrow \frac{b}{\sin(180° - 4A)} = \frac{27}{\sin A} \quad \text{(once more, recall Reflections}$$
on Trig in Chapter 4—sines of supplementary angles are equal)

$$\rightarrow \frac{b}{\sin 4A} = \frac{27}{\sin A}$$

$$\rightarrow b = \frac{27(\sin 4A)}{\sin A}$$

Know that

$$\sin 4A = 4 \sin A \cos A \cdot (\cos^2 A - \sin^2 A) \text{ (again, worth deriving)}$$
$$\rightarrow b = 27 \cdot 4 \cos A \cdot (\cos^2 A - \sin^2 A) \text{ (note that sin A cancels)}$$

$$\rightarrow b = 27 \cdot 4 \left(\frac{5}{6}\right) \cdot \left[\left(\frac{5}{6}\right)^2 - \left(\frac{\sqrt{11}}{6}\right)^2 \right] \rightarrow b = AC = 35$$

Solution 2: Stewart's Theorem

Now have students complete the following steps for a much more creative and interesting solution:

1. Draw cevian CD (see Figure 10.19) to trisect angle C into two angles: R and 2R. (This is possible because the measure of angle C is three times that of angle A.)

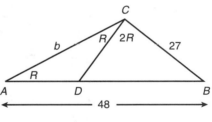

2. Since angle CDB is an exterior angle to ΔACD (see Algebraic Geometry in Chapter 3), the measure of angle CDB = R + R = 2R.

Figure 10.19

3. Notice in ΔDCB how the measure of angle CDB = that of angle DCB = 2R. This makes ΔDCB isosceles; therefore, opposite sides CB and DB must be equal. Since CB = 27, now DB = 27.

4. Along base AB, then, AD = AB − DB → AD = 48 − 27 = 21.

5. The reasoning as to why ΔDCB is isosceles applies to ΔACD as well. Note that the measure of angle CAD = that of angle ACD = R. Therefore, opposite sides AD and CD (the cevian) must be equal. Since AD = 21, now CD = 21.

6. Finally, apply Stewart's Theorem to solve for AC = b:

$$48 \left[21^2 + (21)(27)\right] = b^2 (27) + 27^2 (21) \rightarrow b = AC = 35.$$

LINEAR REACTIONS

<blockquote>

Grades 8–12

It should be apparent by the time a student reaches senior high school that, given different types of information, there seems to be a variety of ways to represent and to graph straight lines. Having a graphing calculator within reach can be a big help to those who wish to complete such assignments in as little time as possible, but if a good sketch of a graph will do, then there is a way to "read" a linear equation and get a good idea of the graph in advance.

This activity correlates to the following highlighted expectation for students:

- Create and use representations to *organize,* record, and communicate mathematical ideas
- Select, apply, and *translate* among mathematical representations to solve problems
- **Use representations to model and *interpret* physical, social, and mathematical phenomena**

</blockquote>

Each student needs the following materials:

- One $8\frac{1}{2} \times 11$-inch piece of paper
- A ruler
- TI-83/84 Plus graphing calculator
- A sharp pencil

Patterns

To begin, have students sketch the graph of $x - y = 0 \rightarrow x = y \rightarrow y = x$ (see Figure 10.20).

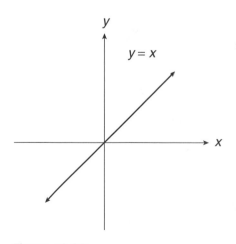

Figure 10.20

NOTE: This activity is adapted from Sally Fischbeck of The Rochester Institute of Technology.

NOTE: The process of sketching every other line graph starts with that of the diagonal line $y = x$.

Now have students employ their graphing calculators as a learning tool to unravel four important transformation patterns from the following four scenarios:

1. Access the "$Y =$" screen, and ENTER the lines $Y_1 = x$ and $Y_2 = -x$. How would you describe the relationship between those two lines?

Answer: $y = -x$ is the reflection ("flip") of the line $y = x$ *over* the x-axis.

2. CLEAR the Y_2 entry, and replace it with $Y_2 = x + \{2, 5, -3\}$. How would you assess the effect that tacking any constant number onto the right-hand side of $y = x$ has on that particular graph?

> **Answer:** $y = x + C$ translates ("pushes") the line $y = x$ up the y-axis, and $y = x - C$ pushes the line *down* the y-axis.

3. CLEAR the Y_2 entry again, and replace it with $Y_2 = (x + 3)$. What do you notice about the movement of the line along the x-axis?

> **Answer:** $y = (x + C)$ translates ("slides") the line $y = x$ *left* along the x-axis.

Now replace the +3 with a −4. How would you describe movement along the x-axis this time?

> **Answer:** $y = (x - C)$ slides the line *right* along the x-axis.

4. CLEAR the Y_2 entry again, and replace it with $Y_2 = \{2, 4\}\ x$. Take note of what effect those coefficients (number multipliers in front of x) have on $y = x$. Then, replace "2, 4" with "$\left(\frac{1}{2}\right), \left(\frac{1}{4}\right)$" and again compare the effect of those fractional coefficients on $y = x$. Perform one more CLEAR and replacement. What happens if you input $Y_2 = 0x$ (which is $Y_2 = 0$)?

Combine all of your findings with different coefficients into one statement.

> **Answer:** When the coefficient $A > 1$, the line $y = x$ rotates ("tilts") toward the y-axis. When $0 < A < 1$, the line tilts toward the x-axis. Moreover, when $A = 0$, the line tilts right onto the x-axis and can be renamed line $y = 0$.

Students may notice a parallel between the upcoming left-to-right transformation concept and the more familiar right-to-left slope-intercept, or $y = mx + b$, process of graphing linear equations.

Without question, precision should remain a primary goal in the teaching and learning of mathematics. However, just as estimation while doing arithmetic gives problem solvers a better idea of where to find an exact solution, so too does the flip-push-slide-tilt sketch notion encourage those same students to become sharper readers by providing more clues for drawing better graphs.

Now, see if students can "read" the following equations and talk through the line sketches with paper and pencil.

Say-and-Sketch Questions

Now have students set their graphing calculators aside, and challenge them to develop a mind's eye while telling a partner how to sketch the following three problems:

1. $y = -2x + 3$

Start with $y = x$ (see Figure 10.21).

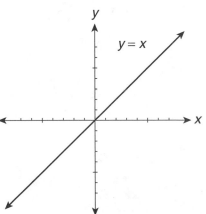

Figure 10.21

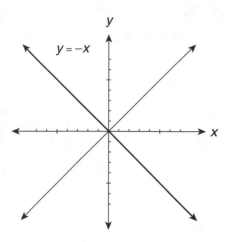

Figure 10.22

Negative: Flip it over the x-axis (see Figure 10.22).

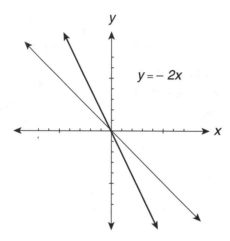

Figure 10.23

2: Tilt it toward the y-axis (see Figure 10.23).

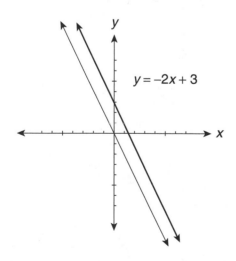

Figure 10.24

+3: Push it up the y-axis (see Figure 10.24, which is the answer to Question 1).

   2. $4x - 3y = 12$

Start by solving for y:

$$-3y = -4x + 12$$

$$\left(-\frac{1}{3}\right) \cdot (-3y = -4x + 12)$$

$$y = \frac{4}{3}x - 4$$

$\dfrac{4}{3}$: Tilt $y = x$ slightly toward the y-axis (see Figure 10.25).

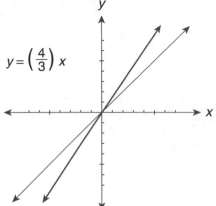

Figure 10.25

−4: Push it down the y-axis (see Figure 10.26, which is the answer to Question 2).

3. $y = -\left(\dfrac{1}{3}\right)(x + 6) + 4$

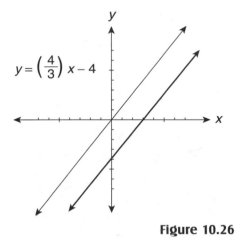

Figure 10.26

Negative: Flip $y = x$ over the x-axis (see Figure 10.27).

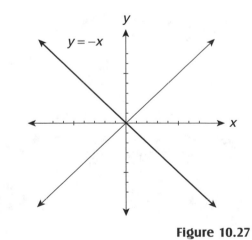

Figure 10.27

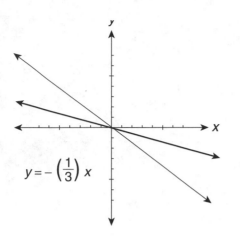

Figure 10.28

$\frac{1}{3}$: Tilt it toward the *x*-axis (see Figure 10.28).

$(x + 6)$: Slide it *left* 6 units (see Figure 10.29).

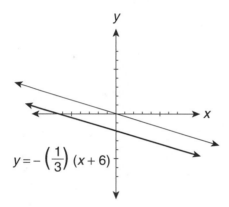

Figure 10.29

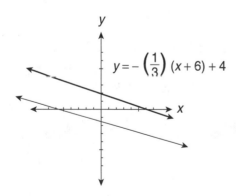

Figure 10.30

+4: Push it up the *y*-axis (see Figure 10.30, which is the answer to Question 3).

4. **(Alternative)** $y = -\left(\frac{1}{3}\right)(x + 6) + 4$

Distribute

$-\left(\frac{1}{3}\right): y = \left[-\left(\frac{1}{3}\right)x - 2\right] + 4$

$y = -\left(\frac{1}{3}\right)x + 2$

$\frac{1}{3}$: Tilt $y = -x$ toward the x-axis (see Figure 10.31).

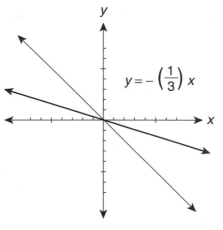

Figure 10.31

+2: Push it up the y-axis (see Figure 10.32, which is the alternative answer to Question 3).

NOTE: The result of the alternative may be the same, but a little algebra, such as distributing $\left(-\frac{1}{3}\right)$, makes for an easier graphing situation for students.

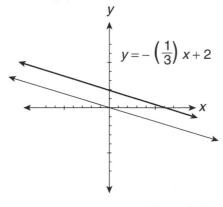

Figure 10.32

One Step Further

The various transformations mentioned in this activity apply to other kinds of graphs as well. For example, have students predict (and then verify with the graphing calculator) what happens to the basic parabola $y = x^2$ when a coefficient *other* than 1 is applied in front of the x^2-term.

What students will find is that for $y = Ax^2$, when $A > 1$, the parabola "pinches" the y-axis from both sides (the equivalent of the line $y = Ax$ tilting toward the y-axis under similar conditions). When $0 < A < 1$, the parabola "fans" away from the y-axis and more toward the x-axis (again, in much the same fashion as the line $y = Ax$ tilted toward the x-axis).

Students will be happy to learn that the rules for flips, pushes, and slides still apply for parabolas and, for that matter, other types of functions (cubic, trig, exponential, logarithmic, rational, and absolute value) as well.

Appendix

Worksheet Blackline Masters

CHAPTER 2: CONSTRUCTING LOGS

Worksheet

Name _____

Date _____

X	$y = \log x$
1	
2	
3	
4	
5	
6	
7	
8	
9	
10	
11	
12	
13	
14	
15	
16	
17	
18	
19	
20	

CHAPTER 3: INTERIOR AND EXTERIOR ANGLES OF A REGULAR POLYGON

Worksheet

Name _____

Date _____

Derive formulas for the Interior and Exterior Angles of a Regular Polygon.

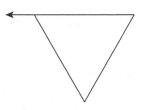 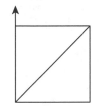 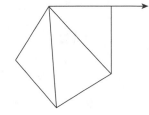

Directions: Fill in the last column (Regular *N*-gon) and the last row of this chart.

Figures	Equilateral Δ	Square	Regular Pentagon . . .	Regular N-gon
1. # of Diagonals Drawn From a Given Vertex	0	1	2	
2. # of Interior Triangles	1	2	3	
3. # of Degrees in Sum of the Interior Angles	180°	360°	540°	
4. # of Degrees in Any One Interior Angle	$\dfrac{180}{3} = 60°$	$\dfrac{360}{4} = 90°$	$\dfrac{540}{5} = 108°$	
5. # of Degrees in Any One Supplementary Exterior Angle	120°	90°	72°	
6. . . . Times the Number of Sides				

CHAPTER 4: EASY AS PI EXPLORATIONS TABLE

Worksheet

Name _____

Date _____

	π Explorations Table				
	π Explorations	*Object #1*	*Object #2*	*Object #3*	*Predict*
Q1	**C** (circumference)				
	d (diameter)				
	$\dfrac{c}{d} = \pi$?				
Q2	**A₁** (inscribed sq.)				
	A₂ (circumscribed sq.)				
	$\dfrac{A_1 + A_2}{2} = A$				
	r (radius)				
	r² (radius squared)				
	$\dfrac{A}{r^2} = \pi$?				

CHAPTER 4: CNS ANGLE FORMULAS

Worksheet

Name _____

Date _____

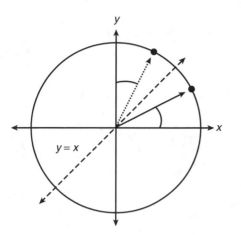

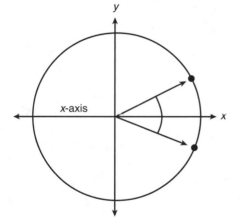

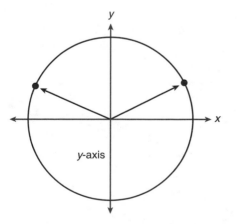

CHAPTER 4: 12-3-6-9 O'CLOCK

Worksheet

Name _____

Date _____

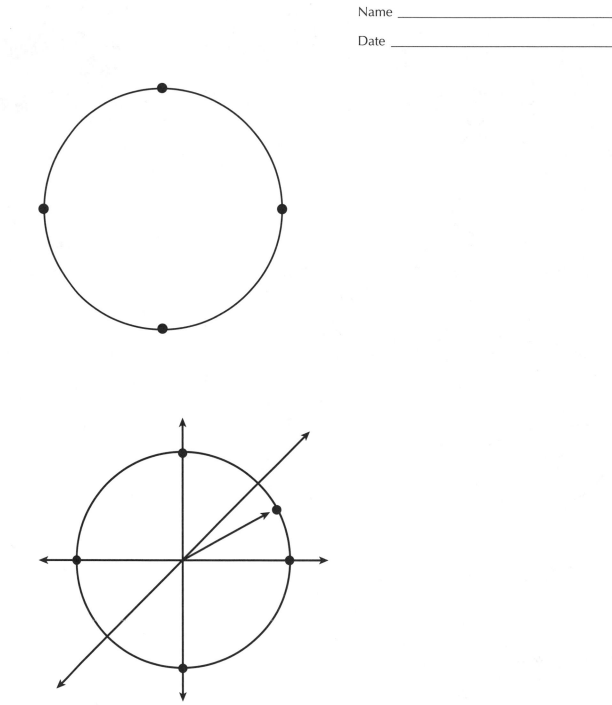

CHAPTER 4: DEGREE TIME TABLE

Worksheet

Name _____

Date _____

Degrees	Time	(1) Over $y = x$	(2) Over x-axis	(3) Over y-axis
0°	3:00			
90°	12:00			
180°	9:00			
270°	6:00			

CHAPTER 4: 1-2-4-5-7-8-10-11 O'CLOCK

Worksheet

Name _____

Date _____

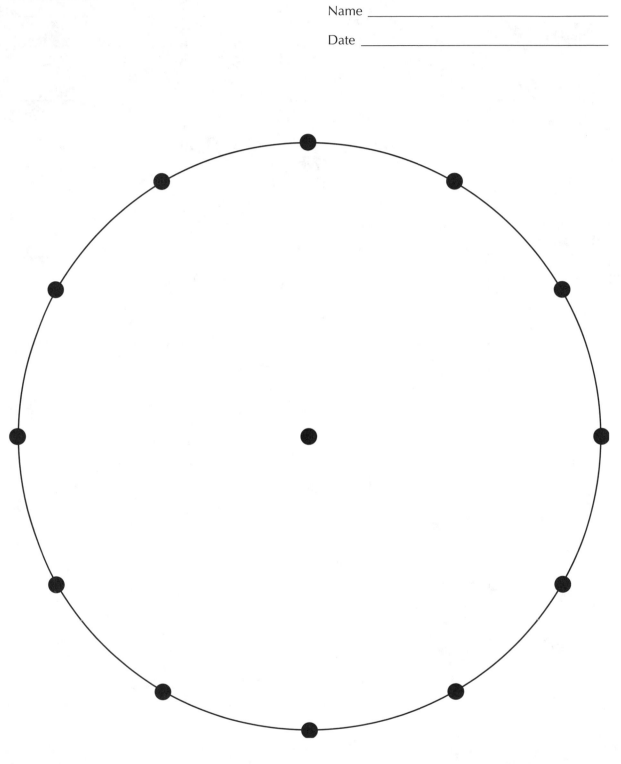

CHAPTER 5: SEEDS-APPLES TABLE

Worksheet

Name _____

Date _____

# of Seeds = x	# of Apples = y	
Totals		

CHAPTER 5: PERMUTATIONS-COMBINATIONS TABLE

Worksheet

Name _____

Date _____

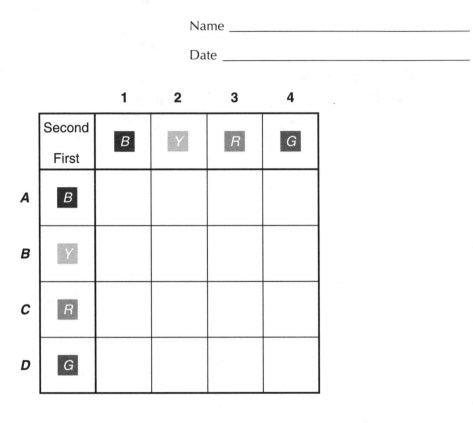

Colors	Permutations	Combinations

CHAPTER 5: GROUP TALLY TABLE

Worksheet

Name _____

Date _____

Trial #	Red	White	Green
1			
2			
3			
4			
5			
6			
7			
8			
9			
10			
Totals			

CHAPTER 5: CLASS SUMMARY TABLE

Worksheet

Name _____

Date _____

Group #	Red	White	Green
1			
2			
3			
4			
5			
6			
7			
8			
9			
10			
Totals			
Probability %			

CHAPTER 5: 1–3–3–1 CHECKERBOARD

Worksheet

Name _____

Date _____

Enter Here

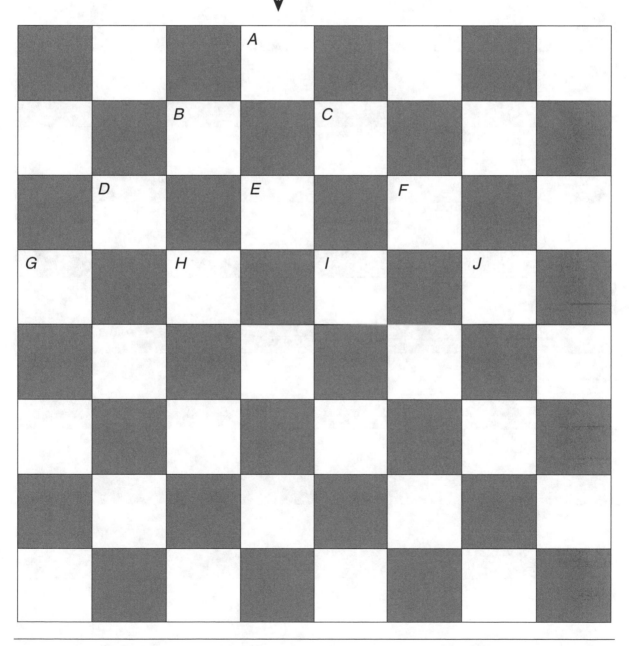

CHAPTER 6: 8-BY-8 CHECKERBOARD

Worksheet

Name _____

Date _____

CHAPTER 6: CHECKERBOARD CHARTS

Worksheet

Name _____

Date _____

Size of Checkerboard	Number of These Squares Within			
	1-by-1	2-by-2	3-by-3	4-by-4
1-by-1				
2-by-2				
3-by-3				
4-by-4				

# of Squares Along One Side	1	2	3	4	5	6	7	8
Total # of Squares on Board								

1st Differences:

2nd Differences:

3rd Differences:

CHAPTER 10: RADICAL DEPARTURE CHART

Worksheet

Name _____

Date _____

	0°	30°	45°	60°	90°
sin	$\dfrac{\sqrt{}}{2}$	$\dfrac{\sqrt{}}{2}$	$\dfrac{\sqrt{}}{2}$	$\dfrac{\sqrt{}}{2}$	$\dfrac{\sqrt{}}{2}$
cos	$\dfrac{\sqrt{}}{2}$	$\dfrac{\sqrt{}}{2}$	$\dfrac{\sqrt{}}{2}$	$\dfrac{\sqrt{}}{2}$	$\dfrac{\sqrt{}}{2}$
tan					

Glossary

Addition Formula

Given two sets A and B, $N(A$ or $B) = N(A) + N(B) - N(A$ and $B)$.

Angle-Angle Postulate

If two angles of one triangle are congruent with two angles of a second triangle, then the triangles are similar.

Apothem

The perpendicular distance from the center of a polygon to any one of its sides.

Bar Graph

A discrete graph that uses the lengths of solid (rectangular) bars to represent quantities so as to allow for a comparison of data.

Cardinality

Refers to the number of items, particularly the number of elements in a set. (*See also* Addition Formula.)

Cartesian Plane (or Coordinate Grid or Cartesian Coordinate System)

A geometric construct wherein ordered pairs of numbers are represented by means of the rules of coordinate geometry.

Cevian (pronounced "SHAY-vee-en")

A segment inside of a triangle that connects a vertex with any point on the opposite side.

Circle Graph

A graph that depicts how a whole is broken into parts (usually accompanied by a relative frequency, or percentage, per each part).

Circumference

The perimeter of a circle.

Circumscribed Square

A square drawn around a circle, each of which sides in turn are tangent to that circle.

Combination

A group or arrangement of numbers, items, or events in which order *does not matter*. (*See also* Permutation.)

Constant of Proportionality

The factor of multiplication in which one number is always a particular multiple of another number.

Cosine of an Acute Angle of a Right Triangle

The ratio (or fraction) of the leg *adjacent* to the acute angle divided by the length of the hypotenuse. (*See also* Sine of an Acute Angle of a Right Triangle, Tangent of an Acute Angle of a Right Triangle.)

Counting Principle

If there are K distinct ways to describe one attribute and L distinct ways to describe another attribute and M distinct ways to describe a third attribute, then the highest possible number of items having all three attributes = $K \cdot L \cdot M$.

Cramer's Rule

A rule found in the study of matrices used for solving certain classes of simultaneous equations. (*See also* Determinant.)

Deductive Reasoning

Moving from generality (formula) to specifics (examples)—the outdated antithesis of the growing amount of "do-math-to-know-more-math" research (National Council of Teachers of Mathematics [NCTM], 2000). (*See also* Inductive Reasoning.)

Degree-Rotator Vector

The representation of a complex number in the form $a + bi$ used for rotating a set of points a certain number of degrees around a fixed point.

Determinant

A square array of numbers having a specific value as determined by stated rule and used for solving certain classes of simultaneous equations. (*See also* Cramer's Rule.)

Diameter

One of the infinite number of chords that pass through a circle's center with the endpoints on the circle itself.

Dimensional Analysis

A series of steps designed to change fundamental measure from one type (e.g., miles per hour) to another type (e.g., feet per second).

Directed Graphs

A connection of various like-directed vectors, each vector representing the time necessary to complete one particular part of a larger task.

Direct Proportionality

When one quantity increases by a certain factor, a second quantity increases by that same factor. (*See also* Inverse Proportionality.)

Discrete Mathematics

A contemporary branch of mathematics that includes (among other things) networking, efficient routing, task scheduling, game theory, election theory, decision making, and matrices.

Even Function

A function that, when graphed, is symmetric to the y-axis. (*See also* Odd Function.)

Five-Number Summary (L-Q1-M-Q3-H)

Given a set of data, the five most important numbers represented in a box-and-whiskers plot (L = the lowest term, or minimum; Q1 = the first quartile; M = the median; Q3 = the third quartile; and H = the highest term, or maximum).

Histogram

A continuous graph that uses the lengths of solid (rectangular) bars to represent how often the given data fall into particular ranges or intervals.

Identity Element

A number that combines with another number without changing it. (0 is the identity element for $a + 0 = a$, and 1 is the identity element for $a \cdot 1 = a$.)

Identity Matrix $I_3 = \begin{vmatrix} 1 & 0 & 0 \\ 0 & 1 & 0 \\ 0 & 0 & 1 \end{vmatrix}$

Inductive Reasoning

Moving from specifics (numbers and observed patterns) to generalities that involve making conclusions (writing and testing formulas similar to the scientific method) based on those observations. (*See also* Deductive Reasoning.)

Inscribed Angle

An angle in which the vertex lies directly on the circle and in which the sides are chords of the circle. The measure of an inscribed angle is equal to the measure of the intercepted arc (the subtended angle of the circle).

Inscribed Square

A square drawn inside of a circle such that any of the square's vertices also represent one of the two endpoints of the radius of that circle.

Inverse Proportionality

When one quantity increases by a certain factor, a second quantity decreases by that same factor, or visa versa. (*See also* Direct Proportionality.)

Isosceles Triangle

A triangle that has two congruent sides (called *legs*).

Law of Large Numbers

Empirical (experimental) probability begins to approach the value of theoretical (predictive) probability the longer a particular experiment is repeated.

Limit

The value of a dependent variable (function) approached while its independent variable is approaching some other value.

Linear Equation

An algebraic equation, $ax + by = c$, in which the highest-degree term between the variables is of the first degree. (*See also* Quadratic [Parabolic] Equation.)

Matrix

A rectangular array of numerical or algebraic quantities in "m-by-n" format that is treated as an algebraic entity (m = # of *rows* [or "across" lines of elements]; n = # of *columns* [or "up-and-down" lines of elements]).

Mean

The sum of a set of numbers divided by how many numbers comprise that set.

Mean Proportional (or Geometric Mean)

If a, b, and c are all positive numbers and $\frac{a}{b} = \frac{b}{c}$, then b is considered the mean proportional of a and c.

Median

1. In geometry, a line segment drawn from one vertex of a triangle to the midpoint of the opposite side.
2. In statistics, the number that falls in the exact middle of a set of data arranged from lowest to highest.

Mode

The data item that is present the greatest number of times in a data set (e.g., a data set may have no mode, one mode, or more than one mode).

Module

A part of a mathematical construction (such as an analog clock) used as the standard to which the rest is proportioned.

Normal Distribution

A theoretical frequency distribution for a group of data, represented by a bell-shaped curve symmetrical to its mean.

Odd Function

A function that, when graphed, is symmetric to the origin. (*See also* Even Function.)

Orientation

The location or position of points relative to one another.

Percentile

A number that corresponds to 1 of 100 equal divisions of the range of a group of data and characterizes a contained value therein as not exceeded by the specified percentage of the data group (e.g., a score higher than 80% of all of those who took the same test is said to be at the 80th percentile).

Perfect Square

Any number that is the product of the same two whole-number factors.

Permutation

A group or arrangement of numbers, items, or events in which order *does* matter. (*See also* Combination.)

Perpendicular Bisector

A line or line segment that is perpendicular to *and* bisects the segment when drawn from its opposite vertex.

Position Vector

A vector that is put into a favorable or advantageous place (such as along the *x*-axis). Other vectors are positioned and identified relative to it.

Quadrantal Angle Values

0°, 90°, 180°, 270°, and 360° (all of which are located along either the *x*-axis or the *y*-axis).

Quadratic (Parabolic) Formula

An algebraic equation of the second degree, $y = ax^2 + bx + c$, in which the value of a does not equal 0. (*See also* Linear Equation.)

Quartile

The value of the boundary at the 25th percentile (first quartile), 50th percentile (second quartile or median), or 75th percentile (third quartile) of a group of data divided into four parts, each containing a quarter of the data.

Radicand

The expression under the radical sign.

Radius

A segment with one endpoint on a circle and the other endpoint at the center of the circle.

Ratio

A comparison of two quantities by division, usually in fraction form.

Reference Angle

The angle (usually acute) from which trigonometry values are computed.

Scientific Method

Principles and procedures for identifying a problem, collecting data through observation and experiment, and forming and testing hypotheses.

Sequence

Any ordered set of quantities in which numbers are generated using some predetermined underlying rule. (*See also* Series.)

Series

The term for the sum of the numbers in a sequence. (*See also* Sequence.)

Sine of an Acute Angle of a Right Triangle

The ratio (or fraction) of the leg *opposite* the acute angle divided by the length of the hypotenuse. (*See also* Cosine of an Acute Angle of a Right Triangle, Tangent of an Acute Angle of a Right Triangle.)

Slope of a Line or Line Segment

Reveals how the value of y changes as the value of x changes. For any two points—(x_1, y_1) and (x_2, y_2)—on the line:

$$\text{slope} = \frac{(\text{change in } y)}{(\text{change in } x)} = \frac{(y_2 - y_1)}{(x_2 - x_1)}.$$

Statistics

The collection, organization, and analysis of data.

Tangent of an Acute Angle of a Right Triangle

The ratio (or fraction) of the leg *opposite* the acute angle divided by the leg adjacent to that same angle.

(*See also* Cosine of an Acute Angle of a Right Triangle, Sine of an Acute Angle of a Right Triangle.)

Tessellation

A pattern of shapes that is repeated over and over to cover some specified area.

Unit Equilateral Triangle

All angles = 60° and all sides = 1.

Unit Square

All angles = 90° and all sides = 1.

Venn Diagram

A pictorial representation using a rectangle and combinations of interlocking and/or separate circles. It is drawn in such a way as to represent operations found in set theory.

Vertical Asymptote

A vertical line considered a limit to the curve in that the shortest (perpendicular) distance between the curve and the asymptote approaches 0 as the value of the curve stretches up and approaches positive infinity or as the value of the curve stretches down and approaches negative infinity.

References

Bartlett, J. (1968). *Familiar quotations* (14th ed.) (E. M. Beck, Ed.). Boston: Little, Brown, and Co.

Brown, S. I., & Walter, M. (1983). *The art of problem posing.* Hillsdale, NJ: Lawrence Erlbaum Associates.

Donovan, R., Lucarelli, E., Sun Park, M., & Rogers, P. (1992). The sound of mathic. *Math Mirror, 2*(1), 23–24. [The *Math Mirror* is an in-house student publication produced by Manhasset High School in Manhasset, New York.]

Fogarty, R. (1997). *Problem-based learning and other curriculum models for the multiple intelligences classroom.* Thousand Oaks, CA: Corwin Press.

Gardner, H. (1983). *Frames of mind: The theory of multiple intelligences.* New York: Basic Books.

Gardner, H. (1993). *Multiple intelligences: The theory in practice.* New York: Basic Books.

Garland, T. H. (1987). *Mystery and magic in numbers.* Palo Alto, CA: Dale Seymour.

Great Source Education Group. (2000). *Algebra to go: A mathematics handbook.* Wilmington, MA: Author.

Great Source Education Group. (2000). *Math on call: A mathematical handbook.* Wilmington, MA: Author.

Hart, D. (1994). *Authentic assessment: A handbook for educators.* Menlo Park, CA: Addison-Wesley.

Houghton Mifflin Company. (1985). *The American heritage dictionary* (2nd college ed.). Boston: Author.

Jurgensen, R. C., Donnelly, A. J., Maier, J. E., & Rising, G. R. (1978). *Geometry.* Boston: Houghton Mifflin.

Loomis, E. (1968). *The Pythagorean proposition.* Reston, VA: National Council of Teachers of Mathematics.

Malloy, C. E. (1997). Mathematics projects promote students' algebraic thinking. *Mathematics Teaching in the Middle School 2,* 282–288.

McClain, K. (1999). Reflecting on students' understanding of data. *Mathematics Teaching in the Middle School 4,* 374–380.

McNamara, T. J. (1997). *ITALICS_math.* Buffalo, NY: Parkside Press.

McNamara, T. J. (2003). *Key concepts in mathematics.* Thousand Oaks, CA: Corwin Press.

National Council of Teachers of Mathematics (NCTM). (1989). *Teaching and learning: A problem-solving focus* (F. Curcio, Ed.). Reston, VA: Author.

National Council of Teachers of Mathematics (NCTM). (2000). *Principles and standards for school mathematics.* Reston, VA: Author.

National Council of Teachers of Mathematics. (1980). *Sourcebook of application of school mathematics.* Reston, VA: Author.

National Council of Teachers of Mathematics. (1989a). *Curriculum and evaluation standards for school mathematics.* Reston, VA: Author.

245

National Council of Teachers of Mathematics. (1989b). *Teaching and learning: A problem-solving focus* (F. Curcio, Ed.). Reston, VA: Author.

National Council of Teachers of Mathematics. (1991). *Professional standards for teaching mathematics.* Reston, VA: Author.

National Council of Teachers of Mathematics. (1995). *Assessment standards for school mathematics.* Reston, VA: Author.

Nelson, R. (1993). *Proofs without words: Exercises in verbal thinking.* Washington, DC: Mathematical Association of America.

Pedersen, J., & Pólya, G. (1984). On problems with solutions attainable in more than one way. *College Mathematics Journal, 15,* 218–228.

Pólya, G. (1951). *How to solve it: A new aspect of mathematical method* (2nd ed.). Princeton, NJ: Princeton University Press.

Sandefur, J. (1995). Discrete mathematics: A unified approach. In C. Hirsh (Ed.), *The secondary school mathematics curriculum: 1995 yearbook of the National Council of Teachers of Mathematics.* Reston, VA: National Council of Teachers of Mathematics.

Schoenfeld, A. H. (1985). *Mathematical problem solving.* Orlando, FL: Academic Press.

Simmons, G. F. (1987). *Precalculus in a nutshell: Geometry, algebra, trigonometry.* Dedham, MA: Janson Publications.

Simon and Schuster. (1964). *The universal encyclopedia of mathematics.* New York: Author.

Sobel, M. A., & Maletsky, E. A. (1988). *Teaching mathematics: A sourcebook of aids, activities, and strategies.* Englewood Cliffs, NJ: Prentice Hall.

Thompson, D. R., Senk, S. L., & Viktora, S. S. (1991). Matrices at the secondary school level. In M. Kenney and C. Hirsch (Eds.), *Discrete mathematics across the curriculum, K–12: 1991 yearbook of the National Council of Teachers of Mathematics* (pp. 104–116). Reston, VA: National Council of Teachers of Mathematics.

Index

CORWIN PRESS